Since 1972, Sue Goldstein has been the author of America's best-selling bargain shopping guidebooks, including *The Underground Shopper*. Value and getting your money's worth is her bargain "buyline." Called America's diva of discounts, she was born to shop at half-price out of necessity. Now she shops at half-price because she's smart. Since launching her publishing career, she has appeared on hundreds of talk shows—"Donahue," "Oprah," "Hour Magazine," "Good Morning America," "Real People," and "CBS News"—and has had countless newspaper and magazine articles written about her, which have appeared in everything from *Money* to *Newsweek*. She lives in a lakefront house outside Dallas with her two dogs and five cats. Her son, Josh, is a college student/photographer/TV grip and waiter in his spare time and is decorating his own apartment with the help of *Great Buys*.

# SUE GOLDSTEIN

## Great Buys

### FOR PEOPLE
### OVER 50

PENGUIN BOOKS

PENGUIN BOOKS
Published by the Penguin Group
Viking Penguin, a division of Penguin Books USA Inc.,
375 Hudson Street, New York, New York 10014, U.S.A.
Penguin Books Ltd, 27 Wrights Lane,
London W8 5TZ, England
Penguin Books Australia Ltd, Ringwood,
Victoria, Australia
Penguin Books Canada Ltd, 2801 John Street,
Markham, Ontario, Canada L3R 1B4
Penguin Books (N.Z.) Ltd, 182–190 Wairau Road,
Auckland 10, New Zealand

Penguin Books Ltd, Registered Offices:
Harmondsworth, Middlesex, England

First published in Penguin Books 1991

1 3 5 7 9 10 8 6 4 2

LIBRARY OF CONGRESS CATALOGING IN PUBLICATION DATA
Goldstein, Sue, 1941–
Great buys for people over 50/by Sue Goldstein.
p.   cm.
Includes index.
ISBN 0-14-013268-6
1. Shopping—United States.   2. Aged—United States—Economic
conditions.   I. Title.
TX336.G64   1991
380.1′45′000844—dc20      90–46526

Printed in the United States of America

Set in Baskerville
Designed by Victoria Hartman

There are two significant shoppers
who helped shape this book and my life:
my darling dad, Bill Elkin—at 81,
the quintessential senior citizen—
and my adorable son Josh, 19, who only shops
when he's hungry and pays retail at that.
This guide, hopefully, will help close
the proverbial generation gap.

"Forty is the old age of youth,
Fifty is the youth of old age."
—Victor Hugo

# Preface

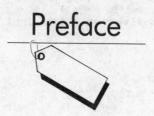

Growing pains even as I approach fifty are minimized by the prospects of all the wonderful discounts ahead. Childhood. Parenthood. And now—whoopee—Seniorhood!

There's no doubt in my mind that we're not getting any older—just better. Better at shopping, for sure. It wasn't so long ago that my toes finally yelled "Enough!" Being squeezed into those pointy Charles Jourdan shoes all those years just in the name of fashion has finally given way to comfort and NATURALIZERS. From bunions to bargains. At least now I can walk a mile or two to snag one.

Slide into fifty with me, if you're not already there, with the momentum of childlike wonderment. Throw away the adolescent devotion to wearing high heels that you can't walk in or that prevent you—God forbid—from looking like everyone else. Remember praying to live through another excruciating algebra test? Forget it. Forget pain. Forget feigning it. Now you can relax, be honest, and go for it.

To be right with your world, at last, it's right that you approach the next decades with ease and excitement. It's time to explore your potential once more. Start a new career. A new family. Even a new life.

It's all possible with *Great Buys for People over 50* as your guide to the myriad of possibilities just waiting to be tried.

Like in the community dressing rooms at Loehmann's,

you'll have plenty of company who would also like to grin and—bare it. Don't be shy. Try it. You'll like it and . . .

Think of all those very many thoughts just waiting to be thought . . .

Sue Goldstein

# Acknowledgments

Since the early 1970s and my *Underground Shopper* days of strictly bargain basements and outlets to today's *Great Buys* and revolution in retailing, we've come a long way, and I thank my agent, Jane Dystel, and my editor, Lori Lipsky, for seeing that difference. Shop 'til you drop . . . only if you don't have to go very far, spend less than you thought, and have fun in the process. *Great Buys for People over 50* is reported, chronicled, cataloged, indexed, and typed by my cohort, Sherry DeBorde, who temporarily gave up her career as a best-selling novelist to address shopping in the senior marketplace. Alongside her, Marilynne Robertson worked with a database to keep the thousands of details straight and helped wade through the mountains of materials and wound up reaffirming her love of senior shopping, even if she was only approaching forty. And last, to the family of friends who helped me make it to 50: Ann and Lonnie, Ellen, Margie R., Margie N., Laurie, Barbara, Judy, Alan E., Alan M., Christy, and the Mumford High School Class of 1959.

# Contents

# Introduction

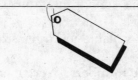

By the year 1995, over 50 percent of the money spent in the marketplace will come from shoppers over 55. Today, there are over 55 million senior shoppers graying and growing.

The U.S. Census Bureau predicts a population explosion of over 92 million by the year 2020. By then, one out of every three Americans will be a part of the senior generation.

Retailers have their work cut out for them. The senior community is by no means homogeneous. Each age segment (50–64; 65–75; 76–84; 85 and over) represents very different needs and disposable incomes.

Hopefully, though diverse, the "empty nesters," the "gray market," the "silver streakers," or whatever you call them, all have one thing in common. They all like to shop. And with plenty of time and plenty of opportunities to check prices, they will know a Great Buy when they see it.

Convenience will be the single overriding consideration of the senior shopper. Customer service, ease in shopping, and clerks who can be understood are the three major concerns of the senior shopper.

In developing a rationale for which merchants, products, or services were chosen to be included in the first edition of *Great Buys for People over 50,* those reflecting a genuine sensitivity to the needs of the senior shopper were foremost. We asked ourselves the following:

- Were stores well lit, products easily accessible and conveniently located?
- Was merchandise well marked, product and care information given, nutritional guidelines detailed?
- Were return policies stated, guarantees and warranties described?
- Was merchandise available in larger sizes, easy to wear and care for?
- Were there toll-free numbers? Were mail and telephone orders accepted?
- Was there delivery (preferably free)?
- Were there rest areas in the store? Restrooms available? Wheelchair access?
- Were food products available in single servings, smaller portions, heart healthy?
- Were there low salt, decaffeinated, and diet portions?
- Were there deals offered to seniors, such as "early bird" specials or discounts on rooms?
- Do they sponsor special senior events or organizations?
- Do they offer specific products and services geared to the senior citizen?

*Great Buys for People over 50* is the culmination of some of the best deals and opportunities offered to the Power Shoppers of the future—the over 50 set. The baby boomers plus! The listings that follow reflect the diversity of retailing that will be (or should be) targeted to the "silver streak" in us all.

# Symbols Key

I. Types of payment accepted

CK    Personal check. A few firms don't accept personal checks. They think that the inconvenience of waiting until the check clears, and the resulting impatience of customers due to the delay in receiving their order, makes checks more trouble than they're worth. Firms that *do* take personal checks have a "CK" symbol in the line beneath the address where types of payment are listed. Certified check, cashier's check, and money orders are all commonly accepted as payment by mail-order companies and won't mean a delay in processing your order.

MO    Money order.

MC    Mastercard. Using a credit card is advisable for orders you want to receive quickly, since there is no delay. It almost goes without saying that credit-card orders are mandatory when you order by phone. A final word of warning: Even when you use credit, it's still a good idea to write down the model and style number of the merchandise, as well as the name of the person you spoke with if you ordered by phone. If a problem arises, this information may prove useful.

V     Visa.

AE    American Express.

D     Discover.

DC    Diner's Club.

CB    Carte Blanche.

COD   Cash on delivery. Firms that accept COD payments usually qualify that with some type of restriction, such as a 25 percent deposit. When you order COD, know that this means CASH on delivery. If you expect to receive your order and pay by check, you'll probably be disappointed. The seller will most likely require some form of "safe" payment.

MW   Montgomery Ward.

II.  Information about the supplier

C     Catalog available. When it costs something to get a catalog, the price will be noted to the right of "C." The charge for a catalog is usually small (if anything), only enough to cover postage and handling, and to discourage catalog requests from people who wouldn't actually order. We have indicated when the catalog price is refundable with your first order.

B     Brochure. A brochure is smaller than a catalog and often folds out. For our purposes, a brochure is eight pages or less.

F     Flier or price sheet.

PQ     Price Quote. Companies with a "PQ" following their write-up will answer telephone queries or letters requesting information about specific merchandise. To get a price quote, you must know the manufacturer's name, the item's stock number, et cetera.

SASE   Requests that you send a self-addressed stamped envelope.

REFUNDABLE Means the costs of the catalog will be discounted from the purchase you make.

*NOTE:* Prices quoted in the write-ups are subject to change and are merely reflective of usual discounted prices.

# Tips for Ordering by Mail

- *Never send cash;* order by check, money order, or credit card.
- Find out the company's policy on warranties, exchanges, and refunds.
- Keep a record of your order: name of company, address, telephone number, and date of order, advertisement.
- Know shipping charges.
- Orders (unless otherwise stated) must be shipped within 30 days of receipt of your order. If there is going to be a delay, the company must notify you.
- You are not required to pay for anything you did not order. Write "Refused" on the package and send it back (no postage needed).
- For complaints or questions regarding warranty policy, misrepresentation, or fraud, contact:
  Postmaster or Chief Postal Inspector
  U.S. Postal Service
  Room 3517
  Washington, DC 20260
  (202-245-5445)
- For questions or complaints about unordered merchandise or delay of your order, contact:
  Consumer Inquiries
  Federal Trade Commission
  Washington, DC 20580
  (202-523-3598)

# Complaints

So, you've got a problem. After attempts at resolution with the merchant in question and you've correctly followed the procedures for complaints covered in the catalog, brochure, or by phone, you can seek outside counsel. If you've written or spoken to the company first and still received no satisfaction, you can turn to the following (it is a good idea to include all of your correspondence and photocopies as documentation when seeking help):

*BETTER BUSINESS BUREAU* (BBB): Always check with the local BBB *before* ordering from a mail-order company. This local BBB is in the area where the company resides, not *your* hometown. If you send a SASE to the Council of Better Business Bureaus, Inc., 1515 Wilson Blvd., Arlington, VA 22209, you will receive a directory of BBB offices. Though the BBBs are funded by the participating businesses, they do maintain files on firms, help resolve consumer complaints, and provide an overview of the firm's selling history. That way, if a firm has hundreds of unresolved complaints on file, chances are they're not a good bet.

*CONSUMER ACTION PANELS* (CAPs): These are third-party dispute resolution programs established by the industries they represent. For example, for a problem with a major appliance, you can write to MACAP (Major Appliance Consumer Action Panel), 20 North Wacker Drive, Chicago, IL 60606 or call 800-621-0477.

*DIRECT MARKETING ASSOCIATION* (DMA): This is the trade association for mail-order merchants and direct-marketing companies. Its Mail Order Action Line (MOAL) helps resolve nondelivery problems with a mail or direct marketer. To get help, send a copy of your complaint letter and documentation to Mail Order Action Line, DMA, 6 East 43rd Street, New York, NY 10017. You may also get your name added to or removed from mailing lists through the DMA's Mail Preference Service. Write to the DMA at the address above to receive the MPS form.

*FEDERAL TRADE COMMISSION* (FTC): Though this law enforcement agency does not act on individual complaints, every letter helps build a case. The Fair Credit Billing Act (FCBA) of 1975 offers mail-order shoppers who use credit cards some leverage if there's a problem of nondelivery. Disputes regarding the quality of goods or services are also covered, but such provisions vary from state to state. It's best to contact your local consumer protection agency for clarification before proceeding to the federal level.

*UNITED STATES POSTAL SERVICE* (USPS): This is probably the most effective of all the agencies; their track record of resolution is almost 85 percent. Send a copy of your final complaint letter and documentation to the Chief Postal Inspector, U.S. Postal Service, Washington, DC 20260. Contacting the local postmaster nearest the firm in question may be even quicker.

# Feedback

We'd like to hear from you! Comments, both good and bad, help shape our next edition and other books in the *Great Buys* series. Of course, we'd like to hear from you, our readers, and from merchants who would like to be listed.

If you've had a problem, and you fail to resolve it with the merchant directly, don't hesitate to state your case to us:

GREAT BUYS
P.O. Box 294042
Lewisville, TX 75029-4042

Be sure to include all the pertinent information and *copies* of any documentation relating to the transaction and what you would like done. Don't forget, too, to give your name, address, and day-time phone number.

# Note to Readers

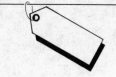

As *Great Buys* goes into the final stages of production, our staff has scrupulously checked and double-checked every detail, making sure that it is current and correct at the time of submission. But as a word of caution, businesses are not stagnant, and ownership, location, and pricing policies can change in a matter of days or weeks. So please keep this in mind as you shop, and call to verify information before sending a check for any of the items or services listed. Wherever possible, we have indicated toll-free numbers for your convenience and savings.

**SPECIAL OFFER TO READERS:** In order to take advantage of any special offers, discounts, gift-with-purchase, etc., be sure to identify yourself as a *Great Buys* reader when calling or writing to order a product or request a price quote.

# GREAT BUYS
# FOR PEOPLE OVER 50

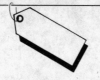

# ADVISORS

"Aging Information Offices" are springing up in cities across the country. These often provide directories of your area's community resources. Check the directory to see if there's an office in your city.

**AARP**
**Office of Communications**
**1909 K Street, NW**
**Washington, DC 20049**
**202-728-1300**

The AARP—American Association of Retired Persons—is a nonprofit, nonpartisan organization dedicated to helping older Americans achieve lives of independence, dignity and purpose.

*DUES:* Membership dues (for you and your spouse) are $5 for one year, $12.50 for three years, and $35 for 10 years. Dues for those outside domestic U.S. mail limits are $7 per year or $18 for three years.

*PUBLICATIONS: Modern Maturity* and the *AARP News Bulletin.*

*RETIRED TEACHERS DIVISION:* The NRTA *News Bulletin* and NRTA edition of *Modern Maturity* magazine.

*AARP PRIORITIES:*

- Health Care Campaign
- Women's Initiative
- Worker Equity
- Minority Affairs Initiative
- Legislative Advocacy
- Member Services:
  Pharmacy Service
  Investment Program
  Travel Service
  AARP Motoring Plan
  Group Health Insurance
  Auto/Homeowner Insurance
- Educational Resources:
  Audiovisuals
  AARP Books
  Publications
  Chapter Activities:

| | | |
|---|---|---|
| Area I | Boston, Massachusetts | (617-426-1185) |
| Area II | New York, New York | (212-758-1411) |
| | Pennsylvania State Office | (717-238-2277) |
| Area III | Alexandria, Virginia | (703-739-9220) |
| Area IV | Atlanta, Georgia | (404-458-1491) |
| | Florida State Office | (813-576-1155) |
| Area V | Des Plaines, Illinois | (312-298-2852) |
| Area VI | Kansas City, Missouri | (816-842-3959) |
| Area VII | Dallas, Texas | (214-361-3060) |
| Area VIII | Salt Lake City, Utah | (801-328-0691) |
| | | (801-328-0692) |
| Area IX | Long Beach, California | (213-417-9611) |
| Area X | Seattle, Washington | (206-526-7918) |

- Community Service
- Consumer Affairs Program
- Criminal Justice Services
- 55 Alive/Mature Driving
- Health Advocacy Services
- Housing Program

- Institute of Lifetime Learning
- Intergenerational Program
- International Activities
- Interreligious Liaison
- Legal Counsel for the Elderly
- National Gerontology Resource Center
- NRTA Activities
- Senior Community Service Employment Program
- Tax Aide Program
- Widowed Persons Service

**AARP AUTO AND HOME INSURANCE**
**1909 K Street NW**
**Washington, DC 20049**
**608-256-2111**
**B**

This well-documented booklet of facts and fiction about insurance from the AARP is yours for the asking. Straight talk about premiums and claims, how to evaluate coverage and determine a fair cost of the policies—even how to reduce your premiums if you are a mature driver. Free, no-obligation quotes.

**AARP HOME EQUITY CONVERSION**
**1909 K Street NW**
**Washington, DC 20049**
**608-256-2111**
**B**

The AARP is devoted to keeping seniors informed. In this continuing effort, they have published "Consumer's Guide to Home Equity Conversion," detailing a wise way to get extra money during hard times. For more information, call or write the AARP today.

**AMERICAN EXPRESS CONSUMER AFFAIRS DEPT.**
**"LIFECYCLE"**
**World Financial Center**
**New York, NY 10285**
**212-640-2000**
**B**

In conjunction with AARP, American Express has developed a series of "Lifestyle Brochures" on many financial subjects and money management. Write for free brochures.

**ARTHRITIS FOUNDATION**
**1314 Spring Street, NW**
**Atlanta, GA 30309**
**(404) 872-7100**

For the most comprehensive *Guide to Independent Living for People with Arthritis,* call your area's local chapter of the Arthritis Foundation. Over 400 pages of how to make it through each day with ease, including a rather hefty resource directory of products, self-help aids, and suppliers to consider. Photos, additional reading suggestions, tips for day-to-day living, and more make this a guide you shouldn't live without. Price per copy varies with each local chapter, but it usually costs around $4.

**ASAP**
**6102 E. Mockingbird Lane, Ste. 194**
**Dallas, TX 75214**
**(214) 321-2990**

The Adult Support and Assistance Program's goal is to provide services to seniors so that they may maintain their independence, including daily check-in service to see if you're all right, companion sitting, shopping, errands, secretarial services, domestic duties, home maintenance—just about anything. It's a nice concept that should gain national attention as the need to provide in-home personal care accelerates.

## CARE RESOURCES
P.O. Box 2692
Dallas, TX 75221-2692
214-263-4281

One call does it all if you want the most comprehensive and current information in the area of senior care and housing. This free source can be for you or your family if you're looking for a referral to a retirement community, nursing home, hospice, adult daycare, home health care, respite care, or durable medical products or equipment. All pertinent information is revealed, including prices and services provided—even owners' comments are thoroughly researched and confirmed. Care Resources can even connect you to someone for help with grocery shopping, filling out Medicare forms, or transporting you to appointments—across the country. Soon to be nationwide, this state-of-the-heart service is currently available only in Texas, Illinois, Florida, California, Delaware, and New Jersey.

## CARE SHARING
c/o Children of Aging Parents (CAPS)
2761 Trenton Rd.
Levittown, PA 19056
215-945-6900

A most useful encyclopedia of care-givers is chronicled by this organization. Listings include community resources, good nursing homes, care managers, home health services, adult daycare centers, and more. Spawned by the often necessary decisions families must make when they are far from the person in need of care, this informational directory is a helpful introduction to private care organizations, support groups, and practitioners. Though short-term care management can be handled by such organizations as area agencies on aging and the social service departments of hospitals, private care-givers provide more personal involvement and more intense management of a person's needs. An appendix of reading material is provided for further information.

**CLAREMONT MCKENNA COLLEGE**
**500 East Ninth Street**
**Claremont, CA 91711-8094**
**714-621-4848**

Programs offered by Claremont College can help you generate income, teach you how to avoid or reduce taxes on capital gains, provide charitable deductions, reduce estate taxes, and eliminate management worries. You may receive substantial benefits from a gift that will help Claremont McKenna College continue its outstanding academic programs for tomorrow's leaders in government and business. Call or write for more information.

**COUNCIL ON AGING**
**600 Maryland Ave., SW**
**Washington, DC 20024**
**202-479-1200**

By calling your local state agency, you will be in direct contact with current information on services, programs, and policies that relate to aging.

## 55 ALIVE/MATURE DRIVING
**AARP**
**1909 K Street NW**
**Washington, DC 20049**

Save lives—yours and others'—prevent injuries, retain your driver's license, and perhaps even lower your insurance rates by participating in the 55 Alive program, available throughout the country. If you're over 50, you should take this course, with its emphasis on safe driving. Obtain detailed information about time and availability of the course in your state by writing to the AARP today. Be sure to include your name, address, and phone number.

## FORTY PLUS CLUBS
**Forty Plus Clubs of New York**
**15 Park Row**
**New York, NY 10038**

Currently located in 15 cities in the United States, this nonprofit organization of unemployed executives, managers, and professionals includes both men and women aged 40 plus. Its objective is to help members conduct effective job searches and locate new jobs. There is a one-time charge of $800 (payable in installments), and members must commit themselves to a weekly meeting and two days a week working at the club. This club may be used as your base of operations during your job search, as they have computers, a reference library, and mail and phone-answering services. This is definitely worth checking out.

## GRANDPARENT VISITATION DISPUTE:
### A LEGAL RESOURCE
c/o American Bar Association Order Fulfillment
750 North Lakeshore Drive
Chicago, IL 60611

The American Bar Association produced this book to provide guidelines to grandparents who seek visitation privileges with their grandchildren following divorce. Doing everything possible to avoid taking the matter to court could be a small price to pay to retain your relationship with the grandkids. Send a check for $22.90, which includes postage and handling, to the American Bar Association.

## HOTLINES
P.O. Box 19405
Washington, DC 20036
$1.25 (SASE)

Ralph Nader's *Consumer's Guide to Toll-Free Hotlines* is a 28-page booklet of toll-free numbers sent upon request (enclose a business-sized, self-addressed envelope and $.25 postage, plus $1 check or money order). You'll soon be calling *toll free* for information concerning cancer treatment, Alzheimer's disease, arthritis, alcoholism, headaches, diabetes, and asthma, as well as problems concerning housing, meat and poultry handling, home product safety, automobile defects, pesticides, workplace safety, and veteran's benefits.

## LEGAL COUNSEL FOR THE ELDERLY HOTLINE
Monday–Friday; 9 A.M.–5 P.M.
800-252-5997 (in Florida); 305-576-5997 (Dade County)

Look for FREE legal assistance via the telephone, as exemplified by Florida's hotline service if you are 60 or older. There's also a legal hotline for older Americans operated by

AARP's Legal Counsel for the Elderly, offering FREE legal counsel on problems such as Medicare and Medicaid, Social Security and other government benefit programs, personal injury, and disputes involving wills and probates.

**LEGAL SERVICES PLAN**
**200 North Martingale Road**
**Schaumburg, IL 60173-2096**
**800-323-4620**
**MC,V,AE,D, MW (Montgomery Ward)**

Have your own personal attorney (not business advisor) for the low price of $6.75 a month. Now you can utilize the services of a licensed lawyer in your local community without astronomical retainers. Unlimited consultations on initial problems or review of legal documents (up to 6 pages) without additional charges (leases, contracts, service agreements, installment notes), and professional advice such as securing your rights and benefits under government programs like Social Security, Medicare, veterans' programs, and more. A simple will is part of the deal. Even posting bail (up to $1000) is available with one toll-free call, at no additional charge. Guaranteed cap of $50 per hour for additional services. All Plan attorneys are closely monitored, and they must adhere to the highest standards of professional excellence, such as returning phone calls. The Plan will go to bat for you if you have any problems with the assigned attorney. You may withdraw from the program at any time, but why would you, when you have affordable representation at last? Available in all states except Mississippi and South Carolina.

First month free to readers of *Great Buys*.

**MATURE INVESTOR**
**QXO Publishing**
**Box 2741**
**Glen Ellyn, IL 60135**

*Mature Investor* is specifically tailored to the unique investment needs of seniors and mature adults. Most seniors have too much money in liquid funds, according to *Mature Investor*. With their expertise, they can help fine-tune your existing investments and establish better use of these funds. You'll be on your way to sound retirement and investment planning with their help. Three months costs $9.95—nothing compared to the money it can generate. More information available upon request.

**NATIONAL ACADEMY OF ELDER LAW**
**ATTORNEYS, INC.**
**655 North Alvernon**
**Suite 108**
**Tucson, AZ 85711**
**602-881-4005**

This association's purpose is to foster the highest standards of practice among attorneys who specialize in the legal needs of older persons. Such areas as Medicare claims and appeals, Medicaid assistance, long-term health issues, and estate planning. Write for more information, including how to be a better "legal" consumer, how to find free or low-cost legal assistance, and more.

**1991 CONSUMERS RESOURCE HANDBOOK**
Consumer Information Center
Pueblo, CO 81009
There are over 2000 sources in this big country to
help with a consumer problem, and this handbook is
FREE for the asking.

## NATIONAL COUNCIL ON SENIOR CITIZENS, INC.
925 15th Street NW
Washington, DC 20005

Born during the struggle for Medicare in 1961, this senior
organization has been an *active* advocacy group for seniors
ever since. Some of their victories include increases in Social
Security benefits, creation of senior centers and nutrition
sites, low-income housing, community employment projects,
and other social services. There are almost 5,000 Senior
Citizen clubs, with a total of over four million members.
Upon payment of annual dues, you'll receive their Gold
Card, making you eligible for low-cost health insurance, their
in-hospital protection plan, direct-mail drug discounts, discounted travel services, discounts at participating hotels
across the country, and car-rental discounts. The *Senior
Citizen News*, an 8-page newspaper, is published monthly and
helps keep members informed. Write to the address above
for more information on membership.

## OCCUPYING THE SUMMIT: THE GUIDE TO
## SUCCESSFUL RETIREMENT PLANNING
**Wordware Publishing, Inc.**
**1506 Capital Avenue**
**Plano, TX 75074**
**214-423-0090**
**800-229-4949**

"Today is the first day of the rest of your life. Don't waste it." This is the motto reflected in this guide to successful retirement planning by Robert Shaffer, whose inspiration springs from his own experience. After a stressful career as president and CEO of General Telephone, he is now enjoying an active, fulfilling retirement. A healthy future does not happen accidentally, but the detailed planning outlined in Section I will help you "occupy that summit." Section II shows ways to achieve satisfaction through volunteering, and Section III covers the all-important aspects of physical, emotional, and spiritual well-being. Shaffer maintains that a positive plan at any stage of life can make the remaining years more useful and enjoyable.

*Great Buys* readers can buy this handy reference for only $11.96 (regular price $15.95) plus postage and handling ($2).

## OFFICE OF PUBLIC RESPONSIBILITY
**American Express Company**
**World Financial Center**
**New York, NY 10285-4700**
**SASE**

"What Do I Want to Be . . . When I Retire?" is a booklet on how you can anticipate your financial needs in the future and start planning now in order to enjoy your life later.

## RETIREMENT INCOME AND EMPLOYMENT
**"Guide to Planning Your Retirement Finances"**
**Select Committee on Aging**
**U.S. Government Printing Office**
**Washington, DC 20402**

Unfortunately, millions of Americans do not know the first thing about financial planning; some don't even know when they are eligible to retire. Fortunately, "Guide to Planning Your Retirement Finances" is available free from the government. It can help lead to a sound, thought-out, and well-planned retirement. Everything from the basics to more sophisticated needs is explained in simple terms. A bibliography at the end is a source of additional information.


## SALVATION ARMY
**P.O. Box 2608**
**Dallas, TX 75221**
**214-353-2731**

Write for the Salvation Army's free booklet "37 Things People Know about Wills . . . That Aren't Really So." It pays to be prepared so no unnecessary or excessive costs are incurred and your estate can be distributed as desired.


## SENIOR SHOPPER INSURANCE PROGRAMS
**800-458-5259; Fax 313-626-1947**
**Mr. Marshall Shanbraun, R.H.U.**

Choose all or select from a menu of national insurance options designed especially for senior needs.

- On the Road Accident Plan
- Cancer, Health & Stroke Indemnity Plan
- In-Home Health Care

- Nursing Home
- Medicare Supplements

*Great Buys* readers: FREE "Guide to Health Insurance for People with Medicare."

**WASHINGTON CONSUMER'S CHECKBOOK**
**806 15th St., NW**
**Washington, DC 20005**
**202-347-7283**

or

**BAY AREA CONSUMER'S CHECKBOOK**
**101 Embarcadero, Ste. 101**
**San Francisco, CA 94105**
**415-397-8305**

This nonprofit organization publishes two quarterlies called *Checkbook* and *Bargains*. Each gives prices and rates the quality of each service or store listed, such as banks, hospital emergency rooms, household movers, or dog kennels. Prices on the most popular items like appliances are also included.

# APPAREL AND SHOES

**AMPLE SAMPLE**
**2825 Valley View, Suite 212**
**Farmers Branch, TX 75234**
**800-633-6964; 214-243-3776**
**PQ**
**MC, V, AE**

Forget the bland, boring, big look. Shop with ease (on your pocketbook and your figure) for the latest name brand and designer fashions at a fraction of the retail price. Save 50 percent and more. If you need a large-size wardrobe, this is your source for "ample samples" in sizes 3X, including one-of-a-kind knockout outfits that are sure to fit you to a tee! Don't settle for the drab and dreary when you're well-endowed. Make a grand entrance and be assured of a standing ovation.

**ANTHONY RICHARDS**
**6386 Engle Road**
**P.O. Box 94503**
**Cleveland, OH 44101-4503**
**800-359-5933**
**C**

Find the same bargains in the Anthony Richards catalog that you would expect to find rummaging through the crowds at the dozens of discount shops in New York's business districts, all without leaving the comfort of home! Affordable prices on women's two-piece outfits and dresses. Ideal for those on a tight budget who are looking for an alternative to pants and sweaters. Most dresses are machine-washable and come in misses, women's, and half sizes. Several shoe styles and a small selection of nightwear and lingerie is also offered.

**ARIZONA MAIL ORDER COMPANY, INC.**
**3740 East 34 Street**
**Tucson, AZ 85713-5305**
**602-745-4500; 602-748-8600 (Customer Service)**
**MC,V,AE,D,DC**
**C $2**

Since 1946, the Arizona Mail Order Company, Inc., has brought proportioned ladies' contemporary and famous-maker fashions, shoes, and lingerie in hard-to-find sizes right to your door. From petites to large sizes, narrow to wide-width shoes, there are items from around the world to wear with panache and flair. Satisfaction guaranteed or your money back. Also available for the asking are catalogs targeted to the hard-to-fit fashion customer. Included are:

- SERENDIPITY: Contemporary fashions and shoes
- OLD PUEBLO TRADERS: Affordable fashions and shoes
- UNIQUE PETITE: Fashions and shoes for women under 5'4"
- REGALIA: Fashions and shoes for fuller figures, half and women's sizes
- NANCY'S CHOICE: Women's shoes in hard-to-find sizes
- INTIMATE APPEAL: Loungewear and lingerie for misses and larger sizes
- SHOPPING INTERNATIONAL: Contemporary and famous-maker fashions, shoes, and lingerie in hard-to-find sizes

## BURLINGTON COAT
**263 W. 38th St.**
**New York, NY 10018**

Burlington Coat sells sportswear, dresses, jewelry, shoes, bags, domestics, baby stuff—it's much more than just the world's largest selection of coats. Headquartered in New York since 1977, they've been growing steadily into a national force to be reckoned with. Off-price is here to stay, so move over, department stores, and say hello to saving 20 to 60 percent at Burlington Coat. Check your directory for the location nearest you or write to the above address.

## CARTAN'S SHOES
**1201 West Magnolia Avenue**
**Fort Worth, TX 76104**
**800-541-8052**
**C**

Request a catalog for those feet that are hard-to-fit. Sizes 2 to 14 and widths 5A to 12E in brand names like OLD MAIN, TROTTERS, SELBYS, and HUSHPUPPIES. The basics in comfort and at prices that even include the box ($45–90).

## CENTER FOR CLOTHING/PHYSICAL DISABILITIES
**Buffalo State College**
**Caudell Hall**
**1300 Elmwood Avenue**
**Buffalo, NY 14222**

Send a SASE (self-addressed stamped envelope) for more information on this volunteer-center clearinghouse where people can find out where to buy and how to adapt clothing that provides comfort and ease in dressing despite their disability. Founded by college professor Colleen Frey and her fashion-tech classes at Buffalo State. Because of her determination to provide contemporary and attractive clothing to the over 37 million Americans who are physically impaired, the center has paid off in great dividends to the recipients. It offers such services as clothing alterations just for the cost of the fabric and supplies, do-it-yourself instructions, and a list of recommended fashions and manufacturers.

## CHADWICK'S OF BOSTON, LTD.
35 United Drive
West Bridgewater, MA 02379
508-583-6600 (Order line)
C

The original off-price catalog is right on target when it comes to fashion. Make a statement in suits, dresses (casual or formal), coats, Ts and tops, sweaters, accessories, sleepwear, activewear, and more. Easy to wear, easy to order, easy to fit (lots of S–M–L), easy to return if you're not satisfied, and, most of all, easy on your pocketbook. Save 20 to 50 percent below department-store prices and see for yourself why they're considered a saving grace for all shoppers, both juniors and seniors.

## THE CHELSEA COLLECTION
Hanover, PA 17333-0018
800-722-7888 (7 days a week, 24 hours a day)
Major credit cards
C $2

With over 50 years of bringing stylish women unconditional catalog satisfaction with hip and priced-right apparel and accessories, you can't go wrong here. Sizes 8 to 18, coordinated to the hilt with fashion jewelry and accessories. You'll go from the board room to the boudoir and not have to borrow from the bank! Great looks plus great prices add up to one of the best bets in this book. Once you've ordered, you're assured of receiving all the year's best offerings. You can even order on THEIR credit card if you qualify.

**CHOCK CATALOG CORPORATION**
**74 Orchard Street**
**New York, NY 10002**
**800-222-0020; 212-473-1929 (in NY)**
**MC,V**
**C $1**

Unmentionables? Not anymore. You'll want to shout from the rooftops about the 25 percent discount on hosiery and underwear for the whole family. Their catalog is chock full of namebrands like CARTER'S, HANES, BURLINGTON, DUOFOLD, VASSARETTE, and CALVIN KLEIN. Women's pantyhose is their main claim to fame, though. Thirty-day exchange or refund period.

**COMFORTABLY YOURS**
**61 West Hunter Avenue**
**Maywood, NJ 07607**
**201-368-0400**
**201-587-1875 (FAX)**
**MC,V,AE,DC,CB,CK,COD**
**C $1**

So many unique and intriguing items, we don't know where to start—or where to stop, so hold onto your hat and bring your shopping list! Lovely lingerie in unusual sizes (30A–48FF), like all CY clothing, chosen with a view toward beauty as well as comfortable fit and in sizes that range from petite to misses to women's, with some large petites. Shoe selections include German-made SPIERS shoes and boots with removable arch supports. Can't bend down to put on those shoes and socks? A frustrating problem solved by the Sock and Shoe

Aid that doubles as a long-handled bath sponge! Not enough room for a recliner? Check out the FOLDAWAY RECLINER that folds compactly when not in use. Like Goldilocks, want a cushion that's "not too soft, not too hard"? Try the PRINCESS AND THE PEA floatation cushion that makes sitting for long periods of time easy. Just a quick mention of some other one-of-a-kind items: fire-escape ladder ready for instant use, oversized watch, volume-boost phone, biocurve pens for comfortable writing, mink-oil hand and foot cream, and a folding reacher that makes your arm longer. Gift certificates available. Money-back guarantee.

**COTTONFIELDS/SUNDANCE**
**215 Forest Avenue**
**Laguna Beach, CA 92651**
**800-444-2383; 714-494-3002 (in CA)**
**MC,V**
**C**

Californians have counted on Sundance for the 100 percent cotton clothing by "Property of" for years. Their promise—"You shrink it, we'll buy it back"—provides a sure-fit guarantee that it'll fit forever. Now you, too, can shop for savings via their catalog of great, casual, and easy clothing with elasticized drawstring waists, back pockets, deep-cut front pockets, shorts, pants, and more. Unisex shorts, bermudas, pants, pullovers, tops, and jackets with an easy-to-read sizing chart. All items made in the USA. For shopping fantasies, don't miss their "talking tops." Shopasauraus Ts or sweatshirts, and the popular aerobisaurus, jogasaurus, anglerasaurus and partysaurus for appropriate devotees, $13–$26. Also the fun talking pillows: "I love you! Prove it!" or "I have a headache . . . I have an aspirin . . ."

**D & A MERCHANDISE CO.**
**22 Orchard St.**
**New York, NY 10002**
**212-925-4766**
**MC,V**
**C $2 (one time fee), PQ**

The Underwear King, Elliott Kivell, has had more than a brief reign—since 1946. Save 25 percent on men's and women's robes, lingerie, and underwear for men, women, and boys. Stellar performers that have held up over the years include LILY OF FRANCE, MAIDENFORM, BALI, VASSARETTE, FORMIT ROGERS. Men can jockey into place with BURLINGTON, CHRISTIAN DIOR, and JOCKEY. Bra sizes to 48 and panties to size 12 should keep the world at large covered.

**DEERSKIN PLACE**
**283 Akron Road**
**Ephrata, PA 17522**
**717-733-7624**
**MC,V,CK,COD**
**B,PQ**

Those who don't run with the herd can let their fingers do the stalking through this brochure. You can fawn over jackets, coats, handbags, shoes, moccasins, sheepskin coats and jackets, gloves and wallets for men and women at 30 to 50 percent off retail. (Talk about saving some bucks! Bargains like that belong on our trophy rack.) Interest is mounting since there is no minimum order and no restocking charge on returns, although there is an exchange-only policy (no refunds). Satisfaction guaranteed.

*Great Buys* readers: Take an additional 10 percent off all merchandise.

## DEMESY AND COMPANY
**5650 North Riverside Drive**
**Fort Worth, TX 76137**
**800-635-9006**

Time is money when you can receive $50 to $50,000 for your vintage wrist watches or pocket watches. Joe DeMesy is looking for antique pocket and wrist watches from the 1900s to 1960s and will pay premium prices for certain types of watches, including moonphase, chronograph (stopwatch), world time, pilot's watches, and watches with a chiming feature. Condition is not important, and offers are based on rarity, maker, and features. Call for a free appraisal Monday through Friday, 9–5 P.M. CST.

## DESIGNER DIRECT, DESIGNS FOR LESS
**Designer Circle**
**Salem, VA 24156-0501**
**800-848-2929**
**MC,V,AE,D,CK,MO**
**C**

Fashion plus fit plus footwear equal savings of up to 60 percent below retail. Shop direct and get fashion first in a full size range (to 18), and choose accessories (belts, bags, jewelry and shoes to size 11½) to complement the look. Lots of contemporary looks for the price, plus easy-fit fashions with lots of elasticized waists or one-size-fits-all. Everything's there to make shopping a breeze. Satisfaction guaranteed and the option of Federal Express overnight delivery, for an extra $5, if you've got a last-minute date.

**DORSETT DISTRIBUTING CO.**
11866 Dorsett Rd.
Maryland Heights, MO 63043
314-291-8565
MC,V,CK
PQ

This Dorsett wins a Tony in the category of men's first-quality suits and sportswear at prices huddling at 30 to 50 percent less than retail. Pinstripes, herringbones, tweeds, solids, plaids, and sharkskin (sorry, no pigskin) line up with a roster of first-string manufacturers. Designer shoes at 25 to 30 percent off in sizes 5 to 16, AAAA to EEE widths. Custom shirts, too. Call for price quote and complete money-back guarantee.

**DR. LEONARD'S HEALTH CARE CATALOG**
74 20th Street
Brooklyn, NY 11232
C

This source for shoes is designed for people with swollen feet or postoperative conditions. Each front lifts to desired height and width, achieving a custom fit. The shoe (for men and women) itself looks like suede but is really machine-washable and comes in black or brown.

**F. R. KNITTING MILLS, INC.**
P.O. Box 4360
Flint Station
69 Alden St.
Fall River, MA 01723-4360
800-446-1089; 508-678-7553 (in MA)
MC,V,CK
C

Straight from this 75-year-old historic New England manufacturer of fine sweaters, pants, skirts, and coordinated separates, bundle up and save a bundle at the same time. Tradition at its best and made to perfection fit, this factory guarantees to keep you warm, as well as completely satisfied. No questions asked, whatever your reason for wishing to return your purchase. Simply return for an immediate refund or exchange. Latch onto savings of 30 to 50 percent for the entire family, with selections available in a rainbow of colors.

**GELBER'S MENSWEAR**
**1001 Washington Avenue**
**St. Louis, MO 63101**
**314-421-6698**
**MC,V,AE,COD**
**PQ**

The inventory of discounted men's clothing changes weekly at this 94-year-old St. Louis–based company. Everything's first quality and discounted 20 to 70 percent off regular prices. Current styles are available in names such as ADOLFO, OLEG CASSINI, HAMMONTON PARK, RAFFINATTI, and PHILLIPE GABRIEL. Factory overruns and salesmen's samples are available at very low prices. They do alterations at little or no charge. Customers usually receive their orders in about ten days.

For readers of *Great Buys*, take an extra 20 percent off their already discounted prices.

**GOLDMAN & COHEN, INC.**
**55 Orchard Street**
**New York, NY 10002**
**800-356-2090; 212-966-0737 (in NY)**
**PQ**

Women's underwear, including intimate apparel by BALI, BARBIZON, CARNIVAL, CHRISTIAN DIOR, LILYETTE, MAIDENFORM,

PLAYTEX, VANITY FAIR, WARNER'S, and other well-known designers and manufacturers. Hard-to-find sizes available, as well as HANES pantyhose. Also a full line of sleepwear. They ship worldwide.

**HANOVER SHOE COMPANY**
**118 Carlisle Street**
**Hanover, PA 17331**
**800-426-3708**
**MC,V,AE,DC,CB,CK,MO**
**C $1**

Men can snare a shoe or two and save about 25 percent from this almost 100-year-old company. Through the 32 pages of their four-color catalog, Hanover's shoes are a shoe-in to other more famous brands. In sizes 6 to 15, widths from AA to EEE, even the most finicky feet can get covered. From classic calfskin brogues, wing-tips, or Oxfords to sportier lizard slip-ons, deerskin golfshoes, or walking shoes by CLARK, NEW BALANCE, or SPERRY, men's feet at last can be neat and cheap!

**HARVARD TROUSER CO.**
**P.O. Box 217**
**2191 S. Main St.**
**Pittsford, MI 49271**
**517-523-2167**
**COD**
**B**

Factory-direct car coats, jackets, and washable and insulated nylon outerwear ride out at less than retail for women in sizes 8 to 34. Men, too, brake for jackets, hunting garb, duck workclothes and snowmobile suits in small to XXXXX-large. Since 1926, this all-American factory is as time-honored as the Model A.

**HTC COAT FACTORY**
**4731 South Main Street**
**P.O. Box 217**
**Pittsford, MI 49271**
**517-523-2167**
**CK,MO**
**B**

Direct-from-the-factory prices with no middleman make these coats the perfect cover for cold-weather activities. HTC Coat Factory specializes in coats that are lightweight and washable in a wide range of sizes. All materials are made in the USA and the coats are manufactured at the Pittsford plant. Add $2.95 for shipping and handling.

*Great Buys* readers: Take off an extra 10 percent discount.

**ISAAC SULTAN & SONS**
**332 Grand Street**
**New York, NY 10002**
**800-999-1645; 212-979-1645 (in NY)**

Suck in your stomach for the good old-fashioned girdles like SMOOTHIS and RAGO, or stretch your savings in hard-to-find bras like 100 percent cotton DO-ALL.

Seniors demand the best for less, according to our man at Isaac Sultan & Sons and for *Great Buys* readers, you can expect an additional 20 percent discount. Cross my heart.

**I. TUSCHMAN & SONS, INC.**
61 Orchard St.
New York, NY 10002
212-226-4318
CK,MC,V
PQ

Everything for the tush and more. Family fun and flair with fantastic prices on namebrand underwear, sleepwear, shirts, jeans, socks, sweaters, and more, at up to 35 percent off. Brands cover the spectrum, from DR. DENTON'S and CARTER'S for the kids to BVD, HANES, and FRUIT OF THE LOOM for men. One of the few places to get the original Grand Slam golf shirts by MUNSINGWEAR, and the size range offered is gigantic (to size 60 and XL to XXXXX). Call or write for price quote.

**JUST RIGHT!**
30 Rozer Road
P.O. Box 1020
Beverly, MA 01915-0720
800-767-6666
MC,V,AE,D
C

Fashions for females sizes 14 and up by Appleseed's doesn't come cheap, but what price, fashion! This beautiful four-color, 40-page catalog can dress you up in designer duds in sizes 14W to 24W (or 1X to 4X), all with the convenience of one-stop shopping, toll free.

**THE KING SIZE COMPANY**
**24 Forest St.**
**Brockton, MA 02402**
**800-343-9678; 617-580-0500 (in MA)**
**MC,V,AE**
**C**

King-size men, whether tall or large, should not have to pay king-size prices for their clothing. Pants in sizes 44 to 60, shirts 17 to 22, are priced within 10 percent of what a 5'8" man would pay. Private labels are previewed, as well as brands such as JOCKEY, PALM BEACH, BOTANY 500, HAGGAR and LONDON FOG. Unconditional guarantee with free catalogs and twice-yearly sale catalogs.

**LAND'S END**
**Land's End Lane**
**Dodgeville, WI 53595-0001**
**800-356-4444; 608-935-2788 (in WI)**
**MC,V,AE,CK**
**C**

A landmark whose never-ending battlecry is value with a capital *V*. And consider them victorious. Winning the war on high prices and quality craftsmanship, Land's End offers traditional quality and 100 percent natural fiber products fit for family fun. Their mainstay of classic shirts, skirts, and pants include the broadloom spectrum of sensible madras, rugby and polo shirts, twill pants, tote bags, shorts, jackets, docksiders, and now, domestics and childrenswear, mate. Satisfaction guaranteed no matter what, or a complete refund. Get onboard their mailing list for a never-ending cotillion of clever and well-priced catalogs.

**LANE BRYANT**
**P.O. Box 8301**
**Indianapolis, IN 46283-8301**
**317-266-3311**
**MC,V,AE**
**C**

For the fuller, but fashion-conscious, female, try on Lane Bryant for size. From bend-over, pull-on pants to oversized, one-size-fits-all, Lane Bryant can get you covered. Choose casual or evening wear, sleepwear or loungewear. And special support is found in both garments and hosiery. For value and quality in fuller-figure sizes, along with selection and service, shop Lane Bryant by mail. Apply for a Lane Bryant charge card and you may be eligible for $250 immediate credit. Don't forget to ask about "telephone specials." Order 24 hours a day, 7 days a week. Most orders are shipped the next day, and shipping and handling are free. Every purchase is unconditionally guaranteed.


**LEE-McCLAIN COMPANY**
**U.S. Highway 60 West**
**Rt. 6, Box 381A**
**Shelbyville, KY 40065**
**502-633-3823**
**MC,V,CK**
**PQ,B**

Fifty-plus years manufacturing its own line of mens' STRATH-MORE suits and sportswear (and other private labels), is sold direct at a savings of 40 to 60 percent over comparable designer brands. An occasional blazer for women is available, though the majority are mens' sizes 36 to 50 in extra-long, long, regular, and short. Just send them your suit size, and they'll send you fabric swatches to choose from. Among the Derby favorites were 100 percent camel's hair sportscoats, navy blazers, and pinstripe suits.

## MARSHALLS
## 800-MARSHALLS

Since 1956, the Marshall plan has been taking the country by storm. Today they are the biggest and one of the best off-price chains linking Americans to the concept of name brands for less. Save 20 to 50 percent (and sometimes more) on a department-store selection of men's, women's, and children's apparel, jewelry, cosmetics, accessories, lingerie, shoes and bags, gifts, and bed and bath items. Larger sizes are not forgotten, either, in their Woman's World collection. A one-stop emporium for an economical statement, where the bottom line is savings without sacrificing style, selection, or service. Call 1-800-MARSHALLS or write to their corporate headquarters (200 Brickstone Square, Andover, MA 01810) for the store nearest you.

## L'EGGS SHOWCASE OF SAVINGS
**P.O. Box 748**
**Rural Hall, NC 27098-1010**
**800-522-1151**
**MC,V,CK**
**C**

Slightly imperfect L'EGGS pantyhose, HANES underwear and socks for men and boys, and UNDERALLS and SLENDERALLS round up the perfectly wonderful savings of up to 50 percent. Sock away the difference, you'll surely have a leg up on your neighbors. Colorful catalogs feature style and size charts for ease in ordering, and you'll even know if you'll be getting a first-quality or an irregular item.

**MATURE WISDOM**
P.O. Box 28
Hanover, PA 17333-0023
800-638-6366
MC,V,AE,D,DC,DB
C $2

Grow old gracefully and in style as this catalog exemplifies. Page after page, you'll see fashions that fit the fuller figure or that fit for comfort, products that make for healthier and easier living, products for the traveling man or his pet, products for the home front and more. Also, there's an exercise bike with a seat that is easy on the rear end, soft-knit shoes with orthopedic arch supports, a take-your-own blood pressure kit, an anti-wrinkle facial pillow, or a four-wheel cart for groceries. If you're a smart shopper and are blessed with mature wisdom, you'll shop by phone and save both time and money. (See also under Gifts and Gadgets.)

Receive 10 percent off your first order just by identifying yourself as a *Great Buys* reader.

**MENDEL WEISS**
91 Orchard Street
New York, NY 10002
212-925-6815; 212-226-9104
B

T-shirts and women's underwear, boasting designers such as BALI, BARBIZON, CHRISTIAN DIOR, FORMFIT, ROGERS, HALSTON, LILYETTE, MAIDENFORM, OLGA, PLAYTEX, WARNER'S, and others. All name-brand T-shirts are available here. Call or write with style numbers to see if the item you want is in stock, and you can also ask about Mendel Weiss's own line of T-shirts and T-shirt dresses, in pure cotton and cotton-poly blends.

**MINNETONKA-BY-MAIL**
**P.O. Box 444A**
**Bronx, NY 10458**
**C $1**

Get the real thing—Minnetonka moccasins and casual footwear for the whole family—at prices comparable to and sometimes lower than the knock-offs seen in local stores each summer. Minnetonka produces several interpretations of the fringed and tied moccasins with beaded "Thunderbird" design, with choice of sole type (crepe, boat, soft and polyurethane, etc.) A 16-page catalog shows off a variety of boots, booties, and mocs at prices from about $11 to $70.

**MS., MISS, AND MRS.**
**462 Seventh Ave (35th St.)**
**(Enter 3rd Floor)**
**New York, NY 10018**
**800-223-6101; 212-736-0557 (in NY)**
**MC,V,AE,CK,MO**

Seventh heaven is on seventh avenue whether you're a Ms., Miss, or Mrs. Almost 500 designer labels in sportswear, dresses, coats and suits are bursting at the seams on two floors which are at least ⅓ off retail in sizes 4–20. Call or write with a magazine photo, an item you've tried on at a retail store, or your favorite label, and I bet they've got it (or will order it for you). Periodic year-long sales will net enough savings to even pay for a flight to New York City. They'll mail your order.

**NATIONAL WHOLESALE COMPANY**
**Hosiery Division**
**400 National Blvd.**
**Lexington, NC 27294**
**704-249-0211**
**CK,MC,V,AE,MO**
**C**

Ever get caught in the "not so tender" trap of spending good money for bad hosiery? Ones that run the minute you walk in them or worse, that sag in all the wrong places. Stop spending hard-earned money on pantyhose that are not worth two cents! National offers a guaranteed personal fit program along with big savings of up to 50 percent. No imperfects or supermarket-type hose, either. Thigh thinners and even "walkin' " socks are also available. So, if you'd like to test-wear hosiery that's "tailor-made" for you—for anybody and everybody—try the National way. All orders are shipped within 24 hours and sold with an absolute money-back guarantee.

Free laundry bag to readers of *Great Buys* with first order. Just identify yourself.


**OKUN BROTHERS SHOES**
**356 East South Street**
**Kalamazoo, MI 49007**
**800-433-6344**
**MC,V,D,CK,MO**
**C**

Get a jump on fashion and put your best-foot-forward for less. Okun's beautiful four-color catalog can complete your feet in name brands for men and women like DEXTER, SOFT SPOTS, ROCKPORT, MINNETONKA MOCCASINS, GRASSHOPPERS, REEBOK, PROWALKER, HUSH PUPPIES, ALLEN EDMONDS, CLARKS, ROCKY, SOREL, LA GEAR, EASY SPIRIT—yes, the list of stellar shoes can carry you for miles. Comfort is the name of the game where savings will never pinch your pocketbook (or your toes). Women's sizes 5–12 in slim, narrow, medium, wide, and x-wide widths; men's sizes 6–16 in AA, B, D, EE, and EEEE.


**ONE SHOE CREW**
**86 Clavela Avenue**
**Sacramento, CA 95828**

There's no business like this shoe business for amputees, anyone with a brace on one foot, different sized feet, clubfoot, or anyone with one-sided foot problems who still wears one regular shoe. The One Shoe Crew helps people in finding partners to share the high cost of shoes. No cost to register for this service, but a small fee is charged when a partner is found. Include the following information when writing: your name, address, telephone number, shoe size, width, and an idea of what you're looking for.


**PAGANO GLOVES, INC.**
**3-5 Church Street**
**Johnstown, NY 12095-2196**
**518-762-8425**
**MC,V,CK,COD**
**C $2.50 refundable**

Let your fingers do the walking, snug in their deerskin leather gloves, and at Pagano's, they'll find coats, jackets, accessories, leather attaché cases, handbags, slippers and moccasins, and even knit hats. Plus billfolds, key cases, tobacco pouches, and handbags, in addition to those wonderful deerskin gloves for the whole family. Custom sizes, linings, and links available at reasonable prices. Exchanges only; no refunds. Shipping is $3 per order, and orders usually arrive in two to three weeks.

Mention that you are a *Great Buys* reader, and get 1990 prices for 1991—a 10 percent savings. The $2.50 catalog fee is refundable with your first order.

**PATAGONIA**
**1609 West Babcock Street**
**P.O. Box 8900**
**Bozeman, MT 59715-2046**
**800-638-6464; 800-523-9597**
**MC,V,AE,CK,MO**
**C**

This scrumptious mail order catalog commits 10 percent of its pre-tax profits to preserving and restoring the environment. Isn't that a breath of fresh air? Furthermore, Patagonia's casual sporting clothing (for men, women and children) is made to last more than a few lifetimes. Their products are useful, long-lasting and lightweight. They will carry you through the coldest of climates, the slopes, a brisk morning walk, or a wind-blown sail in the Caribbean. Face masks, gloves and socks complete the fashion wardrobe of jackets, shirts, pants, and sweaters. They even invite spirited photographers to submit their 35mm slides for use in their catalog (and will pay a fee, if used).

**PE & CO.**
**1812 Main Street**
**Dallas, TX 75201**
**800-899-COAT (2628); 214-653-1993 (in Dallas)**
**MC,V,AE,DC,CB,CK**
**PQ**

The Smith brothers, Jeff and Mitch, take the bite out of coughing up full prices on men's clothing (suits, sportscoats, and trousers—period). You won't sneeze at their service, either. When you deserve the very best, they see to it that they live up to their promise of being one of the country's finest men's discounter. They offer year-round savings of 20 to 50 percent. They don't claim 70 to 90 percent discounts, simply because the best cannot be sold at those prices. What they sell is QUALITY at a price. And that's their guarantee.

**PREMIERE EDITIONS**
**Hanover, PA 17333-0012**
**800-822-9982 (7 days a week, 24 hours a day)**
**Major credit cards**
**C $2**

Contemporary, casual, and chic plus comfort adds up to a full complement of ladieswear available seven days a week. Shoes, jewelry, lingerie—all inexpensively priced for the perfect pairing of apparel and accessories in this value-wise shopping source. Misses 8 to 18 plus larger sizes can have their cake and wear it, too. On the other hand, if the urge to splurge strikes you at 2 A.M., think about a new dress as your "just dessert."

**RAYMOND SULTAN & SONS, LTD.**
**47 Orchard Street**
**New York, NY 10002**
**212-966-3488**
**PQ**

Raymond Sultan & Sons are a study in undercover work. Brassieres in sizes 32A to 50DD win applause from a broad audience. Current and discontinued styles are granted rave reviews. If you know your lines, you'll score 20 percent on lingerie by BALI, MAIDENFORM and a crowd of others. Their supporting cast includes a large selection of black bras and girdles. Send a postcard giving manufacturer, style number, size and color to receive a price quote.

**REBORN MATERNITY**
1449 Third Avenue
New York, NY 10028
(212) 737-8817
MC,V,AE,CK
C $2

Granted, getting pregnant may be the last thing on your mind, but what about your daughter? Or those with fuller figures, have you ever considered maternity clothes as a fabulous fashion option replacing those boring and unstylish half-size outfits still hanging limp in your closet? Minimum orders by mail (even to the stars who shop here) are $20 and you can bet your sweet bippy it won't take 9 months to deliver. Savings to 40 percent on moderate to better sportswear and eveningwear.

*Great Buys* readers get an additional 5 percent off on any purchase.

**RED FLANNEL FACTORY**
73 South Main
P.O. Box 370
Cedar Springs, MI 49319
616-696-9240
C

Nostalgic seniors can turn their clocks back to 1949. The Red Flannel Factory first produced their now-famous pajamas, undergarments, robes and shirts in white and red for the entire family (even the dog). Now past forty, but still going strong, their outlet offers their entire line at 20 to 30 percent less than retail. Write for free catalog and curl up and save right.

**ROAMAN'S**
**P.O. Box 8301**
**Indianapolis, IN 46283-8301**
**800-338-3606 (24 hours); 317-266-8099 (Customer**
   **Service)**
**MC,V,AE,CK**
**C**

Comfort, casual, and chic converge in the 78-page color catalog of mature and large-size fashions. Discounts are interspersed throughout this value-packed and often name-brand array of sportswear, swimwear, lingerie, shoes, dresses, and suits, all with you in mind. Don't leave home without it!

**ROBY'S INTIMATES**
**1905 Samson Street**
**Philadelphia, PA 19103**
**800-878-BRAS**
**MC,V,CK**
**PQ, (SASE),B,C $1**

Roby's is a firm supporter of over 50 brands of lingerie including MAIDENFORM, LILY OF FRANCE, VASSARETTE, LADY MARLENE, FORMFIT, EVE STILLMAN, DANSKIN and many imports. Sizes range from 28AA to 46F and all are first quality. Pantyhose are discounted 20 to 50 percent and Roby's is definitely tops on our list when it comes to underwear, bras, girdles, lingerie, robes, and nightgowns. No returns on special-order merchandise, worn, torn or soiled items or items with the tags removed. $2.50 shipping and handling. SASE for brochure and send manufacturer and style number for price quote.

*Great Buys* readers discount: an additional 5 percent off on any order over $100.

**ROSS STORES**
8333 Central Ave.
Newark, CA 94560
800-345-ROSS; 415-790-4400 (in CA)

A "Dress for Less" success story began in 1982, and with the first chapter was coined the slogan "Why pay department-store prices?" This department-store-size selection of family apparel, accessories, cosmetics, gifts, and more is in store, where 20 to 60 percent off is the everyday bottom line. Call or write to the corporate offices for the store nearest you.

**SAINT LAURIE LTD.**
**Mail Order Department**
**897 Broadway at 20th St.**
**New York, NY 10003**
**800-221-8660; 212-473-0100 (in NY)**
**CK,MC,V,AE**
**C (Swatch Club Membership $10/year:**
   **2 seasons, Fall and Spring)**

Classic looks for men and women in prices ranging from $350 to $475 from the saint's heavenly collection. Top-of-the-line tweeds, silks, midweight wools, linens, cashmeres, worsted wool and camel's hair are crafted and normally delivered in about a week. If you'd rather switch and save, their swatches come twice a year, so you can touch and try before you buy. If you're visiting New York City, factory tours are conducted Monday through Friday from 9 to 4.

**THE S & B REPORT**
112 East 36 Street
New York, NY 10016
212-679-5400

This monthly report of Sales and Bargains (S & B) lists designer showroom sample sales in, where else but the fashion capital of the world, New York City. Accessories and current season clothing, though often limited in selection and size, are sold at prices 50 to 80 percent off. Single issues of the report are available at $5 or on an annual subscription basis for $40 per year. Each report provides all the basics: location, phone, hours, description of items available, sizes, discounts offered, and accepted method of payment.

## SERENDIPITY
**Palo Verde at 34th St.**
**P.O. Box 27800**
**Tucson, AZ 85726-7800**
**800-362-8400 (credit card orders)**

A coordinated catalog of missy and fuller fashions and accessories will tempt even the most tight-fisted clotheshound. Sportswear, career dresses, shoes, after-five, and jewelry complement each of the 36 color pages. Proportioned pants (in petites, too), wearable works of art, lingerie, and more in sizes S–XL, 8–20, and some X-tra sizes. Even fashion dunces have it made page by page, as your eyes focus on the accessories that pull each look together.

## SILHOUETTES
**340 Poplar Street**
**Hanover, PA 17333-3333**
**800-852-2822 (7 days a week, 24 hours a day)**
**C $2**

No, you're not seeing too many 3s. There's a lot of them in their zip code, but your fingers shouldn't tire as you let them do the walking through the pages of this plus-size catalog. Inexpensive women's full-figure apparel with P-jazz including dresses, sportswear, pant suits, and lingerie, all accompanied by dazzling companion accessories like earrings, hats, and shoes to complete the picture. Colorful and sized for easy on and easy care. Their size chart guarantees a perfect fit.

**THE SMART SAVER**
**P.O. Box 105-H**
**Wasco, IL 60183**
**CK,MO**
**C**

Save up to 30 percent from this almost ten-year family-owned business selling bras, girdles, and other female foundation garments guaranteed to give you more than 18-hour support. Write for their free illustrated catalog that also provides a girdle size guide to shopping that is firmly one of their mainstays.

**SOCKS GALORE & MORE**
**220 Second Avenue South**
**P.O. Box 1515**
**Franklin, TN 37064**
**800-626-SOCK; 615-790-SOCK (collect in TN)**
**MC,V,CK,MO**
**C**

Plant savings up to 80 percent on socks for the entire family. Over 1,200 styles are available through their over 40 outlet stores across the country, with the most popular styles featured in their catalog. From CHRISTIAN DIOR and the WORLD'S SOFTEST SOCK to BURLINGTON'S line of hosiery, you can foot the bill for men, women, and children, in support and sport styles, tube socks, all-cotton ones as well as blends, argyles, personalized, and thick ones for outdoor blizzards. So stop paying through the nose for your feet.

**SOFSOLE**
**800-333-7680**

Pamper your feet with SOFSOLE insoles, like no other insole on the market. Your money refunded within 30 days of purchase if not completely satisfied. Call for more information or to place an order.

**THE SOLE SOURCE**
**8400 A Hilltop Road**
**Fairfax, VA 22031**
**800-82-RESOLE (800-827-3765)**
**MC,V,CK,MO**
**B**

If you have concrete feet weighted down with heavy old shoes (leather, casual, or workshoes), pack them off to The Sole Source and they'll send your shoes back with new, lightweight comfort soles. Basic service includes resoling, new laces, cleaning and polishing uppers, minor repairs of eyelet and upper stitching as necessary ($30). The Shoe Source is the only authorized Rockport shoe repair facility in North America.

**SPIEGEL**
**1040 W. 35th St.**
**Chicago, IL 60609-1494**
**800-345-4500 (charge orders)**
**708-954-2772 (customer service)**
**708-954-3379 (accounting/to open a charge)**
**MC,V,AE,SPIEGEL CHARGE**

Fall asleep counting sheets and savings and everything else you buy for bedtime, clothestime, playtime, or worktime. Shop catalogs from Spiegel, the grand dame of all mail-order catalog shopping, which now boasts an entire collection of specialty catalogs: FOR YOU, 56 pp., women's sizes 12W–26W, $2; PROPORTION PETITE, READY TO WEAR (ready to unwind), 56 pp., sizes 2–14 for the under 5'4", $2; MEN, 36 pp., $2; comfortable clothes for men and women, 84 pp., $2; TOGETHER, exclusive but affordable designs that you won't see yourself cloned all over town in, 48 pp., $2; and THE ULTIMATE OUTLET, offering, as its name implies, an avalanche of top-of-the-line and private labels at rock-bottom prices from their "big books." All fees for catalogs are refunded with purchase.

**SUNGLASSES USA**
**469 Sunrise Highway**
**Lynbrook, NY 11563**
**800-USA-RAYS (800-872-7297)**
**MC,V,AE**
**C**

See the USA and more through these rose-colored sunglasses and see clearly ⅓ less than retail. For years, RAY-BAN has been *the* fashion choice for shady ladies and men who want to look chic in the sun without squinting. Their 50th anniversary classics (the famed aviators from WWII and General McArthur's trademark) and the "classic metals" that are soundly engineered and meticulously crafted for rugged wear should be some of your favorites-for-less.

For readers of *Great Buys*, take an additional 10 percent off the printed wholesale price.

**SWEETWATER HOSIERY MILLS/SOCK SHOP**
**P.O. Box 390**
**Sweetwater, TN 37874**
**615-337-9203**
**B, C**

This almost-centenarian manufacturer (established in 1896) socks it to you at their outlet store or through their catalog. Save at least 30 percent on made-in-the-USA women's and girls' pantyhose; queen sizes, control tops, support styles, knee highs, bobby socks—just about anything that's fit for the feet. Men have a selection of socks, briefs, boxers, and T-shirts, too. Write for free brochure and catalog.

Readers can sock off an additional 10 percent at their outlet, the Sock Shop, or by mail simply by identifying themselves as a *Great Buys* reader.

**T.J. MAXX**
**770 Chochituate Rd.**
**Framingham, MA 01701**
**508-390-2000**
**MC,V,AE,D,CK**

Getting the maxx for the minimum has been the buyword of this off-price giant since 1976. Big savings (20–60 percent), big selection, big names in the department-store business, and big on service. From apparel for the entire family, designer fragrances, giftware, shoes and bags, domestics—if you close your eyes and wish for closets full of dreams (with discounts), the magic carpet ride would stop at a T.J. Maxx. Call or write for the location nearest you.

**WILLOW RIDGE**
**421 Landmark Dr.**
**Wilmington, NC 28410**
**919-763-6500**
**MC, V, AE**
**C**

A store that never closes gets high marks in my book. Misses' fashions to size 20, including petites, are covered in versatile and inexpensive fashions from the golf course to the club. Everything's on sale from the first page to the last. Choose from tops, bottoms, sportswear, dresses, and cover-ups, and your budget will not go bust. Everything's under $50.

# APPLIANCES, TVS, AND ELECTRONICS

**C.O.M.B.**
**1405 Xenium Lane North**
**Plymouth, MN 55441-4494**
**800-328-0609**
**MC,V,AE**
**C**

You could scour the country with a fine-tooth comb and still not unearth a better bargain than you would right here. Savings of 50 percent is commonplace on major appliances, housewares, stereos, TVs, phones, computer hardware, exercise equipment, and car accessories. Monthly catalogs arrive in your mailbox, including an insider's hotline with special deals.

**DAMARK**
**6707 Shingle Creek Parkway**
**Minneapolis, MN 55430**
**800-729-9000; 612-566-4940 (Customer service)**
**MC,V,D**
**C $3**

The "Great Deal" catalog is virtually close-out heaven. The full spectrum of namebrand savings from 30, 60, 70, 80, even 90 percent (read product descriptions carefully, as a few select items are factory reconditioned). Speaker phones from COBRA (Reg. $129 for $39.99), stereo systems with CDs from CASIO ($999 for $599.99), REGINA vacuums ($211.99 for $99.95), electronic heat massager ($59.99 for $39.99), graphite shaft golf clubs ($660 for $399), BUSHNELL binoculars ($159.95 for $69.99), luggage, tool chests, car alarms, MR. MEAT smokers, apartment-size washer and dryers, picnic baskets and more. Watch for full page ads in *USA Today* for products to purchase direct without the catalog.

**DIAL-A-BRAND, INC.**
**110 Bedford Avenue**
**Bellmore, NY 11710**
**516-378-9694**
**CK,MC,V**
**PQ**

Dial-a-Brand offers name-brand major appliances, microwaves, TVs, air-conditioners, and more. Just call them up and give the make and model number of the item requested. With large appliances, the savings can sometimes be eroded by the shipping, so do request a price quote that includes freight.

**FOCUS ELECTRONICS**
**1225 39th Street**
**Brooklyn, NY 11218**
**800-223-3411; 718-871-7600 (in NY)**
**C $2/PQ**

Focus on savings from 10 to 50 percent on all makes and models of electronics and electrics—from computers to can openers. Savings range loud and clear in their stereo systems, TVs and VCRs, microwaves, and small appliances. Brand names aplenty, from APPLE to ZENITH. Free catalog with any purchase and bonus gifts with selected items.

**MARYMAC INDUSTRIES, INC.**
22511 Katy Freeway
Katy, TX 77450
800-231-3680 (Orders); 713-392-0747 (in TX)
MC,V,AE,CK
PQ

Compute this: Marymac promises to beat any legitimate advertised price that has brand-name new computer merchandise. Tell them what your computer needs are and receive a free price quote. They pay freight and insurance. Then, use your new computer for home shopping!

*Great Buys* readers: Save 15 percent or more on all Tandy items.

**RADIO SHACK**
Department 083-03
300 One Tandy Center
Fort Worth, TX. 76102
C

Big buttons and built-in amplifiers, all at beautiful prices! Radio Shack's ET-203 telephone has big buttons for easy dialing and an amplifier to boost incoming voices. It is hearing-aid compatible and has handy features, such as hold, redial, and switchable tone for use on any line—cost $49.95. Write for free catalog.

**WISCONSIN DISCOUNT STEREO**
2417 West Badger Road
Madison, WI 53713
800-356-9514; 608-271-6889 (in WI)
MC,V,MO

Calling all audio and stereo aficionados, for nowhere else is there such an extensive inventory of sound and sight equipment. Every brand name fit to print: ADC, AIWA, BOSE, DBS, JBL, JENSEN, JVC, KENWOOD, MARANTZ, NEC, SONY TECHNICS, and more. Savings can soar to 70 percent, but middle of the road is around 35 percent. Wisconsin even guarantees the lowest delivery charge on most items.

# AUTOMOBILE BROKERS

**AMERICAN AUTO BROKERS**
**24001 Southfield Road #110**
**Southfield, MI 48075**
**313-569-5900**
**CK,MO**

Mel Palmer and his brokering crew negotiate deals nation-wide. You can save from $150 to $4,000, depending upon how much margin there is and whether or not the car is in demand. A firm quote in writing costs $3. American Auto Brokers deals in all makes and models, domestic and foreign, as well as trucks and vans. Order is placed upon receipt of deposit, which is refundable if order is cancelled within 72 hours. Delivery to any dealership in the country includes manufacturers' warranty and takes about six weeks. Be sure to have specific information on models and options when placing your order.

Additional $50 discount from usual low-discounted prices for *Great Buys* readers with proof of senior status.

**KEN TOMPOR AUTO BROKER**
**4140 S. Lapeer Rd.**
**Orion, MI 48057**
**313-373-8010; out of Detroit area, call collect**

Ken Tompor, the long-established pro of wheeling and dealing, is your *personalized* car broker connection. A legitimate $50 over dealer invoice on any car can be delivered to you anywhere as quickly as 24 hours. Most custom orders take 4–6 weeks, however, and come equipped with all factory warranties and service guarantees. The only difference is you haven't paid for the dealer's expensive overhead, advertising costs, or salesmen's commissions, but you do pay for the car, period. No hassle, no computer price quotes to pay for, be it a FORD or a FERRARI. Specialty cars are fast replacing art as the collector's choice for investment appreciation—also a specialty service at Ken Tompor Auto Broker Company.

Free price quotes to all readers.

**NATIONWIDE AUTO BROKERS, INC.**
**17517 West 10 Mile Road**
**Southfield, MI 48075**
**800-521-7257; 313-559-6661**
**MC,V,CK**
**PQ**

In business for well over 20 years, Nationwide Auto Brokers is one of the largest and best-known car brokerage firms (trucks and vans, too). Nationwide charges $50 to $125 over factory invoice on American-made cars and $125 to $300 on most foreign makes (certain cars are not available). Most deposits are $100, but on some cars it could go as high as $500. Price quotes are FOB Detroit or delivered to your local dealer. All come with a factory warranty. A friendly staff will be happy to answer your questions over the phone.

# BANKING, FINANCE, AND INSURANCE

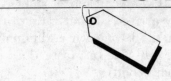

## Special Banking Programs for Those over 55

Today, banks are beginning to recognize the loyalty and buying power in a very special and dedicated group of customers—the 55+. Most banks have recently developed additional services that help seniors benefit even more, from low minimum requirements on checking accounts to organized travel groups. The Emerald Club membership at select First Interfirst banks, for example, offers exclusive benefits such as:

- Free interest-bearing checking accounts
- Preferred rates on CD's
- 50 percent off safe deposit rentals
- Special interest rates on most consumer loans
- Special trips for travelers over 55

Programs vary, so contact your local bank for more information.

## Rating the Banks

Before you put your money in a bank or savings and loan, call Veribanc, 1-800-442-2657, to find out how safe your money is. If you want more detailed information on how they arrived at that rating, it'll cost $10 for the first bank, $3 for each additional bank, and it is charged to your Visa or MasterCard (hopefully from a bank that's solid).

## Rating the Insurance Companies

Send $3 to The Insurance Forum, Box 245W, Ellettsville, IN 47429, for the names of over 200 life and health insurance firms rated A+ by A.M. Best.

**AARP REPORT ON MEDIGAP**
**Consumer Affairs**
**1909 K Street NW**
**Washington, DC 20049**
**B**

A recent study conducted by the AARP in conjunction with the National Association of Attorneys General, found that four out of five Americans who use Medigap health insurance policies to supplement Medicare had better beware. Sometimes overzealous agents lure older folks into buying excessive and costly policies which are totally unnecessary. Seniors have lost over $3 billion in one year due to this abuse and other unscrupulous practices of insurance sales agents. The

AARP report will alert you to warning signs (such as deceptive advertising). Write for more information today.

## AETNA INSURANCE
**Nationwide locations**

If you're over 55 and only drive for your own pleasure, check out the discount of about 10 percent given on liability and collision coverage if you're a good driver, and about 40 percent on fire and theft coverage. At least Aetna knows "you're not getting older, only better."

## ALLSTATE INSURANCE
**Nationwide locations**

If you are retired and 55, you can receive a discount of 10 percent across the board with Allstate on your auto and homeowner policies.

## CHUBB
**Nationwide locations**

CHUBB gives 10 percent off if you're over age 50 on your liability and collision coverage and 20 percent off on comprehensive auto insurance providing your car is used only for pleasure and there are no drivers under 25 in your household.

COLONIAL PENN, GEICO, HARTFORD, LIB-
ERTY MUTUAL, NATIONWIDE, and U.S. F & G
all have special discounted insurance rates for seniors.
Check your yellow pages for their local numbers.

## FEDERAL INCOME TAX GUIDE FOR OLDER AMERICANS
**Select Committee on Aging**
**U.S. Government Printing Office**
**Washington, DC 20402**
**B**

Like other informative pamphlets published by the government, this guide serves as an important tool in helping
seniors with their financial needs. Answers are given about
who must file, filing deadlines, which forms to use, where to
get assistance in preparing forms, Social Security and Railroad retirement taxability, actual tax form preparation and
how to prepare for next year, as well as a final section on
gift and estate taxes. Information is available free upon
request.

## THE HOME PARTNERSHIP
**450 Seventh Street**
**Hoboken, NJ 07030**
**201-963-8765**

The Home Partnership can answer all of your questions
concerning home equity conversion, if you are finding it
harder to pay for home repairs, health care, or rising
property taxes. Through the Home Partnership, you can
receive information on how to acquire additional income

through your home equity to pay for the necessities of life. For more information and eligibility requirements, contact them today.


## HOW TO COLLECT BIG DOLLARS FROM
   UNCLE SAM
R. Emil Neuman
249 South Highway 101
Department RC-11
Solano Beach, CA 92075
$13.95

This book, written by a former federal investigator, tells how to collect Social Security before retirement, education benefits, income supplements, farm and business loans, even welfare and food stamps. With its help, many families are leading a more comfortable existence. This book costs $12.95, plus $1 handling and postage. You may return the book in 30 days if not satisfied for a full refund.


## MATURE INVESTOR
QXO Publishing
Box 2741
Glen Ellyn, IL 60138

*Mature Investor* is specifically tailored to the unique investment needs of seniors. Most often, mature adults have too many liquid funds, according to the *Mature Investor*. This publication is the information source that can help you fine-tune your investments that are already in place or help you establish better use of these funds that are just lying around. You will soon be on your way to sound retirement and investment planning. A three month subscription costs only $9.95; a small investment to maximize earnings.

**SCORE**
**National Office**
**1825 Connecticut Ave. NW**
**Suite 503**
**Washington, DC 20009**
**202-653-6279**
**Service Corps of Retired Executives**

SCORE believes in "helping small businesses SCORE." Since 1964, they have been offering free business counseling by retired successful business men and women. And with counselors standing by to help you in all fifty states, there's no excuse not to call or write to secure free expertise. There is someone close by who can fill your particular business needs, and they'll even come to you.

**SELECT QUOTE INSURANCE SERVICES**
**800-343-1985**
**B**

One call will net you a free written price quote from top-ranked companies that consistently offer the lowest rates for quality protection. Not one of these companies has failed to pay a valid life insurance claim for as long as it has been in business. All rated A or A+ by independent authorities. Allow four to six weeks for price comparisons. Low-cost term life insurance for 70 years or younger provides the simplest and most economical plan if pure protection is what you want.

**SENIOR SHOPPER INSURANCE PROGRAMS**
**800-458-5259, Mr. Marshall Shanbrom, R.H.U.**
**FAX 313-626-1947**

Insurance coordinator Marshall Shanbrom is a registered health underwriter. He and his staff can respond to your special health needs toll free around the country. Deal with a team of professionals and choose all or select from just one of many specialized plans, including:

- On the road accident plans;
- Cancer, health, and stroke indemnity plans;
- In-home health care plans;
- Nursing home plans;
- A variety of Medicare supplement plans;
- Guaranteed-issue life insurance plans;
- Cash-value long-term health care plans;
- Personal care plans;
- Long-term care policies;
- Personal disability plans; and
- Convalescent care plans.

*Great Buys* readers: FREE "Guide to Health Insurance for People with Medicare."

**WOMEN'S FINANCIAL INFORMATION PROGRAM**
**P.O. Box 15**
**AARP**
**1909 K Street NW**
**Washington, DC 20049**

Women who are newly widowed, divorced, or separated and who have minimal financial experience beyond household budgeting will be helped by this course, designed to assist midlife and older women assess their financial situations and options. This seven-session workshop introduces participants to basic financial planning in a step-by-step format. WFIP is sponsored by community-based nonprofit groups at 140 sites throughout the U.S. Write for more information, and take a giant step for womankind.

## WRITING AND CASHING CHECKS: YOUR
### CONSUMER RIGHTS
### BANKCARD HOLDERS OF AMERICA
**560 Herndon Parkway**
**Suite 120**
**Herndon, VA 22070**
**703-481-1110**

"Writing and Cashing Checks" is available for $1 from Bankcard Holders of America. This one-page flier suggests you can protest the practice of giving a credit card number to a salesperson when cashing a check and what to do if there is an objection. Several states are looking at legislation to halt this practice.

# BOOKS AND MAGAZINES

**AARP INFORMATION BOOKS**
**400 South Edward Street**
**Mount Prospect, IL 60056**
**CK,MC,V,MO (payable to AARP Books)**

AARP has joined with Scott, Foresman to create AARP Books and to offer comprehensive guides (written by experts) to help with money management, choosing where to live, estate planning, saving on insurance and helping seniors to lead a better life. Some of their titles include: *Planning Your Retirement Housing* ($8.95), *The Essential Guide to Wills, Estates, Trusts, and Death Taxes* ($12.95), *What to Do with What You've Got: The Practical Guide to Money Management in Retirement* ($7.95), *The Over Easy Foot Care Book* ($6.95), and others. Add $1.45 shipping per order. These titles are also available at your local bookstore.

**B. DALTON BOOK\$AVERS CLUB**
**B. Dalton Booksellers**

Join the B. Dalton Book\$avers Club for a small fee at any one of the 750 locations across the country and read at 10 percent less (except magazines, newspapers, and gift certificates). Access over 100,000 titles at all times, even if the book you want isn't in the store. Receive advance notification of special sales and events, plus B. Dalton's new magazine featuring reviews of all the latest books.

**BARNES & NOBLE**
**126 Fifth Avenue**
**New York, NY 10011-5666**
**800-242-6657**
**C**

" 'Tis nobler to pay less for Shakespeare's sonnets than to ever pay full price again" should be every reader's motto. An education in itself since 1873, this barnes-storming mail-order bookseller will save you plenty of bucks. History books, the classics, how-to's, science, reference, humor—even the stackable shelves to store all those books after you've finished the last chapter are available at incredibly low prices.

**BON APPETIT**
**140 East 45 Street**
**New York, NY 10017**

This gourmet magazine contains scrumptious recipes, mouth-watering photos, practical columns, shortcut menus, plenty of nutritional advice, plus travel and entertaining tips for the gracious gourmet. A recent offer featured one free issue plus seven additional, for a total of eight for $6, or half the regular subscription rate.

**CHOOSE LATIN AMERICA:**
**A GUIDE TO SEASONAL AND RETIREMENT LIVING**
**John Howells**
**Gateway Books ($9.95)**

Planning to live abroad? Let John Howells help you *Choose Latin America*. Escape the high prices and harsh climate of North America and experience anything from European sophistication to a casual tropical lifestyle. Live for less, full or part time, in Costa Rica, Argentina, Uruguay, Mexico, and several other Latin American countries, with up-to-date information on prices, housing availability, legal requirements, and lots more for $9.95. Check your local bookstore or write directly to the publisher, Gateway Books, 31 Grand View Ave., San Francisco, CA, 94114 (415-821-1928).

## CHOOSE MEXICO: RETIRE ON $400 A MONTH
John Howells and Don Mervin
Gateway Books ($9.95)

Thousands of Americans living today in Mexico owe their retired contentment to the first edition of *Choose Mexico*, which is now revised, updated, and expanded. This retirement guide is packed with helpful information about every aspect of retirement living, from finances to health care to housing. It shows how, for as little as $400 per month, a couple can live in a two-bedroom house and have regular domestic help and ample and delicious food. Additional chapters discuss new communities that have recently become attractive to Americans, RV travel for comfortable living in Mexico, and recreation areas for golf, tennis, and sports fishing. Check your local bookstore for a copy or write directly to the publisher, Gateway Books, 31 Grand View Ave., San Francisco, CA 94114 (415-821-1928).

## COMPLETE GUIDE TO HEALTH AND
## WELL-BEING AFTER 50
Columbia University School of Public Health

This very helpful, informative book written by Dr. Robert Weiss is published by the Columbia University School of Public Health, one of the first universities to develop a specific division of Geriatrics and Gerontology. Dedicated to the idea that each individual is his/her own best health care provider and that knowledge is good medicine, the book covers in-depth subjects such as "Emotional Well-Being and Relationships," "A Preventive Approach to the Diseases of Aging," "Health Resources for Older People" and "Coming to Terms with Mortality." Handy reference sections in each chapter provide further reading material, as well as pertinent organizations and how to contact them for help. An appendix includes medical prefixes and suffixes, a metric conversion chart, and recommended adult immunizations. An extensive, thorough index follows the text.

## COMPLETE RETIREMENT PLANNING BOOK
**Peter A. Dickinson**
**44 Wildwood Dr.**
**Prescott, AZ 86301**
**$11.95 (includes postage)**

Learn to make your retirement plans early with this book that discusses the five major concerns to potential retirees (housing, legal, health, finance, and, last but not least, leisure).

## THE DISABILITY BOOKSHOP CATALOG
**P.O. Box 129**
**Vancouver, WA 98666**
**206-694-2462**
**206-696-3210 (FAX)**

What a boon to anyone seeking assistance and information about their particular disability, be it vision or hearing impaired, physical or mental limitations, or problems of a general health nature. Helen Hecker, a registered nurse and author, compiled her exhaustive search to catalog books about pain, aging, general medical topics, sexuality, home nursing care, starting a business at home, or books that are just pure fun. Some in large or larger type.

FREE to *Great Buys* readers, plus $1 postage and handling.

## DOUBLEDAY LARGE PRINT HOME LIBRARY
**501 Franklin Avenue**
**Garden City, NY 11535**
**516-294-4000**

At last, you can see it clearly when you join this "large print" bookclub. Write for free brochure and receive one free book and two more for only $1. If not completely satisfied, simply return the books within ten days at Doubleday's expense, and you will get to keep the free book and a canvas carry-all tote. From bestsellers like Danielle Steele's *Star,* Judith Viorst's *Forever Fifty,* Debbie Reynolds' *Debbie,* or the *8 Week Cholesterol Cure,* you'll be able to see what's fit to print.

## DOVER PUBLICATIONS
**31 East 2nd Street**
**Mineola, NY 11501**
**C**

Do you have an elderly parent or friend who might get a lot of pleasure out of coloring books designed for adults? Write to Dover for adult-oriented coloring books with fine renderings of such subjects as birds, animals, horses, flowers, military uniforms, antique cars, trains, Victorian architecture, etc. Free catalog.

**EATING WELL**
**Ferry Road**
**P.O. Box 1001**
**Charlotte, VT 05445-9977**
**$12/1 year subscription; $18/Canada**

Save $12 over the newsstand price by subscribing to this luscious new magazine of food and health. This is the first consumer magazine dedicated to exploring the vital relationship between what you eat and how you feel. Includes in-depth reports on nutrition and medicine, recipes that are appetising, appealing, and healthy, reviews of new products, food trends, and more.

**GOLDEN YEARS MAGAZINE**
**Box 537**
**Melbourne, FL 32902-0537**

Bring a little extra sunshine into your life with *Golden Years:* a periodical designed with the active, modern senior in mind; a periodical in search of those very special readers who make up the population of the age group between 50 and 64 and who are interested in a good deal! Nowadays, who isn't?

*Golden Years* is offering readers of *Great Buys* one whole year absolutely FREE. There is no obligation and nothing to buy.

**HOW TO LIVE TO BE 100—OR MORE**
**Putnam & Sons**

George Burns shares his secrets for a long and happy life, telling you how to exercise, diet and stay sexy and maintain your *joie de vivre*. This is a priceless guide to levity and longevity, which will have you charging on, and laughing all the way. Favorite chapters include: "If It Wears Out, You

Can Order a New One!" followed by "Sex Can Be Fun After 80, After 90 and After Lunch!" Available from the publisher, or your local bookseller or library.

## THE ILLUSTRATED DIRECTORY
## OF HANDICAPPED PRODUCTS
c/o Trio Publications, Inc.
297 Cameron Way
Buffalo Grove, IL 60089
708-253-9426
708-394-0712 FAX
$12.95/CK

Publisher Monte Mace's own personal experience in shopping for "just THE right stuff" resulted in this veritable gold mine for the handicapped shopper. For $12.95, a bargain in itself, this 4-color emporium highlights products from A to Z, giving photographic and descriptive information on what's available in manual or power wheelchairs, specialized wheelchairs, power scooters, pressure sore prevention, lifts, elevators, ramps, adaptive vehicles, eating utensils, communication assistance, exercise and sporting goods, clothing, hygiene, and safety—your needs are covered!

## LEARS
655 Madison Avenue
New York, NY 10021
212-888-0007

Founder and editor-in-chief Frances Lear (Norman's ex) delivers the diva of mature magazines. Stories are featured elegantly coiffed and crafted and columns from glamour to gutsy get you going. This magazine is fit to be tried. 12 issues are $18.

## LIFELINE: A GUIDE TO WRITING YOUR PERSONAL RECOLLECTIONS
**Betterway Publications**
**P.O. Box 219**
**Crozet, VA 22931**
**804-823-5661**

Send a check for $8.95 (includes postage and handling) and receive *Lifeline: A Guide to Writing Your Personal Recollections.* This book will help you start the flow of ideas and get started writing your own autobiography. Consider reflecting on the many memorable events in your life and write a line or two for posterity. At last, your life's tour can be a best-seller (maybe even a mini-series, who knows?)

## MATURE HEALTH
**Haymarket Group, Ltd.**
**45 West 34 Street**
**Suite 500**
**New York, NY 10001**
**800-435-0715**

Chock full of good ideas and articles to make your life longer and healthier, the basic message of this magazine is that poor health is not inevitable with age. A recent issue spelled out "Sexual Secrets of Happy Couples," elaborated on the benefits of psyllium, and described seven steps to the management of diabetes. Regular columns feature nutrition, books, foods, and a variety of health-related subjects. People with an optimistic "can-do" attitude and who wish to maintain an active, healthy lifestyle will add years of enjoyment with a subscription to *Mature Health* (10 issues, $15).

**METACOM, INC.**
**Adventures in Cassettes**
**1401-B West River Road North**
**Minneapolis, MN 55411**
**800-328-0108**
**MC,V,AE,CK,MO**
**C**

Return to yesteryear with the comedy classics of Fibber McGee and Mollie, Baby Snooks, Jack Benny, and Will Rogers, plus the mysteries and dramas of that time when radio was king. Staying tuned to the Green Hornet was part of life in those days. Recapture the sounds on tape from $3.98 to $9.98. Catalog is free and includes dollars-off coupons. Rounding out their audio selections, rock hits from the 50s and 60s are now included.

**PREVENTION**
**Rodale Press**
**33 East Minor Street**
**Emmaus, PA 18098**
**215-967-5177**

This digest packed mega-book is just what the doctor ordered. Manageable features are easy to digest and tailored to a quick-read mature customer. Regular beauty, health and fitness blurbs are always an added prescription to good health.

**PUBLISHERS CENTRAL BUREAU**
One Champion Avenue
Avenel, NJ 07001-2301
201-382-7960
MC,V,AE,CK,MO
C

Books, books, and more books wind up for "Last Call" at up to 90 percent off. Be it a publisher's overstock or a producer's overrun of a video or record, it winds up in this catalog at gigantic savings. Monthly catalogs offer the full array of reading pleasure. From art books, gardening, diet and health, beauty, children's books to classics, cookbooks to computers, classical records and tapes, golden oldies, old radio shows— PCB is the last word in reading pleasure.

**REIMER PUBLICATIONS**
5925 Country Lane
Box 572
Milwaukee, WI 53201
MC,V,AE,D,CK
800-344-6913 (Orders)

Order a sample copy and you'll want a subscription to one of these four magazines: *Country Woman,* exclusively for women who enjoy country living; *Country,* for *anyone* who loves country living; *Country Handcrafts,* a craft magazine written especially *for* crafters, *by* crafters; and *Farm and Ranch Living* that lets you "tour" 70 farms and ranches every year without ever leaving the comfort of your easy chair. Sample issues are $2.98 each. Subscription rates: One year (6 issues) $14.98; two years (12 issues) $24.95; three years (18 issues) $33.98. They make great gift subscriptions too.

## RETIREMENT CHOICES FOR THE TIME OF YOUR LIFE
John Howells
Gateway Books ($10.95)

All across this great land, seniors can enjoy gracious yet affordable retirement with the information provided here on retirement alternatives. What an enjoyable way to learn about hundreds of places with something special to offer the retiree. Avoid the common pitfalls of retirement by discovering how climate can steal up to half your retirement income, why a bad job market can be good news for retirees, cities where you can safely stroll the streets, day or night, without fear, and how your home equity can raise your standard of living. The answers to many of your unanswered retirement questions are found here, for $10.95. Available at bookstores or write to Gateway Books, 31 Grand View Ave., San Francisco, CA 94114 (415-821-1928).

## RV TRAVEL IN MEXICO
John Howells
Gateway Books ($9.95)

John Howells uses his 40+ years of experience in living, travel, and study in Mexico to share concise information in this how-to-do-it guide to RV travel in Mexico. It includes a directory of 400 cities, towns, villages, and beaches with RV parks, tips on how to avoid tourist traps, and how to save 40 percent on insurance costs. A helpful appendix gives Spanish terms especially for RV maintenance and repair, as well as a listing of Mexican tourist offices. If you have an RV and dream of heading south, don't leave home without *RV Travel in Mexico*. The price is $9.95 at your local bookstore, or order directly from the publisher at 31 Grand View Avenue, San Francisco, CA 94114 (415-821-1928).

**SENIOR POWER NEWS**
**1515 N. Federal Highway, Ste. 300**
**Boca Raton, FL 33432**
**407-392-4550**

Founder Anita Finley, gerontologist and talk-show hostess, has launched a colorful addition to any senior's nightstand. From personal columns looking for Ms. or Mr. Right to an article by Charles Sparks, chairman of the National Council on Senior Housing, on considerations for retirement communities, this easy-to-digest edition is one of a few tabloids catering to the senior market. Annual subscription is $10. Also priced separately is Finley's corporate package, *Senior Power Action Manual,* especially designed for companies (banks, malls, and hospitals) desirous of reaching and relating to the needs of the senior community.

**SPECIAL EDITIONS**
**14232 Marsh Lane**
**Suite 332**
**Dallas, TX 75234**
**214-828-5400**
**C**

Write for your free catalog detailing NEW and quality USED large print books. No clubs to join, no hidden shipping or handling charges, but a pure and valuable service to special readers.

**SPICES OF LIFE**
**P.O. Box 19367**
**Washington, D.C. 20036**
**CK/$8**

*The Well-Being Handbook for Older Americans* is *the* resource compendium for retirement, by Ruth Fort & Associates, with a foreword by Ralph Nader. In this day and age of an "ageless" lifestyle, this book guides the reader through the many opportunities open to the older adult. From the valuable system of service credits (called Time Dollars) conceived by law professor Edgar Cahn to whom to call when you've been wronged, this is a wonderful way to wade through your options.

**SR/TEXAS**
**11551 Forest Central Drive**
**Suite 305**
**Dallas, TX 75243-3916**
**214-341-9429; 214-263-5435 (Metro)**

With one of the few visionary publications foreseeing the need for a seniors-oriented newspaper, publisher Shirley Schwaller and editor Frank Kelley have a decided edge on the market. Current and contemporary issues are revealed and explored and residents of Texas are kept abreast of the seniors' scene. A monthly magazine format for Texas' "most experienced generation" should be required reading for any senior. Wonderful features like FREE work wanted, personal ads and relevant reading throughout.

Readers of *Great Buys* can receive three months FREE. Then, if you decide to subscribe, readers will save 14 percent off the subscription rate for 12 issues ($12 instead of the regular $15).

**SUBSCRIPTION SERVICES, INC.**
**29 Glen Cove Ave.**
**Glen Cove, NY 11542**
**800-SAY-MAGS; 516-676-4300 (in NYC)**

No reading between the lines here. This is THE source for ordering magazine subscriptions at THE lowest prices. Write or call for their list of magazines and a price quote for specific subscriptions. What a great gift idea for your grand-children. Typical costs for top children's magazines are $9.97 to $15.97. They'll even enclose a personalized card with each subscription.

Special to *Great Buys* readers: A personalized file of all your subscriptions will be kept, and you'll be notified when it is time to renew.

**TARTAN BOOK SALES**
**500 Arch Street**
**Williamsport, PA 17705**
**800-233-8467, Ext. 507 (Orders)**
**717-326-2905 (Inquiries & PA orders)**
**MC,V,CK,MO**
**B,C**

This mail-order division of the Brodart Company offers at substantial savings hardbound books returned for whatever reason from libraries. No paperbacks, reference texts, or children's books, but adult fiction, nonfiction, romance, science fiction, Westerns, and mysteries line up at up to 75 percent off. Free catalog and brochure upon request.

**WALDENBOOKS, WALDENBOOKS & MORE**
**800-322-2000**

Book your "Preferred Readers" membership for $10 (FREE if you're already a 60+ club member) and save 10 percent (except on magazines, newspapers, gift certificates). No more reading the fine print, as the 10 percent includes even the already discounted merchandise, such as the top best-sellers.

Shop, too, for audio, video, gifts, software, large print titles, and receive periodic special interest mailings with additional money-saving offerings. For every $100 spent, you can expect a $5 coupon in the mail. Annual renewals are free. Now, that's something to write home about.

## WHERE TO SELL IT DIRECTORY
**Pilot Books**
**103 Cooper Street**
**Babylon, NY 11702**

Like most of us, you probably have a host of items you don't want to keep, but may be too valuable to throw away. The next time you clean out that attic, garage, or basement, stop and consult this handy guide before tossing anything out! Like all Pilot books, this compact volume gives quick insight into resources and information, listing nearly 800 dealers and collectors who'll buy just about anything—old or new—some 95 categories in all. From A to Z: Animal and Art items, Books and Baseball, Catalogs and Comics, Dolls and Games, Guns and Glassware, Letters and Lunchboxes, Newspapers and Photographs, Shaving and Smoking items, Toys and Weapons, just to name a few! Categories of collectible items constantly increase. For example: when an airline ceases operation, all items connected with it become collectibles. This applies to schedules, souvenirs, travel bags, pencils, pens with logos, promotional items, et cetera. This holds true of defunct department stores, sporting organizations, and periodicals that are no longer published. This unique directory also contains a section with useful hints on how to deal with buyers by mail. $3.95 per copy and $1 postage and handling.

# BUYING CLUBS
## AND SERVICES

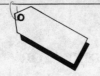

The warehouse club concept was founded in 1976 in San Diego by the Price family and aptly called The Price Club. Its appeal and growth has spawned numerous competitors, like Wal-Mart's Sam's.

The basic idea is simple. As a member, you pay a small annual membership fee and purchase goods at a discounted price. The discount varies whether you're a small- or medium-size business, or whether you are an employee of a certain organization, government unit, or credit union.

Be prepared for a warehouse environment with forklifts and cartons stacked high. Merchandise is often limited in certain categories, and many food products are sold in institutional size quantities. (Having a carton of Doritos on hand is too tempting for me.)

Warehouse clubs generally stock family apparel, office supplies and furniture, small and major appliances, TVs, radios, home entertainment items, cameras, books, and such, within 50,000 to 100,000 square feet.

Sam's is experimenting with an even larger store concept called the Hypermart, where employees skate around to replenish stock.

Warehouse clubs are one of the "hot" retailing phenomena and should reach into many more metropolitan areas in the 1990s.

Here are a few to watch for. Call or write to their corporate offices for the location nearest you.

Pace Membership Warehouse
3344 Moline
Aurora, CO 80010
303-360-8124

The Price Club
2657 Ariane
San Diego, CA 02118
619-483-6600

Sam's Wholesale Club
702 S.W. 8th St.
Bentonville, AR 72712
501-273-4668

If warehouse clubs are not appealing, and shopping from home and saving substantial amounts of money are, then these buying services are for you.


**LVT PRICE QUOTE HOTLINE**
**P.O. Box 444-DFS 91**
**Commack, NY 11725**
**516-234-8884**
**CK,MO**
**B**

Write for their free brochure listing over 4,000 name-brand appliances and electronics. Established in 1976, they combine the convenience of home shopping and low prices. Their huge purchasing power enables them to offer nationally advertised items at "warehouse" prices. All major appliances, vacuum cleaners, microwaves, televisions, air conditioners, camcorders, VCRs, telephones, answering machines, calculators, typewriters, and radar detectors. Just call them with model numbers. One call does it all. Gift shipping is available at no extra cost. All shipping costs are paid by LVT. All manufacturer's warranties are in effect with extension service contracts available upon request.

**MAIL-ORDER-DEALS (M.O.D.)**
**6494 Pumpkin Seed Circle**
**Boca Raton, FL 33433**
**CK or MO**

Join the M.O.D. (Mail-Order-Deals) squad and write for the best buys by mail or by phone in the following categories (1) apparel; (2) appliances; (3) bed and bath; (4) boating supplies; (5) cameras and other photographic equipment; (6) carpets and rugs; (7) china, crystal, and silver; (8) computers and electronics; (9) furniture and accessories; (10) handbags and luggage; (11) hardware and tools; (12) housewares; (13) jewelry; (14) office supplies; (15) plants, flowers, and gardening supplies; (16) shoes; (17) sporting goods; (18) stereo and video; (19) windows and walls; (20) spas; (21) travel; (22) pet supplies; (23) gifts; (24) time shares; (25) cars; (26) toys; (27) fabric. Why shop 'til you drop? This is your one-stop resource for the most commonly asked for merchandise. Save 20–80 percent on name brand quality items without leaving home.

Originally $4 per brochure (one category per brochure), *Great Buys* readers save 50 percent—$2 per brochure. Includes postage and handling.

**MATURE OUTLOOK**
**6001 North Clark Street**
**Chicago, IL 60660-9977**
**800-336-6330**

Join Mature Outlook and never pay full price again. For example, if you are 50 or over, you can save 20 percent on your Holiday Inn rooms and 10 percent on your Holiday

Inn meals. Truly, growing older can mean you're just getting better, enjoying life more, looking for wonderful new experiences and discovering new ways to save money. Mature Outlook, a member of the Sears family, is specifically designed to bring an exciting combination of privileges, benefits, services, and money-saving discounts exclusively to people aged 50 and over. Dramatic travel savings on fabulous trips, tours and cruises, car rental discounts, motor club memberships at reduced prices, no fee travelers checks and travel insurance at no additional cost. In addition, there are special discounts at Sears stores nationwide, a 20 percent discount on quality eyewear products at Sears Optical Departments and low prices on mail order pharmacy prescriptions. Also, you will receive the *Mature Outlook* magazine six times per year, along with *Mature Outlook* newsletters filled with timely articles of vital importance to the changing needs and goals of people over 50.

**THE Y.E.S. CLUB**
**200 North Martingale Road**
**Schaumburg, IL 60173**
**800-421-5396 (Member Help Line) M–F 8–4 (CST)**
**Great Buys for People over 50 I.D. #006701005**
**MC,V,AE,D,MW,CK**

Say "yes" to this club offering years of extra savings (Y.E.S.) if you're 55 and over. Save on a variety of goods and services under the Montgomery Ward banner of bargains. For starters, say Y.E.S. on Tuesdays to an additional 10 percent off on all merchandise (including sale items); an additional 10 percent off on routine car maintenance charges at the Montgomery Ward Auto Center (good on Tuesday, Wednesday, and Thursday). Have a "do" at 20 percent less at their hair salons; see the 20 percent off clearly at their optical centers; 10 percent will be etched off engraving or key duplicating service; 10 percent off income tax service; 10 percent off flowers and silk plants; save $50 on hearing aids,

PLUS they offer you FREE gift wrapping. And if that's not enough, say Y.E.S., Y.E.S., Y.E.S. to a 5 percent rebate on domestic airline tickets (certain restrictions may apply but all terms and conditions are explained fully in the membership handbook), tours and rail passes; a 10 percent rebate on rental cars and hotel/motel accommodations; 20–40 percent off pharmaceutical prescriptions; 50 percent off magazine subscriptions; pay up to 30 percent less for steaks; save 3–6 percent on long distance telephone charges, and more. Stay tuned-in through their *Vantage* magazine providing both money-saving reading and money-saving coupons. Say "no" to high prices and Y.E.S. to this club where you get lots more . . . for less. Membership $34.80.

Readers of *Great Buys* can expect a special gift with membership.

**OVER 50 GREAT BUYS BUYING SERVICE**
**8117 Preston Road, Suite 100**
**Dallas, TX 75225**

Who needs a brother-in-law in the business when you can be a member of the OVER 50 *Great Buys* family? For $49.95 a year (with the first 30 days FREE), you'll get the following:

- Savings of up to 50 percent on over 60,000 brand-name products and a *guarantee* of the absolutely lowest price (or receive double-the-difference price refund on most purchases)
- Double-warranty protection on most purchases
- *Directory of Name Brand Manufacturers*—from CANON, PANASONIC, SEIKO, WHIRLPOOL, ZENITH, you name it, as a member of the *Great Buys* Buying Service, you'll get it, at the lowest guaranteed price!
- A supermarket coupons savings plan

- *Over 50 Travel Discount Club* (a $49.00 value by itself) is waived because you're a *Great Buys* reader
- Personalized membership card

*NOTE:* You must have a valid MasterCard or Visa to respond to this offer. You are under no obligation to continue your membership beyond the FREE 30-day trial period. However, unless you cancel your membership during the trial period, you agree to continue the membership, and the $49.95 annual fee will be automatically billed to your credit card. To insure uninterrupted service, your annual membership will automatically be renewed upon expiration. If you are ever unhappy with your membership at any time during your subscription period, you may cancel and receive a full refund of your annual membership. All services and benefits are provided by AmeriShop.

So much service. So much savings. For such a low price.

Detach (or make a copy) and mail to:

_____

For your FREE three (3) month membership, send $3.95 to cover membership kit, shipping, and handling along with your:

name _____

address _____

city _____ state _____ zip _____

phone _____

Which charge card do you prefer to use?

Visa _____ MasterCard _____

Charge card account number _____

Expiration date _____

Signature _____

to:

**OVER 50 GREAT BUYS BUYING SERVICE**
8117 Preston Road, Suite 100
Dallax, TX 75225

# CAMERAS

**B & H PHOTO**
119 West 17 Street
New York, NY 10011
800-221-5662 (Orders); 212-807-7474 (Customer Service)
MC,V,COD
PQ

Light up your life with flash systems by NIKON, CANON, HASSELBLAD and a host of others. Everything's discounted and the prices are enough to make anybody's eyes shine. Fourteen day exchange or refund policy; no restocking charge. Most orders delivered in about ten days.

**EXECUTIVE PHOTO AND SUPPLY CORPORATION**
120 W. 31st St.
New York, NY 10001
800-223-7323 (orders only)
800-882-2802 (computer hotline)
212-947-5290 (NY,AK,HI and all inquiries)
MC,V,AE,D,COD
C, PQ

You'll smile when you see the savings of 40 to 50 percent flashing across their 50-page catalog. Cameras, lenses, film, paper, and photographic accessories from names like CANON, MINOLTA, NIKON, and HASSELBLAD are part of their photographic inventory. Minimum order is $45, and it's usually delivered in 7–10 days. All manufacturers' warranties are included.


**GARDEN CAMERA**
**345 Seventh Ave.**
**New York, NY 10001**
**800-223-5830 orders only; 212-868-1420 (residents,**
  **inquiries)**
**MC,V,AE**
**C**

Tip-toe through the bargains at Garden Camera and pick between cameras, videos, calculators, electronic games, computers, and telephones at savings from 30 to 50 percent. NIKON and CANON are their biggest camera sellers, alongside their darkroom equipment center, which is abloom with such items as enlargers, meters, CIBACHROME paper and chemicals, color drums, and analyzers. Brands include HASSELBLAD, CANON, NIKON, MINOLTA, PENTAX, OLYMPUS, KODAK, RCA, POLAROID, SEIKO, PANASONIC, PHONE-MATE, and CODE-A-PHONE. A $50 minimum order is required, with a 10-day limit on returns.


**INTERSTATE/FLORIDA, INC.**
**P.O. Box 6536**
**Clearwater, FL 34618-6536**
**813-447-7766**
**F**

Record memories of that once-in-a-lifetime vacation and those very special outings with the grandchildren in 3D photographs that will delight the family. The revolutionary new NISHIKA 35mm 3D camera will give you breathtaking shots with standard 35mm color print film that can be enjoyed without special glasses or viewers. One-year unconditional warranty. Also available: tripod, deluxe camera bag, camera strap, lens cleaner kit, and NISHIKA film.

*Great Buys* readers deal: 5 percent discount off the price of the camera.

**SOLAR CINE PRODUCTS, INC.**
**4247 South Kedzie Avenue**
**Chicago, IL 60632**
**800-621-8796 (Orders only); 312-254-8310 (Inquiries)**
**MC,V,D,DC,CK**
**C**

Solar Cine's stellar selection of 35mm accessories will save you up to 40 percent. Film for both movies and cameras is undoubtedly their best buy. Brands to focus on are KODAK, PENTAX and POLAROID. Solar also carries screens, camera bags, photo finishing, processing, film and video transfers. Catalog is free.

**WALL STREET CAMERA EXCHANGE**
**82 Wall Street**
**New York, NY 10005-3699**
**800-221-4090**
**212-344-0011**
**MC,V,AE,DC,CK,COD**
**C**

For the best insider information on Wall Street, shop Wall Street Camera Exchange and save from 35 to 75 percent on NIKON, ROLLEI, HASSELBLAD, MAMIYA, OLYMPUS, and ROLEX. And if it's a LEICA you're likin', they're one of the largest LEICA dealers in the country. Their wall-to-wall collection includes cameras, lenses, accessories, camcorders (big), video cameras, personal copiers, typewriters, radar detectors, and more. A new division specializes in 35mm equipment for those "before and after" shots. Call for estimate. Trade-ins are welcome; they purchase outright or apply to a new purchase. Manufacturers' warranties where applicable and extended warranties available.

# CATALOG SHOWROOMS

**BEST PRODUCTS**
P.O. Box 25031
Richmond, VA 23260
800-777-8220
C

Either by mail or in person, you can count on the best from Best. Their 400-page catalog offers thousands of name-brand items from ATARI to ZENITH. Being one of the largest watch dealers in the United States, you can count on savings day in and day out. Take the time, too, and wander down their aisles of housewares, appliances, and gifts without wasting a minute paying retail elsewhere.

**SERVICE MERCHANDISE**
P.O. Box 24600
Nashville, TN 37202
800-251-1212; 800-342-8398 (in TN); 615-366-3900
CK,MC,V
C

You can count on Service, of course, selection, and savings at this powerhouse catalog showroom. You'll have the pick of the glitter in their jewelry department and ring in the savings on gifts, exercise equipment, toys, luggage, lawn and outdoor furniture, electronics, small appliances, TVs, and radios. Shop at any one of the 330 locations of Service Merchandise stores in the country (they're in 40 states) or order by phone with the flip of a page. Catalog and sale fliers are free.

# CRAFTS AND KITS

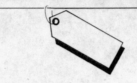

**ALLEN'S SHELL-A-RAMA**
**P.O. Box 291327**
**Fort Lauderdale, FL 33329**
**305-434-2818**
**CK,COD**
**C $1 (receive $2 gift certificate)**

Shark's teeth, sea horses, and sand dollars among your passions? Do you find shells and exotic tropical air plants irresistible? You can add to your collection, at wholesale prices, with decorator, collector, and specimen shells, all from Allen's Shell-A-Rama. There are over 1,000 gifts, novelties, and original kits (unavailable anywhere else) to choose from to craft away the hours.

**AMERICA'S HOBBY CENTER**
**146 West 22 Street**
**New York, NY 10011-2466**
**212-765-8922**
**212-633-2754 (FAX)**
**CK,COD ($15 min.)**
**C ($2.50)**

Does your interest "run" to scaled-down airplanes, railroads, ships or cars? Then America's Hobby Center is for you! If it floats, flies, swims, sinks, roars, or runs, you can bet this place has it, in its over 100,000 catalog items . . . and no doubt, it's on sale. There's even a selection of books on your favorite hobby. Order by mail or by Fax or phone for faster service. Though there's an exchange policy, they will refund your money if they can't deliver.

**ART SUPPLY WAREHOUSE, INC.**
**360 Main Avenue**
**Norwalk, CT 06851**
**800-243-5038; 203-846-2279 (in CT)**
**MC,V,CK,MO**
**C**

Paint the right way at up to 60 percent off name-brand art supplies, including FREE shipping. The full-color spectrum of supplies includes oil and acrylic paints, pigments and fixatives, solvents, oil pastels, chalks, markers, colored pens and pencils, inks, palette knives, brushes, paper, and boards. Do you think Grandma Moses knew of this source?

**AUGUSTA HERITAGE CENTER**
**Davis & Elkins College**
**100 Sycamore Street**
**Elkins, WV 26241-3996**

Appalachian heritage . . . lively fiddle tunes, sparks from a blacksmith's anvil, and the rhythm of dancing feet on a wooden floor. For one week in April, five weeks in the summer and one week in October, the campus of Davis & Elkins College buzzes with the sights and sounds of the traditional arts. Come to study blacksmithing, bookbinding, basketry, log house construction, weaving, stonemasonry, Irish folklore and storytelling, but leave with so much more. You'll be back every year to take advantage of their unique study opportunities or to visit festivals and concerts throughout the year.

## BRANFORD CRAFT VILLAGE AT BITTERSWEET FARM
**779 East Main Street**
**Branford, CT 06405**
**203-488-4689**

Enjoy the serenity of the old Connecticut countryside and discover the splendor of unique and original gifts, crafts and artwork year-round. This working farm is over 150 years old. In 1972, the outbuildings were renovated and converted to low-cost gallery space for artists and craftsmen. From those humble beginnings, the Village is now home to more than thirty shops, galleries and studios. There are even home-grown herbs and flowers sold in the old family farmhouse. Take a shopping picnic and hit the road to one-of-a-kind savings.

## CHERRY TREE TOYS, INC.
**P.O. Box 369-140**
**Belmont, OH 43718**
**614-484-4363**
**MC,V,CK,MO**
**C $1**

Save as much as 50 percent on a rainy-day project for you or your grandkids. Cherry Tree's 64-page catalog makes the "I'm bored" syndrome a thing of the past. Kits to make any number of projects—from whirligigs to nursery characters, wooden wagons to pull toys, dollhouses to vintage cars. Plans, patterns, and books make the how-to portion as simple as A-B-C. Their factory outlet in Belmont offers catalog surplus and irregulars at up to 75 percent off. Even if you're not traveling to Ohio, the catalog stands in a close second.

## CLOTILDE
1909 SW First Avenue
Fort Lauderdale, FL 33315
305-761-8655
MC,V,CK,MO
C

Have a "notion" to sew up something tonight? Clotilde will keep you in "pins and needles." Have trouble finding glass-head steel pins, Teflon iron covers, magnetic pincushions? No more. In Clotilde's catalog, you'll find all this plus pressing aids, patterns and books for smocking . . . even French hand sewing. Discounts run about 20 percent. Enclose $1 shipping and handling on all orders.

## COATS & CLARK, INC.
P.O. Box 1010
Taccoa, GA 30577

Write for their "educational" order form sew you can select from their many FREE how-to sewing booklets.

## DANIEL SMITH
4130 First Avenue South
Seattle, WA 98134
800-426-6740; 800-228-0458 (in WA)
206-223-9599
MC,V,CK,MO
C $5

Fine artists everywhere were united on their praises for Daniel Smith's catalog (by artists, for artists). Save 25 to 30 percent across your canvas and expect colorful and knowledgeable service from a pro. Their catalog is over 200 pages, a mighty hefty tome to wade through but worth its weight in hours of productive pleasure.

**ELDER CRAFTERS**
405 Cameron Street
Alexandria, VA 22314
703-683-4338

An arts-and-crafts emporium for works of artisans 55 years or older, this nonprofit retail outlet is a testimony to handcrafted talent. A full compendium of creativity, from braided rugs to bread baskets, handmade dresses and scarves. There are about seventy-five of these stores around the country.

**ENTERPRISE ART**
P.O. Box 2918
Largo, FL 34649-2918
813-536-1492 (mail-order customers);
813-531-7533 (local)
CK,MC,V
C

Enterprise has been providing crafty customers a vast selection of materials and supplies to keep the nimblest of fingers busy for over ten years. Save by buying in bulk for jewelry-making projects (findings, rhinestones, mirrors, pearls), crafts (doll parts, miniatures, floral supplies), wearable art (tie-dye, metallic foil, fabric paint, bandannas), beads, and much more. Raffia straw for door wreaths, sequins to dress up sweatshirts, or yarn to turn you on to any number of knitting pleasures. When in Florida, you can visit their mail-order warehouse seven days a week at 2860 Roosevelt Blvd., Clearwater, FL 34620.

**FROSTLINE KITS**
**2512 West Independent Avenue**
**Grand Junction, CO 81505**
**800-KITS-USA (800-548-7872); 303-241-0155 (in CO)**
**MC,V,AE,CK**
**C $1**

You don't have to know a thing about sewing to complete a Frostline kit! All you need is a sewing machine and one of Frostline's money-saving, superior quality kits that come complete with everything you need—precut. Just sit down and sew according to their easy step-by-step instructions. If you do have a problem or question along the way, call their answer line (303-241-0155) for help. Mountain parkas and biking gear are their biggest sellers, but they also have kits for making baby-bunting and clothes for hunting, bed quilts, booties and robes, even tents. Allow three to four weeks for delivery. There is a six month refund period with refunds in the event of faulty material.

To really warm you up, readers of *Great Buys* take an additional 10 percent off any item in the catalog.

**GREAT TRACERS**
**3 North Schoenbeck Road**
**Prospect Heights, IL 60070-1435**
**312-988-0731; 312-255-0436**
**B**

You can "trace" tremendous savings (up to 50 percent) straight to Great Tracers! They provide made-to-order letter stencils in a variety of sizes, for use in labeling, addressing, identification, signs and posters. NEW—they now offer a golden, all-metal permanent Social Security card ($3.50) engraved with your name and Social Security number. It comes with a lifetime guarantee. You can be sure it will create a good first impression when you apply for a new job or government benefits.

Mention you're a *Great Buys* reader and receive an additional 20 percent discount!

## HAYSTACK MOUNTAIN SCHOOL OF CRAFTS
**Deer Isle, ME 04627-0087**

"She'll be comin' round the mountain . . ." Haystack Mountain, that is, if she's looking for a scenic location and crafts, all in one package. Overlooking the Atlantic from an awesome, wooded slope, this gem-in-the-Haystack is easy to find. From mid-June through mid-September only, roughly 80 students of all ages and degrees of skill, come together in two and three week sessions to study the arts of clay, fibers, glass, metals, wood, and wicker, in studios that stay open for inspiration around the clock. Charges include room, board, shop fees, and tuition. Accommodations range from open bunkhouses to twin-bedded rooms with private bath. Combine your next vacation with mastering your choice of folk art in this truly beautiful location.

## HEARTLAND CRAFT DISCOUNTERS
**941 South Congress Street**
**Geneseo, IL 61254**
**309-944-6411**
**MC,V,CK**
**C $2**

Over 6,000 items at 30 to 50 percent off will carve out some pretty handy and crafty items. Just about anything for the craft hobbyist: florals, glues, ribbon, wood cutouts, paints, needlecraft, doll parts—the works—for endless creative pleasure.

**HERRSCHNERS, INC.**
Hoover Road
Stevens Point, WI 54492
800-441-0838; 715-341-0560
MC,V,AE
C

Twenty-four hours a day, 7 days a week, you can outfox even the craftiest. Since 1899, this has been one of the oldest and largest quality catalogs of craft kits in the country. Plenty of cross-stitching with a cat theme, afghans, baby items, calendars, crochet items, fabric, frames, needlepoint, paint, pillows, stitchery, threads, yarn—the works—to keep you up to your elbows in projects. When in Stevens Point, stop and shop first hand at their catalog store.

*Great Buys* shoppers take $1 off any order of $5 or more.

**HOBBY SURPLUS SALES**
287 Main Street
P.O. Box 2170
New Britain, CT 06050
800-233-0872 (Orders); 203-223-0600 (Customer Service)
203-346-6592 (FAX)
C $3 ($1 to GREAT BUYS readers)
MC,V,CK,MO

The 1991 edition of the Hobby Surplus Sales catalog is your complete hobby store through the mail. Reading through this catalog is like getting lost in the back aisles of an old-time hobby store. You'll find building kits and supplies for all sorts of hobbies and projects, such as electric train sets, accessories and repair supplies for all types of new and antique scale model railroads, plastic and wooden kits to build models of planes, boats, and cars, dollhouse furniture kits, finishing supplies, wooden toy kits, wooden ship models for the beginner or craftsman. With 128 pages and over

6,000 items, something can be found to interest everyone. This family owned and operated business with over 59 years of experience offers 100 percent satisfaction or your money back. Guaranteed.

As a special introductory offer to *Great Buys* readers, the 1991 Hobby Surplus Sales Catalog will be available at 66 percent off the cover price of $3. To receive your copy of this new catalog, send $1 to the address above.

**HOLCRAFT COMPANY**
P.O. Box 792
Davis, CA 95616
916-756-3023
MC,V (minimum $20), CK
C $2 (two-year subscription)

This yummy catalog specializes in chocolate molds at reduced prices (what a delicious gift-giving idea) and nifty gifty novelties for Christmas, like wreath holders, canvas and blown-glass ornaments, Christmas coasters, and stocking holders.

**HUSTON DOLLS**
7969 U.S. Route 23
Chillicothe, OH 45601
614-663-2881
C $2

What a doll! Sixty years ago, Melvina Huston turned her hobby into one of the grandest doll collections in the world. Still run by her children, this catalog sells both kits and fully dressed dolls. For example, the Melvina doll is $60 but as a kit is $19. Over 250 dolls to dress up (or down), babies to Madame Butterfly, clowns to cherubs, and all crafted with precision and pride.

## MCKILLIGAN INDUSTRIAL AND SUPPLY CORP.
435 Main Street
Johnson City, NY 13790-1998
607-729-6511
CK,MC,V,COD
C $5 (Refundable)

Selling to industries and high-school shop teachers is the main business of McKilligan, but individuals can purchase hardware, tools, electronics, graphic supplies, and craft materials at up to 35 percent off list prices. The encyclopedic catalog costs $5 (refundable) and lists over 70,000 items. Kits for stained glass, model cars, model rockets, and miniature houses are available. When it comes to variety, McKilligan's is one of the best.

## MEISEL HARDWARE SPECIALTIES
P.O. Box 70
Spring Park, MN 55384
800-441-9870
MC,V,CK,MO
C $1

This crafty carpenter's catalog is a 64-page "projects for a lifetime," one-stop source for shopping. Save up to 40 percent on woodworking ingredients, plans for toys, household accessories, gifts, dolls, shelves, hardware for knockdown furniture, and missing parts for furniture.

## MELODY BY MAIL
P.O. Box 830
Glen Allen, VA 23060
CK,MC,V,MO

Join the kings, soldiers, astronauts and cowboys who have enjoyed making melodies on a harmonica. You can learn to play quickly and easily with the 134-page beginner's guide and instructional cassette tape. Start to play your favorite tunes in minutes, even if you've never had a musical lesson before. The complete musical package to get you started is only $24.95, plus $2.50 postage and handling. The package also makes a unique gift. Satisfaction is guaranteed or your money refunded. CA and VA residents add sales tax.

**MICHAELS**
**P.O. Box 612566**
**DFW, TX 75261-2566**
**214-580-8242**

Michaels is THE arts and crafts store and a whole lot more. Call or write for the store nearest you. Outwit the craftiest of foxes with a do-it-yourself work of art, from scrumptious homemade candy to porcelain flower arrangements. Stitchery to specialty T-shirts, create a one-of-a-kind masterpiece and save big bucks over ready-made counterparts. Free custom framing (you only pay for materials), a kids' club for bored grandchildren, and the creative camaraderie of others sew inclined.

**PEARL PAINT**
**308 Canal Street**
**New York, NY 10013**
**800-221-6845; 212-431-7932 (in NY)**
**C $1 (Refundable)**

Pearl Paints has 20 to 40 percent in the can. Call this gem for any of your art or craft materials. Sable brushes, artist's acrylics, plus much more; their inventory could help you paint the town red, and allow you to save green at the same time. Their beautiful catalog has been the source of supplies for artists like Peter Max and Andy Warhol.

**PUEBLO-TO-PEOPLE**
**800-843-5257; 713-523-1197 (in TX)**
**C**

This nonprofit organization has cataloged wonderful and imaginative handmade Latin American crafts, and 40 to 45 percent of the proceeds go to the creators. Items available include handmade clothing and belts, bookshelves, decorative items for your home, wall hangings, toys, and even fruit and coffee. Catalog is free.

**QUILTS UNLIMITED**
**P.O. Box 1479**
**440 Duke of Gloucester Street**
**Williamsburg, VA 23185**
**804-253-8700**
**C $5 (Refundable)**

Where's there's a quilt, there's a way to buy it for less at America's "largest antique shop," selling to more than 1,000 mail order customers each year, including Bette Midler and Lauren Bacall. If you appreciate the fine crafting and fascinating colors found in America's unique quilts, send for the Quilts Unlimited catalog. In addition to listing prices, sizes, and any flaws the quilt may have, the catalog describes quilt colors, fabric and design elements. Prices are about 20 to 30 percent less than antique quilt dealers.

**SAX ARTS AND CRAFTS**
**P.O. Box 51710**
**New Berlin, WI 53151**
**800-558-6696; 800-242-4911 (in WI)**
**414-784-1176 (Fax)**
**MC,V,AE,CK,MO**
**C $4 (Refundable)**

For everything your art desires, consult this full-color catalog and you'll be creating custom jewelry and wonderful wearables, painting canvas dolls and toleware, and stitching up fresh new ideas for gifts and for yourself. Even learn to make baskets and porcelain flowers. Craft accessory supplies, too. Order toll free 24 hours, 7 days a week. Orders are shipped within 48 hours. Free freight with orders of $100 or more. Complete satisfaction is guaranteed.

**SEWIN' IN VERMONT**
**84 Concord Avenue**
**St. Johnsbury, VT 05819**
**800-451-5124; 802-748-3803 (in VT)**
**MC,V,CK,COD plus $2.50**
**B,PQ**

Sew up a good deal on major European and Japanese sewing machines with sew low prices. Don't forget their most popular brand, though: SINGER. You'll save about 30 percent off retail on most models. Credit card orders are shipped the same day they're received; check orders, however, are shipped after the check clears. Write for manufacturers' brochures and price lists.

**STU-ART SUPPLIES**
**2045 Grand Avenue**
**Baldwin, NY 11510**
**800-645-2855; 516-546-5151 (in NY)**
**MC,V,CK**
**C**

No need to "stu" any longer about the high cost of framing and presentation supplies. Not when you can get up to 50 percent off on Nielson metal frame sections, five varieties of mats, D'Archs watercolor paper and all-media art boards. Orders over $250 are shipped free in UPS delivery area only. Satisfaction is guaranteed.

## VETERAN LEATHER COMPANY, INC.
**204 25th Street**
**Brooklyn, NY 11232**
**718-768-0300**
**MC,V,CK,COD**
**PQ,C $1.50 (Refundable)**

Even a novice can find suede, leather, and a large assortment of leather-working accessories and tools at Veteran Leather Company, including OSBORNE, LEXAL, ORIGINAL mink oil, CRAFTOOL, MIDAS, and BASIC. Discounts of up to 30 percent. The minimum order is $25 and there is a 10 percent restocking charge on returns, unless the material is defective.

## WORLD ABRASIVE COMPANY
**1866-S Eastern Parkway**
**Brooklyn, NY 11233**
**718-495-4300**
**CK**
**C,F**

The only thing abrasive about this company is the rub they put on full retail prices. For the hobbyist looking for sanding belts, discs, sheets, rolls, and other sanding or grinding accessories, look no further. Save 30 to 50 percent and expect prompt delivery in one to two weeks.

*Great Buys* readers can grind another 10 percent off all abrasives and tools.

**YANKEE INGENUITY**
**P.O. Box 113**
**Altus, OK 73522**
**405-477-2191**
**MC,V,CK,COD**
**B**

Save up to 70 percent if you're interested in saving money
and your time (piece). This wholesaler will deliver clock
parts in record time (within 48 hours), and all parts are
guaranteed for life against factory defects. Their 8-page
illustrated brochure now is free to readers.

**ZIMMERMAN'S**
**2884 34th Street North**
**St. Petersburg, FL 33713**
**813-526-4880**
**MC,V,CK,MO**
**C $2 (refundable)**

A home crafter's haven for "Have they got a deal for you!"
This is the Ben Franklin of discount craft-supply sources.
Beads, ribbons, yarns, macramé, dolls, books, crocheting and
knitting supplies, and anything else to get the job done. Free
UPS shipping anywhere in the USA.

# DEEP DISCOUNT DRUG STORES

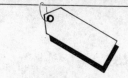

A one-stop drug store shopping phenomenon called "deep discounting" has driven the small neighborhood pharmacies into seclusion. Today's shoppers, driven by price and time constraints, prefer to shop for practically everything they need on a regular basis with one-stop convenience and at savings up to 50 percent. Enter this new wave of retailing. Before, the typical drug store stocked a limited health and beauty aid selection and prescription/over-the-counter drugs. Deep-discounters, on the other hand, combine an expansive inventory of general merchandise such as non-perishable grocery items, paper and party goods, housewares, health and beauty aids, office supplies and equipment, toys, best-selling books, magazines, videos, designer fragrances, pet supplies and more in 30,000 to 60,000 square feet of selling space.

**DRUG EMPORIUM**
**7792 Olentangy River Road**
**Worthington, OH 43085**
**614-846-2511**

Nationally advertised health and beauty aids are found nestled next to designer cosmetics and perfumes at savings of 20 to 35 percent. Prescription drugs will save you up to

40 percent and there's often similar savings on paper products, greeting cards, housewares and non-perishable food
items. Franchise locations in many states including Ohio,
Arizona, Florida, New York, Nevada, Kansas, Missouri,
Minnesota, Texas, Indiana, California, and Washington. Call
or write for location nearest you.

**F & M DISTRIBUTORS**
**25800 Sherwood**
**Warren, MI 48091**
**313-758-1400**

Send a SASE to corporate headquarters listed above for
location nearest you. This deep discounter is jam-packed
with an A to Z collection of cleaning aids, cosmetics, beauty
supplies, baked goods, pet supplies, perfume and lots in-
between. Save up to 50 percent.

**PHAR-MOR**
**P.O. Box 400**
**Youngstown, OH 44501**
**216-746-6641**
**B**

Phar-Mor is the largest and fastest growing company-owned
deep discount chain in the country. House and beauty aids,
pharmaceuticals, designer fragrances, video rentals, car care
products, cosmetics, housewares, non-perishable food items,
office supplies, and greeting cards are available at prices up
to 50 percent off competitor's retail and all products are
name brand. Its concept of "power buying"—buying in huge
volume only when they get a "deal" and passing those savings
on to the consumer, for example, is one of the *Power Buying*

*Tips* available free to *Great Buys for People over 50* readers by writing to Power Buying Tips at the address above.

Other deep discount stores across the country include Freddys, Pic 'n Save, Marc, Rock Bottom, and A.L. Price.

# EDUCATION AND EMPLOYMENT

**ACADEMY OF LIFELONG LEARNING**
University of Delaware
Continuing Education Department
2800 Pennsylvania Ave.
Wilmington, DE 19806
302-573-4433

**ACADEMY OF SENIOR PROFESSIONALS**
Eckerd College
P.O. Box 12560
St. Petersburg, FL 33712
813-864-8834

Choose your studies, on campus or from your home (even a nursing home), and audit year-long required courses. One way to bridge the generation gap, as exemplified by this college, is to participate with the younger students on campus or on field trips to locations around the world.

## CLOSE UP FOUNDATION PROGRAM FOR OLDER AMERICANS
1235 Jefferson Davis Highway
Suite 1500
Arlington, VA 22202-9950
800-232-2000

Since 1972, the Close Up Foundation (nonprofit, nonpartisan, educational organization) has provided a first-hand learning adventure in the nation's capital city. In cooperation with the AARP, take this week-long, behind-the-scenes look at Congress at work (or not at work, as the case may be) and experience the intricacies of both the cultural and social activities of Washington, DC. Discounts available to groups of 10 or more.

## ELDERHOSTEL
80 Boylston Street
Suite 400
Boston, MA 02116
617-426-8056

Cicero, computers, politics, poetry, Maine, Manitoba, Wollogong, Wales . . . all are in the pages of the Elderhostel catalog, inviting you to partake in an educational travel experience of a lifetime. Their motto: Studying THERE is half the fun! One look at the variety of listings and you'll agree. In Canada, study historical pioneer quilting; in Egypt, learn of gods, kings and temples and about Cairo, past and present. Courses are in the liberal arts and sciences and set in exotic locations around the world. These learning vacations are specially geared for older adults (60 and over), but a companion 50 or older may accompany a partner who is at least 60. Some courses are provided for hearing impaired as well. So, browse the catalog, pick the vacation spot that most intrigues you, and start packing!

## GREEN BRIAR JAM KITCHEN
**6 Discovery Hill Road**
**East Sandwich, MA 02537**
**508-888-6870**

Join the Thornton W. Burgess Society to receive discounts in both gift shops, mail-order purchases, programs and more, by supporting the cause of conservation and preservation of our natural and historical heritage. This society has created, among other things in memory of writer Thornton Burgess, the 200-year-old restored house featuring the landmark Green Briar Jam Kitchen. Special cookshops throughout the year teach participants how to make such delectables as apricot-raisin chutney or carrot marmalade. Green Briar Jam Kitchen is a delicious detour in historic Cape Cod. Giftshop is open to the public.

## INSTITUTE OF LIFETIME LEARNING
**c/o AARP/Program Department**
**1909 K Street, NW**
**Washington, DC 20036**
**202-662-4895**

Write for their nationwide listing of peer learning and teaching programs across the country. What you can't get from coffee klatches and country-club living, you can get from this creative college environment for intellectual and social stimulation, which is often lacking in a retiree's life.

**INTERHOSTEL**
University of New Hampshire
6 Garrison Avenue
Durham, NH 03824
800-SEE-WORLD (800-733-96753); 603-862-1147 (in NH)

Do you enjoy travel and believe education is a lifelong process? If so, and if you're an intellectually "with it" adult over the age of 50, Interhostel can bring an enhanced awareness and richness to your life. Participants will gain personal appreciation for other lands and peoples through an overseas university or educational institution, featuring expert presentations on topics including history, politics, economics, literature, arts, and music. Excursions to sites of historic or cultural significance enhance what is learned in the classroom, and planned activities allow interaction with local residents. The fixed price for the program includes all meals and accommodations, lectures and presentations, field trips to museums and points of interest, transportation for all program activities, ground transportation and group flight transfers. Some of the locations have included New Zealand, Puerto Rico, Portugal, Costa Rica, Germany, Greece, Italy, Holland, Spain, Austria, and even a cruise to Alaska! Catalog available upon request.

**JUSTICE FOR AGE DISCRIMINATION
  IN EMPLOYMENT**
Box 6220
Annapolis, MD 21401

The JADE newsletter is published monthly with topics of interest to older workers. For a sample copy, send a $2 check to the address above.

## NORTH AMERICAN UNIVERSITY
3760 Highland Drive
Suite 500
Salt Lake City, UT 84106
801-272-4800
C

North American University's accelerated degree program is geared to mature adults, since past academic work and life experiences count toward Master's and Doctoral degrees in most disciplines. For free eligibility guide and catalog, write now, or if your degree needs are urgent, call for telephone consultation.

## PRIME TIMERS
3550 LBJ Freeway
Suite 150
Dallas, TX 75240
214-386-8040

Some people do their best work after 40. If you, like Abraham Lincoln, are one of these, but find the job market tough to break into because of your age, Prime Timers can break down doors for you, since their clients recognize the value of the mature worker. If you have experience in data entry, accounting, receptionist, general office, or bookkeeping, Prime Timers can have you working again, and it may be easier than you think. Check local directory for employment agencies in your town catering to the older "prime time" workers.

## RECAREERING INSTITUTE
Dr. Roger Axford
Arizona State University
Division of Curriculum & Instruction
Tempe, AZ 85287-1911
602-839-2255

Join the Pepsi generation and discover that retirement is the "first day of the rest of your life." The Recareering Institute helps seniors discover this exciting life principle. Dr. Roger Axford of Arizona State University encourages "recareering" or switching to a job that suits your talents and interests. He often sees people in their 50s, 60s and older happily pursuing a second or even third career. "Be all you were meant to be" is the message of his book, *Recareering*. He continues to encourage readers, like his Institute participants, to reach out in new directions and know that it's not too late to step out and try a new field of endeavor. For more information on the Institute or to purchase the book (cost $15), write to the University at the address above.

## UNIVERSITY OF NORTH CAROLINA/ASHEVILLE
## NORTH CAROLINA FOR CREATIVE RETIREMENT
Asheville, NC 28804-3299

The University of North Carolina/Asheville has developed some new and trend-setting programs for older adults. The Senior Wellness Program is designed to help seniors, retired or working, to improve the quality of life through enhancement of physical and mental well-being. Leadership for Seniors encourages participation in volunteer activities. Life Journey, College for Seniors, and the Research Institute are all vital parts of the University's outreach for seniors.

# FOODS

**ALMOND BOARD OF CALIFORNIA**
**Dept. CA-GH**
**P.O. Box 15920**
**Sacramento, CA 95852**

Write for their free "Heart Healthy Recipes with Almonds." Fourteen tasty dishes made with almonds that follow the recommendation of the American Heart Association, and include a list of nutrients per serving. Be sure to send a SASE.

**APLETS & COTLETS**
**P.O. Box "C"**
**Cashmere, WA 98815**
**C $1 postage & handling (refunded with first order)**

Okay, so you have no idea what an aplet or cotlet is. Well, these folks will be happy to send you their secret recipe sample box FREE (except add $1 for postage and handling), and you can sample these 100 percent pure fruit and nut candies. Made from absolute pure apple and apricot juices and big crunchy walnuts, they are all 100 percent natural flavors with absolutely no preservatives. Christmas gift catalog and discount coupons available upon request.

## ARIZONA CHAMPAGNE SAUCES
## SUGAR'S KITCHEN
**660 East 19 Street**
**P.O. Box 41886**
**Tucson, AZ 85717**
**800-342-9336; 602-624-3360 (in AZ)**
**602-629-0119 (FAX)**

Sugar's Kitchen has developed a winning combination with their full-bodied flavor of Arizona Champagne Sauces with NO SALT. Their three famous mustard sauces are hot, Cajun style and regular, any one of which makes a great topping for cold cuts, cheeses, sandwiches, or a spread for fish, chicken, roasts and ham before cooking. The Vegetable Dip is tops on crackers, chips, cheeses and raw veggies. Sugar's Kitchen also makes a dry Arizona Southwest mix— to which you can add crushed tomatoes and green chilies for a fresh salsa, or use in soups, and they have a dry Herbal Spice Dip mix for making dips, almost from scratch!

*Great Buys* offer: Free sample jar of mustard with any order.

## BALDWIN HILL BAKERY
**Baldwin Hill Road**
**Phillipston, MA 01331**
**508-249-4691**

Sourdough bread in the European tradition comes straight to you from Baldwin Hill Bakery. This 100 percent whole-wheat bread is made from organic stoneground flour and pure well water, leavened with natural sourdough and baked over a wood fire in a brick oven. Sound good enough to eat? It is! Minimum order is twelve large breads, or the equivalent in large and small breads (about $19). Orders will be shipped UPS collect unless you send a check in advance and avoid the $2.25 UPS charge for collect shipments. Orders must be

received by noon on Friday before the week you would like
your bread shipped.

**BEGINNINGS, ENDINGS, ETC.**
**14524 Benefit Street**
**Sherman Oaks, CA 91403**
**818-340-2801; 818-995-9265**
**CK,MO**
**PQ**

Judy and Toby have cooked up some of the freshest, most
natural-tasting preserves with absolutely no sugar, honey, or
artificial sweetener added. What you get is pure fruit sweet-
ened with natural fruit juices (concord grape, strawberry,
boysenberry, orange-cranberry, raspberry, apricot, and apple butter). These TOTALLY FRUIT PRESERVES are thick
and rich in color and handsomely packaged in 10 oz. jars
and gift box trios. (3 jars are $13.50 and the price includes
UPS.) In case you're wondering what comes under the
heading of Etc., consider "Golly, It's Garlic," an aromatic
blend of fresh garlic, herbs and salt, and the unforgettable
taste of their unique "Jalapeño Pepper Jelly," delicious as an
appetizer on crackers or toast rounds or as an omelette
filling.

For *Great Buys* readers: with your order, mention the book
for an additional 10 percent off!

**BEST FOODS**
**Division of CPC International, Inc.**
**P.O. Box 8000**
**International Place**
**Englewood Cliffs, NJ 07632**
**B**

Write for this free cooking with Mazola oil "Eating Tips for
a Healthier Heart" brochure. Recipes like orange-bran muf-
fins help reduce cholesterol levels and are straight from the

heart. Also, a handy guide for heart-healthy ingredient substitutions is also included.

## BUTTERBROOKE FARM
78 Barry Road
Oxford, CT 06483
203-888-2000
B

Lettuce help you unlock the pleasures of gardening. Butterbrooke Farm has quality seeds for your garden at low, low prices ($.45). Every order is carefully packaged and shipped the same day it is received. You are invited to join the Butterbrooke Farm Seed Co-op (details in a brochure provided free upon request, but please send SASE).

For our very special *Great Buys* readers, Butterbrooke has agreed to add a 15 percent discount off their already low wholesale prices on standard sized packets of vegetable seeds.

## CAVIARTERIA
29 East 60 Street
New York, NY 10022
212-759-7410
MC,V,AE,CK
C

You can have fresher caviar than you could get from local gourmet shops and at savings of about 50 percent by shopping through the mail at Caviarteria. Send for the luscious catalog and you will soon be serving Scotch salmon, caviar and other delicacies. Over 35 years at the same location, this family-owned business has been providing fine gourmet foods, including Russian, Iranian and American caviar at discount prices. Shipped to your door within days, their selection, besides caviar, also includes a wide assortment of unique specialty items such as truffles, patés, caviar servers and spoons, as well as 25 varieties of "freezer pac" snacks.

For readers of *Great Buys*, Caviarteria is making a special, first-time (or one-time, if you're already a customer) discount offer of an additional 15 percent off!

## 100% COLOMBIAN COFFEE SAMPLE OFFER
**P.O. Box 8545**
**New York, NY 10150**

Get your FREE sample of Colombian coffee. Allow at least 8 weeks for delivery, but don't expect it to be piping hot.

## CONSUMER INFORMATION CENTER
**Department 81**
**Pueblo, CO 81009**
**CK**

The following pamphlets from the U.S. Department of Agriculture's Human Nutrition Information Service are designed to help you incorporate the USDA-recommended dietary guidelines into your meal-planning:

- "Eating Better When Eating Out" (Item No. 123W; $1.50) offers menu-reading clues, myths about fast foods, and how to order food your way.
- "Making Bag Lunches, Snacks and Desserts" (Item No. 124W; $2.50) offers bag-lunch ideas, a guide to healthy snacks, and low-fat, low-sugar desserts.
- "Preparing Foods and Planning Menus" (Item No. 125W; $2.50) offers nutritious cooking tips, a guide to food choices, and how to fit menus to your family.
- "Shopping for Food and Making Meals in Minutes" (Item No. 126W; $3.00) offers quick-meal hints, how to read labels, and an aisle-by-aisle shopping guide.

- "Fish and Seafood Made Easy" ($.50) explains how to select, store, and prepare fish and seafood and includes several sauce and marinade recipes, as well as seafood main-dish recipes.

Order any of these pamphlets from Consumer Information Center. Specify item number where given and make check payable to Superintendent of Documents.

## DANNON 100
**P.O. Box 5809**
**Kalamazoo, MI 49003-5809**

Write for their 10-page booklet "100 Tips for Cooking with Yogurt," which reveals how you can use yogurt as a healthy substitute for ice cream, sour cream, cream cheese, mayonnaise, and other foods with a higher fat, cholesterol, or sodium content. Price is $.50.

## DINNERS À LA FEDERAL EXPRESS
**900-820-2EAT**

The galloping gourmand has spread its wings to include overnight delivery via Federal Express for your favorite foods or restaurant meals. Call for your FREE directory and only pay for the phone call. How about a full-course lobster dinner for two from Legal Sea Food? Or a gourmet gift from Frieda's Finest or Harry & David? Pining for some downhome Memphis barbecue from Germantown Commissary or melting away for a scoop of Whitney's ice cream? Start drooling and call for your dinners or desserts today and bon appetit tomorrow. The menu brochure is free. You do, however, pay extra for the phone call to order it.

**DUNDEE ORCHARDS**
**P.O. Box 327**
**Dundee, OR 97115**
**503-538-8105**
**B,PQ**

Write for their free brochure/price list for "Yummy in your Tummy" Oregon Hazelnut butters (creamy or crunchy). Try these 100 percent dry-roasted Oregon hazelnuts (no salt, sugar, or stabilizers) in a pancake batter or a pasta salad for a taste sensation. You'll go nuts over their walnut peanut chocolate or mocha hazelnut butter.

And then, *Great Buys* readers, take 20 percent off mail-order brochure prices with your first order.

**FARMS OF TEXAS COMPANY**
**TEXMATI RICE**
**P.O. Box 1305**
**Alvin, TX 77512**
**800-232-RICE (800-232-7423); 713-331-6481 (in TX)**

Rice is nice when it has the appetizing aroma of popcorn and a subtle nutty taste when eaten, and TEXMATI rice is all it's cracked up to be. Cooks up fully in 15 minutes (brown varieties take 45 minutes) but, m-m-m good. Their rice is grown domestically and modeled after the Indian basmate rice and the American long grain. They even make Texmati Lite Bran—the perfect blend of convenience of the white-mulled kind, but packed with the nutritional punch of brown or whole grain. Call toll-free for cooking tips from their in-house home economist as well as the location nearest you to buy TEXMATI rice.

## FRANK LEWIS' ALAMO FRUIT
100 North Tower Rd.
Alamo, TX 78516
800-477-4773

Vine-ripened to perfection, cantaloupe is one of the best fruits for you. Low in calories, high in vitamins and minerals, these are Texas's finest sweets (but only available in midsummer). You'll get six field-fresh melons, each weighing two pounds plus, guaranteed to arrive in flawless shape, for $21.98 plus $3 shipping and handling.

## GRACE TEA COMPANY
50 West 17 Street
New York, NY 10011
212-255-2935
CK
B

Grace Tea Company provides a "connoisseur's cup of tea" and has devoted its efforts to these superb and rare teas for over 25 years. This family business prides itself on hand-blended, hand-packed teas such as high-grown fancy Ceylon Earl Grey superior mixture, Pinhead Gunpowder Pearl, Winey Keemun English Breakfast and others. Teas are packed in elegant black metal canisters that can be used for other decorative purposes when empty or can be refilled from the less costly canister refills at attractive savings. Brochure (free upon request) gives information on the selection of Grace teas as well as helpful hints on gift giving, tea making, serving, and storing. Satisfaction is guaranteed. Prices range from $8.40 to $22.50 for a sampler tray of five teas.

**HARRY & DAVID**
Medford, OR 97501
800-547-3033 (Orders)
800-648-6640 (FAX)
MC,V,AE,CK
C

Make your life a little brighter and your heart a little healthier with the finest fruits and health-conscious foods from Harry & David. From Valentine amaryllis in a Portugese ceramic cachepot to a sweetheart cheesecake, you have to love the selections in their colorful catalog. Also, bone china tea sets, cobblers and strudels, petits fours, cheeses and smoked turkeys. Gifts galore for that special person on your list. Gift certificates available. Federal Express is an additional $5.95 each item and there is overnight delivery for $25, if you're really "Harryed." They offer the "strongest guarantee in the business." (Full refund or replacement.)

**HOLLYWOOD DIET BREAD**
1747 Van Buren Street
Hollywood, FL 33020

Write for your FREE "Calorie Counter & Carbohydrate Guide" if you're serious about your health and controlling your weight.

**INCREDIBLE EDIBLE EGG #31**
Box 755
Park Ridge, IL 60068-0755

The American Egg Board has published a leaflet of prize-winning recipes using its product. SASE.

## JACK SPRAT'S LEANING OF AMERICA
**800-EAT-LEAN**

The man who could "eat no fat" shows you how to trim the fat out of your diet. Information on label reading, shopping, cooking, and dining-out tips.

## JAFFREY MANUFACTURING COMPANY, INC.
**P.O. Box 23527**
**Shawnee Mission, KS 66223**
**913-849-3139**
**B**

If an apple a day keeps the doctor away, can you imagine what a glass of hand-pressed apple cider would do? Once you invest in the grinder kit, the entire family can get into the act. Set up your own "appleade" (no lemons, please) booth and go to work. Even if your name's not Granny Smith, you can still expect pure, clean cider with no preservatives or chemicals. This is a proven healthy drink (why else would more doctors than any other group buy the press?) A free gift certificate is often enclosed with every order for the grinder.

## JUDYTH'S MOUNTAIN, INC.
**1737 Lorenzen Drive**
**San Jose, CA 95124**

Pasta sauces, garlic butters, jellies, and perhaps the best part of all, they're SALT-FREE or LOW-SALT. Indulge with no guilt (well, almost no guilt). Quality, versatility, and uniqueness are bywords of Judyth's Mountain. Your choice of Hot Pepper, Ginger, or Coffee Almond Jelly in 10 oz. jars for $3.25 each; Creamy Garlic Butter or Pepper Olive with Walnuts are $7.25 for 16 oz. or $6 for 10 oz. jars. The three-jar gift pack can be packed into a mailable decorator box and, as an added bonus, they'll send you recipes with your order.

## KELLOGG'S COOKING HEALTHY BROCHURE
**P.O. Box 5017**
**Battle Creek, MI 49016-5017**
**B**

Write for your free "Cooking Healthy," a 12-page brochure providing fiber-rich, low-fat recipes, some with microwave instructions. Send postcard with your name, address, and ZIP to Kellogg's.

## LE GOURMAND
**Box 433**
**Route 22**
**Peru, NY 12972**
**518-643-2499**
**CK,MC,V**
**Newsletter**

*Parlez vous français?* If not, they also speak English, but in any language, the meaning's the same. Feast for the least on all natural gourmet herbs, spices, oils, vinegars, teas, coffees, pastry products, and more. Balsamic vinegars aged over 25 years are the rage for health-conscious palates whose taste buds are spoiled rotten. In fact, a dab of lemon and balsamic vinegar is the most delicious salad dressing imaginable (besides being good for you). Champagne and black currant vinegars are not to be overlooked either. Write for free newsletter.

**LONE STAR FARMS**
P.O. Box 685
Mercedes, TX 78570
800-552-1015
V,MC

Winner of the sweetest raw onion challenge, their onions
will bring more than tears to your eyes. Farm-to-you during
limited onion season, April to mid-May, for 20 lbs. was $20;
40 lbs. was $35 (includes freight and handling). Free recipe
booklet with order.

**MANGANARO FOODS**
488 Ninth Avenue
New York, NY 10018
800-4-SALAMI (800-472-5264); 212-563-5331
MC,V,AE,CK,COD
C

Mama mia! Founded in 1893, this family-owned Italian food
company can impress even the pickiest palate with home-
delivered imported hams, cheeses and provoletti. Choose
from their extensive menu of olive oils, pasta, Italian delicacies like pesto, baby mushrooms, Swiss gruyere, Bel Paese
or fontina cheeses, expresso coffee and delicious desserts,
besides their infamous Italian-style salamis. Gift baskets, too.
Catalog free upon request. Yummy for your tummy.

**MODERN PRODUCTS, INC.**
3015 West Vera Avenue
Milwaukee, WI 53209
414-352-3333

Enclose a SASE and receive one each of SPIKE, VEGE-SAL,
and lo-cal VEGIT. Season several soup pots with the natural
salt-of-the-earth seasonings in each packet.

## MOONSHINE TRADING COMPANY
P.O. Box 896
Winters, CA 95694
916-753-0601
B

Forget prohibition and indulge until you're in a drunken stupor over this delicious family-owned company's mouth-watering delectables. For love or honey, this is a humdinger. Taste their gourmet honey collection. Let's bee specific: all natural flavors, richness of color and intense aroma like "Florida 'certified' Tupelo" with a unique flavor and non-granulating characteristics or Eucalyptus mineral-rich with a mild and wonderful flavor from the San Francisco Bay area. Or wallow in their gourmet butter spreads like California Almond Butter or Nut Crunch. Don't forget the chocolate spreads and gift packs, too. Free brochure and price lists.

*Great Buys* readers can expect 5 percent off initial order and any subsequent gift order.

## NATIONAL LIVESTOCK AND MEAT BOARD
444 North Michigan Avenue
Chicago, IL 60611

"Facts about Versatile Veal" can be yours for only $.50 and will help you to cook veal in healthy ways. Includes recipes.

## NATIONAL PORK PRODUCERS COUNCIL
P.O. Box 10383
Des Moines, IA 50306

"Tasteful Options with Pork." Low-calorie and flavorful recipes using pork. Send SASE.

**NEW BEDFORD SEAFOOD COUNCIL**
**Promotional Department**
**17 Hamilton Street**
**New Bedford, MA 02740**
**617-994-3457**

Free fishy items to make your head swim. Included are iron-on transfers for you or your first mate's T-shirts, blue and gold stickers (both with the council's logo—a sailor boy with a background of a rope and nets), plastic litter bag and recipe folder of delicious seafood dishes. Limit your request to three items and include SASE.

**NEW YORK BEEF INDUSTRY COUNCIL**
**P.O. Box 250**
**Westmoreland, NY 13490**

"Lean on Beef" will teach you how you can eat beef and keep your cholesterol and fat levels down. $.50

**NORTHWEST SELECT**
**14724 184 NE**
**Arlington, VA 98223**
**206-435-8577;**
**206-435-3799 (FAX)**
**B**

Spice up your life with this spicy, hot, or really fresh complete gourmet salad. This community lives on a 300-acre farm and produces all of its own produce. They also offer a complete line of every conceivable vegetable, fruit or berry which are picked fresh daily and shipped overnight. Imagine the pleasure a holiday centerpiece basket would bring, as well as decorated garlic braids and grapevine wreaths. Call for free brochure and samples.

*Great Buys* readers: Take 10 percent off purchase price of your order.

**PINNACLE ORCHARDS**
**P.O. Box 1068**
**Medford, OR 97501**
**800-547-0227**
**C**

Comice pears are their specialty, though they are tops in other gourmet fruit and gift baskets, too. A Harvest-of-the-Month Club gift certificate is a yummy and fruitful way to remember someone (or yourself). Candies, bakery items, smoked meats and preserves round out their delicious offerings. Free catalog upon request.

**QUAKER FULFILLMENT CENTER**
**847 West Jackson**
**5th Floor**
**Chicago, IL 60607-3018**

Write for their free "Cholesterol Control through Diet from Quaker Oats," a colorful 10-page booklet containing 7-day fold-out menu selections as well as survival tips for staying in control while eating out or traveling. Recipes included.

**REFUNDLE BUNDLE**
**Box 9605**
**Clinton, IA 52736-8605**

You can receive America's leading sample, coupon, and cash refund publication with hundreds of dollars' worth of grocery offers plus lots of free tips for only $8.95 for 6 issues or $14.87 for 12 issues. For only pennies per month, you can literally save hundreds of dollars at the grocery store.

## RICE COUNCIL OF AMERICA
P.O. Box 740123
Houston, TX 77274
713-270-6699

Send a SASE and write for their complete list of brochures and leaflets. A multitude of "ricey" subjects are revealed from "cooking with rice for persons with allergies," to "rush-hour recipes." Recipes even come in large type and Braille versions.

## RIGHT COURSE
Department 928
P.O. Box 94816
Cleveland, OH 44101-4816

Write for this free 14-page menu and exercise program from Stouffers called "The Right Course." For women and men, this program was designed to help reduce fat, cholesterol, and sodium in your diet. It also includes three store coupons.

## ROCKY TOP FARMS
Route 1, Essex Road
Ellsworth, MI 49729
800-862-9303; 616-599-2251 (in MI)
CK,MO
B

Love the old time flavor and taste of homemade jams and jellies? Then Rocky Top Farms is the place for you. Good ole' Rocky Top! They specialize in Michigan grown and produce products made in small batches to control final quality, and pure ingredients with no preservatives. They boast old-time recipes and a lower level of sweeteners. It's hard to choose a favorite from their Berry Preserves and

Toppings, Fruit Preserves, Fruit Butters and Toppings. You'll drool over the Apricot Butter and Gram's Rhubarb Chutney. Their gift containers of Michigan white cedar will have your lucky friends or relatives pining for more. You are invited on a personal tour of Rocky Top if you're ever in northern Michigan. All orders shipped UPS. Prices range from $10 for 3-jar redwood gift crate to $31 for the 12-jar family pack.

**ROMAN MEAL COMPANY**
**P.O. Box 11126**
**Tacoma, WA 98411**
**B**

If bread is the staff of life, start at least with a slice from Roman Meal. Send for their free list of brochures and publications and enclose a SASE to begin your collection of dieter delight, low-calorie recipes using their Roman Light Bread or their menu/calorie controlled diet plan for delicious but balanced and healthy meals.

**SAN FRANCISCO HERB COMPANY**
**ATTN: GB**
**250 14 Street**
**San Francisco, CA 94130**
**800-227-4530; 800-622-0768 (in CA)**
**MC,V,CK**
**C**

You might have left your heart in San Francisco, but you'll bring home botanicals like Egyptian chamomile, pine nuts, tapioca pearls or tropicana orange pekoe blended teas from now on. Your nose will know by the heavenly scents of potpourri from the San Francisco Herb Company, and the prices will be an aromatic 50 percent off. Buy in bulk and save (more if you're a reader) on spices, teas and natural foods. Minimum order $30.

*Great Buys* readers: be sure to code address: GB, so you will get an additional 10 percent on orders of $200 or more; 15 percent on $500 or more.

**SCHAPIRA COFFEE COMPANY**
**117 West 10 Street**
**New York, NY 10011**
**212-675-3733**
**B,PQ**

Coffee, tea, and you and me, too, can find the best cup of fresh brew. Just write for their free price list and start your morning with a cup of lapsang souchong (tea) or Kenyan AA water-processed decaf coffee. Favorite blends available by the pound or ½ pound or ¼ pound, such as Brown Roast ($5.50), Costa Rican ($5.75), or Jamaican Blue Mountain ($14.75 for 6 oz.) shipped the day it's roasted to your specifications. Beans ground to order for drip percolator, Melitta, or vacuum packed. Naturally flavored teas like raspberry or black current are packed 50 teabags for $3.30.

*Great Buys* readers will receive a FREE scooper with first order.

**SCHOONMAKER/LYNN ENTERPRISES**
**4619 NW Barnes Road**
**Portland, OR 97210**
**503-222-5435**

Bee the first on your block to try Peter and Karen Lynn's lavender honey straight from their hives in the remote fields of southern France. You can buzz about the clarity of their liquid honeys, the promised long shelf-life and the flavor and aroma of each of the nine honeys they produce. Sample the nectar of their Orangier, Montagne, Tournesol, Acacias, and Printemps, and savor the savings.

*Great Buys* readers offer: Two 8 oz. jars shipped anywhere in the U.S. for $10 postpaid. (Save shipping charges of $2.40.)

**SIMPSON & VAIL**
**P.O. Box 309**
**Pleasantville, NY 10570**
**914-747-1336**
**MC,V,CK ($15 minimum on credit cards)**
**C**

Ah, get a whiff of the wonderful aromas that have been filling coffee and tea cups since 1929, and for sure you'll drink to the last drop. Save 10 to 15 percent on the same fine blends that are served at New York's Russian Tea Room. Your hosts, owners Joan and Jim Harron, sweeten the pot with delectable gift canisters filled with teas, teaballs, teapots, sugar and creamer sets, maple syrups, pancake and muffin mixes, pure seafood soups, Louisiana spices—yum-m-m. Over 80 varieties of teas, including an herbal line and over 52 hard bean coffees to select. Their 16-page mouth-watering catalog is free.

*Great Buys* readers can take 10 percent off their first order.

**STEEL'S OLD-FASHIONED FUDGE SAUCE**
**425 East Hector Street**
**Conshohocken, PA 19428**
**800-6-STEELS (800-677-3359); 215-828-9430 (in PA)**
**CK,COD**
**B**

Fudge sauces, fruit sauces, gift baskets—all come in the LO-CAL SUGAR-FREE variety. Since 1919, fudge has been a Steel family tradition. Making sauces in small batches by hand with the finest ingredients and using the finest old-fashioned recipes results in the exceptional quality of these sauces. Then, the sauces are packaged in appealing, old-fashioned style. In addition to the thick, rich dark fudge sauces, they offer praline, huckleberry, strawberry-rhubarb and fresh apricot sauces to make your mouth water. Shipping by UPS. Until credit is approved (three trade references and bank account information), terms are prepaid or COD.

**SUGAR ASSOCIATION**
**1101 15th Street NW**
**Washington, DC 20005**

"Taking It to Heart" and "What Have You Got to Lose?" These two pamphlets are offered together and contain information on diet and health, as well as heart-healthy recipes. SASE.

**SUGARBUSH FARMS**
**RFD 1, Box 568-50**
**Woodstock, VT 05091**
**802-457-1757**
**MC,V,AE,DC**
**B**

Since 1945, the Ayres family business has been delivering naturally good cheese, not processed or colored, at reasonable prices. Even Mom (at almost 80) is down at the farm helping out. If you want to tap into something delicious, their pure maple syrup can't be beat. Sample any one of their seven kinds of Vermont cheeses packaged in foil and wax. Imagine—aged sharp cheese (you'll never know what two years of aging can do to fresh, whole milk cheese), naturally smoked cheese or hard-to-find sage cheese (rarely made today).

Each time you order, mention you're a *Great Buys* reader and expect a 5 percent discount (excluding shipping and handling).

**SULTAN'S DELIGHT, INC.**
**P.O. Box 140253**
**Staten Island, NY 10314-0014**
**MC,V,CK**
**C**

Delight in those Middle-Eastern delicacies that will melt in your mouth, not your pocketbook. Their 16-page catalog lists sumptuous specialties like couscous, bulghur, tahini (sesame butter), cheeses, chick peas, spices, cashews, pistachios, packaged gift items, candied and dried fruits, filo dough, baklava, Turkish coffee, cookbooks are also available. Savings of 10 to 70 percent throughout. Response time is

72 hours (except cheeses). Send SASE, please, to receive FREE catalog.

*Great Buys* readers can take another 10 percent off their first order. Be sure to identify yourself as such.

**TIMBER CREST FARMS**
**4791 Dry Creek Road**
**Healdsburg, CA 95448**
**707-433-8251**
**707-433-8255 (FAX)**
**MC,V,AE**
**C**

Like to eat well and healthy, but not willing to give up on taste-tempting aromas and lip-smacking good taste? Timber Crest Farms has the best of both worlds: nutrition and taste. Most of their products are organically grown and not subjected to chemical fertilizers or detergents. Sugar is never added and every product is unconditionally guaranteed. The ready-to-eat pasta sauce has the classic Italian flavor of parmesan, soybean and olive oil, lemon juice and herbs and spices added to dried Roma tomatoes. The addition of almonds in the savory sauce is just the right touch to make it stand out above the ordinary. Recipes are enclosed with every order and holiday gift boxes are featured in the color catalog.

**TIPS**
**P.O. Box 1144**
**Rockville, MD 20850**

Send an SASE for "Ten Tips to Healthy Eating," a booklet that focuses on maintaining a healthy weight, balancing food choices, and gradually improving your eating habits.

## TOMATO LOVERS—FLORIDA TOMATO COMMITTEE
**928 Broadway**
**New York, NY 10010**

Write for your free "Tomato Lovers' Recipes" and receive 7 terrific recipes from different tomato-loving areas of the world. Send a SASE.

## U.S.A. DRY PEA & LENTIL INDUSTRY
**5071 Highway 8 West**
**Moscow, Idaho 83843**

"Cooking with Lentils and Split Peas" includes nutritional information on these legumes, which are high in protein, vitamins, and minerals, along with inventive, nutritious recipes. Send SASE to above address.

## WAKE UP
**Box A-2424**
**Young American, MN 55399-2524**

"Wake Up to Breakfast" is a free brochure whipped up by Carnation using its Coffee-mate Liquid Non-Dairy Creamer. SASE.

## WALDEN FARMS
**c/o WFI Corporation**
**P.O. Box 1398**
**Clifton, NJ 07015**

For a free copy of their quarterly newsletter, send SASE, and if you haven't dressed a salad with one of their reduced-calorie dressings, you haven't been dressing in good health. Found in the produce section of the supermarket, Walden Farms dressing has no chemicals or artificial preservatives.

**WISCONSIN MILK MARKETING BOARD**
**8418 Excelsior Drive**
**Madison, WI 53717**

"Wisconsin Cheese in a Flash." Write to Wisconsin Milk Marketing Board for 16 delicious recipes using cheese that can be microwaved.

**ZABAR'S**
**2245 Broadway**
**New York, NY 10024**
**212-787-2000**
**CK,MC,V,AE,DC**
**C**

The good news is that Zabar's is still booming and brimming with delectable delicacies. The bad news is that it'll cost you to call and place your order—but then gluttons should not have a free ride. Feast on gastronomical goodies from Russian coffee cakes to milk-fed white veal, coffees from around the world, and so many gourmet goodies and gadgets that you'll need a wheelbarrow for both you and your bounty. Prices on most items, exclusive of select foodstuff, are 20 to 40 percent less than retail. Write for their free catalog. Yum-m-m!

# FREEBIES

**ANNOUNCEMENT BY WILLARD SCOTT**
**The Today Show, Room 304**
**30 Rockefeller Plaza**
**New York, NY 10012**

Celebrate your wedding anniversary of 75 years plus or your 100th birthday (or beyond) on The Today Show on national TV. Charitable events are also highlighted by NBC's own weatherman, Willard Scott. Just send in name, address, date, and type of event or celebration at least 3 to 4 weeks in advance. Even if you don't make the airwaves, Willard always remembers you with a card.

## Free Calendars

Call 202-224-3121 or write to your congressman for beautiful photo wall calendars (scenes of Washington, DC, of course).

## CONSERVATION TREES
**National Arbor Day Foundation**
**100 Arbor Avenue**
**Nebraska City, NE 68410**

Trees do more than provide shade and beauty. They also produce needed oxygen, reduce noise, attract songbirds, and save energy. Find out how to maximize these benefits with a free copy of "Conservation Trees."

## GREETINGS FROM THE PRESIDENT
**The White House**
**Washington, DC 20500**
**Attn: Greetings Office**

Greet your 80th birthday (or more) or your 50th wedding anniversary (or more) with a congratulatory note from the President. Allow at least four weeks' advance notice.

## HOME IS WHERE THE HEALTH HAZARD IS
**(D13749)**
**AARP Fulfillment (EE104)**
**1909 K Street NW**
**Washington, DC 20049**
**B**

Learn how to protect yourself from scam operators trying to make a quick buck out of environmental bad news. Here's information on what to do if you suspect there really *is* a health hazard in your home. AARP's Consumer Affairs Department, in cooperation with the National Association of Attorneys General, offers this free brochure. Simply address a postcard to the address above and allow 6 to 8 weeks for delivery.

## Free Tickets to TV Shows

Many TV shows have live audiences, and if you plan to be in New York or Los Angeles, write to the network's guest relations department:

ABC
7 West 66th Street
New York, NY 10023
   or
4151 Prospect Ave.
Hollywood, CA 90027

CBS
524 W. 57th Street
New York, NY 10019
   or
7800 Beverly Blvd.
Los Angeles, CA 90036

NBC
30 Rockefeller Plaza
New York, NY 10020
   or
3000 W. Alameda Ave.
Burbank, CA 91523

**NEW ENGLAND LOCK COMPANY**
**Box 544**
**South Norwalk, CT 06856**

Write for this FREE "Home Security Test" from the maker of Segal locks, just to see how secure your home is.

# Posters

Free posters are available on related subjects from the following:

U.S. National Arboretum
3501 New York Ave., NE
Washington, DC 20002
202-475-4857 (Flowers)

Department of Energy
P.O. Box 62
Oak Ridge, TN 37831
615-576-1301

Environmental Protection Agency
Public Inquiry Center
401 M Street, SW Room 211B
Washington, DC 20460
202-382-7550

# Presidential Message

Call 800-424-9090 (or 456-7198 in DC) to hear a recorded message of the latest news from the White House. Sometimes, though, a member of the Press Corps tells you "There's no news."

## SIGNATURE COLOR FILM
**5311 Fleming Court**
**Austin, TX 78744**

Write for two FREE 35mm rolls of the new Signature film (made by Eastman Kodak), good for slides or prints. Send $2.00, however, for postage and handling.


## SWOPE'S ECONOMY HUT
**632 Pine Street**
**Johnstown, PA 15902**

A great little life-saver miniflashlight on a keychain is yours FREE for the asking. Especially helpful in opening car and front doors in the dark. Send $1.00 for postage and handling.


## "WHERE DID I PUT MY KEYS?"
**AARP Fulfillment EE140**
**1909 K Street NW**
**Washington, DC 20049**

"I know they're here somewhere . . ." This free booklet (D13829) can help you learn more about memory loss and how to improve your memory. Allow 6 to 8 weeks for delivery.

# GIFTS AND GADGETS

## AT&T CONSUMER DIRECT PRODUCTS & SERVICES
**800-222-8800**
**C**

Reach out and shop (for less) 24 hours a day with one call to this phone-to-home connection. A wide selection of touch-tone audio and video products, outdoor and travel items, kitchen gadgetry at its finest, games for young and old, and more. An easy 10-payment plan for purchases on a major credit card that exceed $149 and an unconditional 30-day full refund policy are just some of AT&T's amenities when you shop direct. One ringy-dingy and you'll save a hum-dinger: i.e., PIERRE CARDIN 5-piece luggage collection was regularly $399, their price was $149 (plus delivery $14.90). A SOLAR NIGHT LIGHT listed for $54.95 sold for $29.90 (plus $3.90 delivery); a MR. COFFEE iced tea pot at retail was $49.94, but their price was $34.90 (plus $3.90 delivery). Any way you call it, it can save your day. And you won't get a busy signal, either.

## BORIS RICE
**11319 Wickersham Lane**
**Houston, TX 77077**
**713-496-7152; 713-496-2290**

Sell your old pens, especially fancy ones with gold, silver, or pearl overlays. Call, mail description, or photocopy for price quote.

## CHERYL FOREMAN COMPANY
**260 South Lake Avenue**
**Suite 226**
**Pasadena, CA 91101**
**C,F**

Write for "Price Break" fliers for this company's super-duper discount deals such as the set of ten closet hangar organizers for $5.99, or the amazing multi-purpose 7½" high lantern for $7.95, or the deluxe book lights for $7.95 that will keep you reading all night long without disturbing anyone. When you order, you also get a free copy of their "Gift World" catalog.

## DESCRIPTIVE VIDEO SERVICES
**WGBM**
**125 Western Ave.**
**Boston, MA 02134**
**617-492-2777 ext. 3490**

DESCRIPTIVE VIDEO, a new TV service for the blind, was introduced on PBS and should be an integral part of TV viewing. What it does is describe characters' movements, body language, and scenes during pauses in the dialogue. Those with stereo television or videocassette recorders can receive the additional broadcast signal by pressing a multi-channel stereo button, known as MTS, on the control panel of the stereo or VCR. Contrary to what many people think, a study by the American Foundation for the Blind reported that the visually impaired watch TV up to 6 hours a day, the same as the sighted.

**FINGER MATE**
**Box 607**
**Hallandale, FL 33008**

Have a hard time getting your ring to fit just right? End the problem of ring twisting and sore knuckles. Finger Mate expands over the knuckle and then contracts for a perfect fit. From $200 at your jeweler, or write for the name of an authorized dealer near you.

**HANDI-GRIP**
**c/o Newline, Inc. Dept #3**
**9381 Fletcher Drive**
**La Mesa, CA 92041**

Get a grip on things (jars, caps, and lids) easily with this great gadget. Simple to use and recommended by doctors and therapists (even handymen carry them in tool boxes) for sufferers of arthritis. For that little extra twist-assist, this is an ideal answer to those too-tight tops and caps.

**HARRIET CARTER**
**North Wales, PA 19455**
**215-361-5151 (Orders); 215-361-5122 (Information)**
**C**

You'll cart off some fun as well as fabulous and useful little gadgets and gifts from this catalog; you'll laugh and learn a thing or two. Some favorites include a battery-operated flexible massager to massage areas you can't reach ($24.98), a bathtub safety rail (special at $7.95), a kit to dry flowers in your microwave ($7.98), a spray to make too-tight clothes fit more comfortably ($5.98), a fat separator for removing cholesterol-laden fats from soups and things ($6.98), a pet vacuum, a whistle to find lost keys, a way to preserve the grandchildren's footprints or handprints and more.

**LA VIE EN ROSE**
**82 Christopher St.**
**New York, NY 10014-4252**
**212-266-4010**
**MC,V**

A rose by any other name wouldn't smell as cheap. Order a dozen long-stemmed or 2-dozen medium-stemmed roses for $29.99, anywhere in the continental United States, and they'll be shipped Federal Express. Many other varieties, including dry roses, are available in the store, but you'll have to negotiate the price.

**LIFESTYLE RESOURCE**
**921 Eastwind Drive**
**Suite 114**
**Westerville, OH 43081**
**800-872-5200**
**MC,V,AE**

Where else can one find a portable Sound-Conditioner that masks sounds? From a snoring spouse to the roar of traffic, you can replace those annoying noises with the gentle patter of rain sounds or the soft rush of a waterfall. This device comes with a 6-foot cord and uses regular household current. It's compact and lightweight, with its own travel case, and it has a one-year limited warranty ($99.95). Or you may choose other valuable aids, such as exercise balls to stimulate the hands and fingers, a lifeline gym, an overnight travel bag, or even a wooden-beaded car seat with massaging action. Most orders are shipped within 48 hours. There is no risk with the 30-day return privilege.

**LILLIAN VERNON**
510 South Fulton Avenue
Mount Vernon, NY 10550
914-633-6400; 914-633-6300 (Charges)
MC,V,AE,D,DC
C

This treasure of a specialty mail-order company is almost 40 years old and nary a wrinkle in sight. A wonderful addition to your "must" shopping list for gifts, household, gardening, children's, and holiday items. Over 136 million catalogs in 16 editions will be mailed in 1991. At the helm, founder Lillian Vernon Katz has sold to millions of customers whose battlecry is "Never pay retail!" Of special note to seniors: "Send a Gift" for $2 extra can deliver gifts to children and grandchildren, boxed and giftwrapped without the hassle of a trip to the post office. All products from soup dishes to sundials, goodies for holiday decoration to gourmet items to nibble all year long, all with a 100 percent money-back guarantee—even years after the purchase.

**LONG DISTANCE ROSES**
P.O. Box 7790
Colorado Springs, CO 80933
800-LD-ROSES; 303-537-6737 (in CO)
MC,V,AE,DC,CK
C

Say it with flowers for less than you might expect anywhere in the U.S., shipped Federal Express. Choice of colors in red, pink, and yellow for standard flora, with other color variations occasionally. Orchids are from Hawaii and are guaranteed delivered in two days fresh, or you'll be entitled to a complete refund or replacement.

**MARKLINE**
**P.O. Box 13807**
**Philadelphia, PA 19101-3807**
**800-992-8600 (Orders); 800-225-8390 (Customer Service)**
**215-244-9447 (in PA)**
**MC,V,AE**
**C**

Markline is full of neat gift ideas and personal treasures you'll just love, backed by their 60-day guarantee. Special perks like $5 worth of "Markline dollars" redeemable toward a purchase promise you the full satisfaction they claim and you deserve. Call today for their catalog and check out products like their remote light control system that turns on the lights in your house before you go in or other unique items such as the folding toboggan, a clothes shaver to bring new life to worn sweaters, a bathroom telephone with AM/FM radio and toilet tissue holder, a Vegas slot machine, a SILENT NIGHT pillow that helps stop snoring and migraine headaches, a battery-powered closet light that turns on automatically when the door is opened, a KEYFINDER keychain that lets you find your keys simply by pushing a button, and JUMP START that gives you the luxury, safety and convenience of starting a "dead" car without leaving the driver's seat! They also have a wonderful selection of gift ideas for the grandchildren. Receive a free gift with every order and ask about express delivery.

**MATURE WISDOM**
**P.O. Box 28**
**Hanover, PA 17333-0023**
**800-638-6366**
**MC,V,AE,D,DC,CB**
**C $2**

Grow old gracefully and in style as this catalog exemplifies. Page after page, you'll see fashions that fit the fuller figure or that fit for comfort, products that make for healthier and easier living, products for the traveling man or his pet, products for the home front and more. Also, there's an exercise bike with a seat that is easy on the seat, soft-knit shoes with orthopedic arch supports, take-your-own blood pressure kit, an anti-wrinkle facial pillow or a four-wheel cart for groceries. If you're a smart shopper, you'll shop by phone and save both time and money. (See also under Apparel and Shoes.)

**NEWLINE PRODUCTS**
**200 West 14 Street**
**Wilmington, DE 19801**

Have trouble opening those pesky milk cartons? Well, never again with the "Pouring Pal." It snaps over the top of the container, is easy to use and stops those messy drips and leaks. Dishwasher safe, it comes in pint, quart and half-gallon sizes. Either size is $2.99 plus .95 shipping and handling, or order two and save at $4.95 plus $1.25 shipping and handling.

**PERSONAL CREATIONS**
**375 W. 83rd Street**
**Burr Ridge, IL 60521**
**800-326-6626 (7 A.M. to 7 P.M. CST)**
**708-655-3299 (FAX 24 hours a day)**
**CK,MC,V,AE,MO**
**C**

Baring your own creation, this catalog takes care of everything else with that personal touch. Either call toll free or fax for the fast track. For her, for him, for the bath, wedding or anniversary presents, special occasions, outdoor living, your pet, or your grandkids. For the golfer, you'll score big with a monogrammed silverplated golf-bag tag; for after the shower, a plush, initialized terrycloth robe; a car classic, monogrammed car mats; or stack the deck in your favor with card deals with a 3-initial or family name 2-deck card set. Names grace personal popcorn bowls, coasters, wine or cookie bags, picnic baskets, mailboxes, doggie bowls, birth pillows—even little red wagons. All with the personal touch of a thoughtful gift giver. Most items are shipped within 7 to 10 working days and are shipped anywhere in the United States with a gift card enclosed. Most even come gift-boxed with ribbon.

Special: Identify yourself as a *Great Buys* Reader and receive 10 percent off on all orders.

**PORT-A-PEDIC AIR SEAT**
**7057 South Verbena Circle**
**Englewood, CO 80112**
**CK,MO**

Developed by a chiropractor, this patented vinyl air seat can end back or hemorrhoidal pain from sitting. It suspends the tail bone in the air to prevent painful pressure and is sure to give relief for anyone who sits, rides, travels, or works in a sitting position for extended periods of time. Regular (14″ × 14″) for $15.95 or Kingsize (18″ × 18″—recommended for persons 190+ lbs. or wheelchair bound) is $22.95. Money back guarantee. Colorado residents add sales tax and an extra $2 for air mail.

**POTPOURRI**
**120 North Meadows Road**
**Medfield, MA 02052**
**800-225-9848**
**MC,V,AE,CK**
**C**

As the name implies, this beautifully crafted free catalog is full of clever and imaginative gift items in a smorgasbord of categories. "Cat"-egories and "Dog"-egories are the most fun for the pet fanciers . . . like natural rawhide chewable slippers ($12.95), the First Lady faux pearl adjustable necklace/collars, or their gift canisters of "junk food." Also their "grandma" sweatshirt was appliqued to a tee ($49.95); golfer car mats should fit most cars and would be loved by golfers everywhere ($34.95) and a golf T-shirt for those "who don't get enough frustration during the week" ($15.95).

**RENAISSANCE GREETING CARDS**
**P.O. Box 845**
**Springvale, ME 04083**
**800-341-0375; 207-324-4153 (in ME)**

Send for their catalog . . . it's a card! In fact, thousands of them (cards!) can be had for a 10 percent savings if you're a Great Buys reader. Buying them at full price is no laughing matter. But their cards are ("I was your age once . . . in fact, I've been your age a number of times. Happy Birthday.") and some are more serious. ("Happy Birthday, Grandson . . . you brighten the lives of all of those who know you.") Also National Audubon Society cards that are too breathtaking to part with, Christmas and Hanukkah, Easter, Passover . . . all important holidays, Thank You's, Get Well, Birth Announcements, Congratulations, Anniversary, Wedding, Friendship, and Birthdays—enough to fill an entire year's worth of events. Further discounts with quantity purchases; over $25, take another 5 percent; over $40, 10 percent; over $75, 15 percent, and over $125, 20 percent.

*Great Buys* readers take 10 percent off their quoted prices.

**REPLACEMENTS, LTD.**
**302 Gallimore Dairy Road**
**Greensboro, NC 27409-9723**
**919-668-2064**

Send a SASE for these sleuths to track down both active and discontinued fine crystal, china, and flatware. Set a perfect table for 8 with a matched set and only pay for the missing piece.

**SIGNATURES**
**19465 Brennan Avenue**
**Perris, CA 92379**
**714-943-2021**
**C**

Signatures signs their mailings with individual two-sided color products to choose from, lots of promotional pricing and an incentive of $100 to send in your order promptly. Envelope offerings come monthly, including a "Help Wanted" pitch to try out their products (for free) and evaluate, for $50. Of course, to qualify, you must enclose the application with an order. Still, the products are impressive and run from satin pillowslips (as low as $10) so you can sleep and not muss your hairdo to "no-lines," a temporary wrinkle remover ($14), a coin sorting bank ($13), safe money pouches ($8) for traveling, hand-stitched aprons ($19), tapestry steering wheel cover ($12), travel videos ($19), or a wooden-beaded car cushion to help massage your back while you drive ($30). Products with a more "manly" orientation can be ordered via their "Handsome Rewards" free catalog with a separate request.

**SOUTHPAW SHOPPE**
**803 West Harbor Drive**
**Suite D**
**San Diego, CA 92101**
**MC,V,AE,CK**
**C**

Give this shoppe your paw and they'll send you a free catalog. The camaraderie among lefties is evident by the number of T-shirts, bumper stickers, buttons, and other paraphernalia having to do with being left-handed. Functional items such as scissors, cooking utensils, musical instruments, how-to books for calligraphy, embroidery, guitar, golf, writing and even ego-boosting ("The National Superiority of Left Handers") won't leave you feeling "left out."

## THE NEW SPENCER GIFTS CATALOG
500 Packets Court
Williamsburg, VA 23189
804-220-5966 (Mon.–Fri., 8–8)
MC,V,AE
C

Introducing this all new but still the same tried and true Spencerian fun catalog you've grown to love. Since 1947, Spencer Gifts has been a mainstay in the gift-giving genre. Lots of gifts and gadgets galore, some to keep and some to give. Ice bags ($3.98) to keep your picnic basket chilled to perfection or a pocket-sized electronic mosquito repellent ($7.98) to keep the guest list limited to those you've invited. An infralux heat lamp ($39.98) rubbed us the right way, and that 4-in-1 sit-up seat that you've seen on TV a million times ($19.98) is an exercise thriller (or killer)! The Interplac toothbrush bristled at $30 LESS than most other sources ($69.98), and a tooth polish ($5.98) will make you smile brighter for less. Even a denture-cleaning machine ($5.98) can keep you talking clean for hours. Orthopedic pillows ($12.98), acupressure slippers ($7.98), or Chinese earrings ($4.98) to help you lose weight are all part of the joy of shopping. Clothes, kids' stuff, tools, and more help you double your pleasure with Spencer.

## STARCREST OF CALIFORNIA
19465 Brennan Ave.
Perris, CA 92379
714-657-2793
C

Talk about gadget-city. This is a whole world's worth of fun and valuable knick-knacks that will make your life easier (and cheaper), safer, healthier and more beautiful. JACK

FROST's cold or hot pack ($6.99), slimming poly-pants
($9.99–$11.99), walk-a-matic clip-on meter that counts the
miles as you walk (or shop) for $2.99, a pedal exerciser to
work out while you read a book or watch TV ($13.99), a
microwave coffee maker that brews just one cup in 60 seconds
($9.99), or a portable door lock ($2.99) should ring a bell.
When you get your catalog sheets, you'll receive a confidential
price list for even *lower* prices. Sh-h-h!

**STURBRIDGE YANKEE WORKSHOP**
**Department H**
**Blueberry Road**
**Westbrook, ME 04092-1596**
**800-343-1144**
**CK,MC,V,AE**
**C**

Even after 37 years, their annual sale catalog of Americana
is worth waiting for. From Shaker reproductions of fine
furniture to faithful replicas of accompanying accessories,
you'll save and savor their time-tested appeal. Brass for the
boudoir or braided rugs for the hallway, your best bets are
their once-a-year sales events.

**WHITEASH GIFTWARE**
**P.O. Box 904**
**Pottsville, PA 17901**
**C $3 (Refundable)**
**CK,MO**

Though perfect for your Christmas shopping, this catalog
fits all seasons and for all the right reasons. Send for the can
dispenser to stop the can clutter in your fridge or try the
best companion to take to the shower, the massaging shower
mate that gently scrubs your back, shoulders, knees, and
feet. Then, there are fishing lures and a combination scale

and tape measure to weigh in those big ones! Even a whole line of chain burglar alarms and the "Intruder Alert" that can be hung on any door for protection. Buy one, get one free and you get a full 25% discount off every item and there is a 100% guarantee. Allow three weeks for delivery.

For readers of *Great Buys*, a free mystery gift with orders of $25 or more will be sent, and postage is free!

**WINNING IDEAS**
**AIRPILLOW**
**P.O. Box 1417**
**Snohomish, WA 98290**
**800-82-RELAX (800-827-3529); 206-568-9782**
**B,PQ**

An inflatable airpillow designed by flight attendants is sure to hug and fit any size neck and guaranteed to provide the user comfortable rest with head and neck support in an upright position. Perfect for the seasoned traveler, by air, rail, bus, or car. Write for free brochure and price quotes, including quantity orders for your entire travel club. Prices: one pillow, $8.95; two pillows, $16.95; 5–11 pillows, $6.80 each, plus $2.50 shipping and handling.

*Great Buys* readers can take 10 percent off the quoted retail prices, but should add $2.50 for shipping and handling.

# GRANDCHILDREN

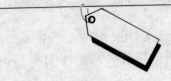

**ASHTON-DRAKE GALLERIES**
**212 West Superior Street**
**Chicago, IL 60610-9948**

Beautiful dolls of superior artistry and craftsmanship in limited series can begin a priceless collection for your favorite grandchild. These dolls are guaranteed for up to one full year (refund credit for full purchase price, including postage). Many of the dolls in this series have increased dramatically in value over a short period of time.

**DALLAS BABY WAREHOUSE**
**4617 S. Buckner**
**Suite H**
**Dallas, TX 75227**
**(214) 388-1201**
**CK,MO**
**B (include SASE)**

Everything for the baby can be delivered here (except the baby) with savings up to 60 percent from this manufacturer. Appliqued fabric crib sets and baby accessories from comforters, diaper bags, totes, to those adorable pillow shams that boast "Grandma's Angel" (or "Grandpa's," too) and "Thank Heaven for Little . . . Girls" (or Boys) are all custom-crafted at these artisans' factory. It doesn't take 9 months to deliver; just 3–4 weeks and a little longer for monogramming. Wall letters by the letter ($4.50 includes freight), baby back rests, balloon or heart wall hangings, terry bibs and Josh's favorite toy, Noah's Arc complete with five stuffed animals.

Special to readers: Free gift with orders over $30.

**DESIGNER DUDS**
**4288 Spring Valley**
**Dallas, TX 75244**
**800-229-7472; 214-458-8029**
**MC,V,CK**
**B**

Save gelt without guilt and get your grandchildren (or others)—infants, girls to size 14, and boys to size 10—outfitted in these specialties of the house. Darling classic European styles for little girls and guys found in your better specialty and department stores at 30 to 40 percent less than retail. Perfect for parties, portraits, school, weddings, and christenings. Matching brother-sister outfits, knicker sets, bubbles, and dresses will make the perfect gift come true for grandkids.

**FOSTER GRANDPARENTS PROGRAM**
**ACTION**
**806 Connecticut Ave. NW**
**Washington, DC 20525**

If you're lacking in the grandchildren department, long no more. Adopt them! Men or women over 60 and in good health (may be handicapped) may volunteer. Along with love, you can receive a yearly stipend of $2,296 for 20 hours of service a week. Write today for information.

## GRANDTRAVEL: THE TICKET COUNTER
6900 Wisconsin Avenue
Suite 706
Chevy Chase, MD 20815
800-247-7651; 301-986-0790 (in MD)

Do you long to have your grandchild/grandchildren all to yourself? To strengthen those ties and generate lifelong memories, take them along as Grandtravelers! What a delightful way to bridge the generation gap and to link a family's past with its future, preserving values for coming generations. These very special vacations provide itineraries that stimulate curiosity and encourage exploration and discovery as well as private time together; meals are well-balanced and delicious, and peer activities with other children and grandparents are planned. Exotic excursions to the castles of England and Scotland, Viking Scandinavia, Holland's waterways and canals, and also popular domestic trips to the western National Parks, our nation's capital or to those perennial favorites, Sea World, Disneyland and Hollywood are all part of GrandTravel's *modus operandi.*

## HANNA ANDERSSON
1010 Northwest Flanders
Portland, OR 97209
800-222-0544; 800-346-6040 (Customer Service)
MC,V,AE,D
C

Swedish quality, brightly colored 100 percent cotton sweaters, knit pants, jackets, caps, gloves, socks, et cetera, all just perfect for the grandkids! Clothing that is meant to be worn, washed, worn and washed again, while retaining fit and good looks. A very special offer called "Hannadowns" is also available. It works like this: If the clothes you order can't be passed down, send them back in "good used condition." Hanna Andersson promises to make sure someone who can't afford them gets them and will give you a 20 percent credit on the purchase price for returned items which can be applied to the purchase of any current catalog item. And if you want to make this a special present, simply include an extra $3 and your gift will be delivered in an exclusive gift box with a handwritten gift card. Gift certificates available, as well, if you're not sure of the size or style. For an extra $5, your package can be sent Federal Express and arrive in two days. There is, of course, a full money back guarantee. Shipping (a flat $4, regardless of order size) the day after your order is received, but your charge account is billed only after the order is shipped.

**HEIR AFFAIR**
**625 Russell Drive**
**Meridian, MS 39301**
**800-332-4347; 601-484-4323 (in MS)**
**C $2 (Free to readers)**

For all those heirs and heiresses, it's apparent that this catalog is made expressly for them. Grandparents whose urge is to splurge will delight in this collection, like a custom monogrammed chair, a complete theater for all of their performances, a tricycle built for two, a beach cabana for an infant including mosquito netting, a sterling dumbbell rattle, Wizard of Oz hand puppets, a ski sled or any other adorable, essential or plain and simple loving gift from your house to theirs.

Mention that you are a *Great Buys* reader when ordering the catalog and you will get the catalog FREE, plus a 10 percent off certificate.

**INTO THE WIND**
1408 Pearl Street
Boulder, CO 80302
303-449-5356
MC,V,CK
C

The next time your grandkids tell you to "Go fly a kite," go
directly to this catalog. No strings attached, either. This is
probably the largest collection-by-mail of kites and wind
socks in the world. They feature traditional Chinese silk
birds and butterflies to high tech space-age nylon airfoils,
boomerangs and wind chimes, too. Write for their free
catalog for hundreds of flight hours of fun and entertainment.

Mention you read it in *Great Buys* when you order and you
can expect a 10 percent discount off your first order (excluding shipping).

**MORTON SALT**
111 North Wacker Drive
Chicago, IL 60606-1555
B

So, what's there to do on rainy days when you're stuck with
the grandkids? Write to Morton's for their free "Saltcrafts"
brochures on how-to-create masterpieces with the salt of the
earth and with a little imagination, you'll have hours of fun.

**RUBENS & MARBLE, INC.**
P.O. Box 14900-A
Chicago, IL 60614-0900
312-348-6200
B (SASE)

Outfit your newest grandchild from top to "bottom" with
infants' clothing and bedding from Rubens & Marble, Inc.
Baby shirts in snap or tie double-breasted and slipover styles

in sizes from newborn to 36 months with short, long, or mitten-cuff sleeves. Many are seconds to save you money, but they also offer first-quality cotton-wool blends and preemie-size cotton shirts. Also, Rubens can cover you with fitted bassinet and crib sheets, training and waterproof pants, kimonos, drawstring-bottom baby gowns, and terry bibs.

**SMALL FRY
CHILDREN'S SAMPLE SHOP
330 Sunset
Denton, TX 76201
817-387-9915
MC,V,CK
PQ**

There's nothing small about this kid's shop near big D. They'll get 'em covered at a whole lot less in brands from out-of-this-world manufacturers and designers. Boys and girls, infants to pre-teens, will love 'em and never leave 'em until they've outgrown 'em. Save from 30 to 50 percent on items from their inventory that's stacked a mile high. Call for a price quote/or write, giving size and budgetary considerations. Since 1969, this mini-mecca is considered one of the best-kept shopping secrets in America and should be a lifesaver for those last-minute gifts for the grandkids.

*Great Buys* readers will receive, off their already discounted prices, 20 percent off any one item (plus shipping) on their first order.

**SUPERCLUBS'
Superclubs' Boscobel Beach Resort
Ochio Rios, Jamaica**

What could be better than grandparents traveling with their grandkids? Children's programs in hotels around the world make this a more interesting and exciting possibility than ever before. Planned activities for the children make the vacation enjoyable for both generations, and these trips are beginning to rival the traditional summer camp, with people choosing resorts like Boscobel instead. Parents (or grand-parents) however, must accompany the children! For more information, contact your travel agent.

**WILTON 1991 YEARBOOK OFFER**
**2240 West 75th Street**
**Woodridge, IL 312-517-0754**
**MC,V,CK,MO**

Birthday cakes to please the most discriminating youngster, along with hundreds of cake, cookie, candy, and dessert ideas for year 'round. New designs and step-by-step instruc-tions will help you meet any occasion—anniversaries, birth-days, or holidays. Make the next party or get-together even more special with a creation of your very own. It's $5.99 for a full-color 196-page book. Order now and get a $6 certificate to use on any Yearbook mail-order purchase over $25.

**WOODEN SOLDIER**
**Apparel for Children**
**Klearsagr Street**
**North Conway, NH 03860**
**603-346-7041**
**C**

If you've been looking for the "perfect" clothes for those perfect grandchildren, try these on for size. They are ador-able, with the most precise attention to detail you've ever seen. They'll look like angels in Wooden Soldier's sweet dresses and fun little rompers and pantsuits. Write or call for a catalog today. This little gem will become a treasure, just like those special little people in your life.

# HEALTH AND BEAUTY

**BEAUTY BOUTIQUE**
6836 Engle Rd.
P.O. Box 94519
Cleveland, OH 44101-4519
216-826-3008
MC,V
C

Ah-h- the sweet smell of . . . ESTEÉ LAUDER, GIORGIO, ANNE KLEIN, OPIUM, GUCCI, L'AIR DU TEMPS or OSCAR DE LA RENTA! Save up to 90 percent on nationally recognized cosmetics from drug store varieties such as CUTEX nail color pens (4 for $1.95—retail $4.25) or MAYBELLINE (mascara for $1.95—retail $4.25). Beauty, skin, and nail care accessories, and lots of inexpensive gadgetry round out this catalog's collection.


**BEAUTY BY SPECTOR**
McKeesport, PA 15134-0502
412-673-3259
MC,V,CK,MO
C

If the only part of you that's thinning is your hair, these wigs, toupées and hairpieces should be at the top of your list, if not your head. All catalogs are free and all the items by Spector are sold at 50 percent off suggested list price. Wash and wear, hang out to dry, at half off for hair today and not gone tomorrow.

## THE BODY SHOP
45 Horsehill Road
Cedar Knolls, NJ 07927-2003
800-541-2535

Finally, this British-based cosmetic company has spread its ecological wings to America and we are now all smelling like a rose (or grapefruit, or banana). Luscious soaps, makeup, fragrances, massage oils, moisture creams and more were all created from plant extracts, herbs, honey, and fruit oils. None of THE BODY SHOP's products have been tested inhumanely on animals and this company insists that even their suppliers follow the same ethical standards. Their recyclable bags and bottles also state: "The question is not, can they reason? Nor, can they talk? But, can they suffer?" A little dab will do "ya" of their alluring White Musk fragrance made from an actual synthetic musk.

## CARE-TECH LABORATORIES
3224 South Kingshighway Blvd.
St. Louis, MO 63139-1183
800-325-9681; 314-772-4610 (in MO call collect)
C

Care-Tech recently released their first-ever catalog featuring those tested health and skin care products formerly used only by patients in hospitals and nursing facilities. Now available for home use, every product is 100 percent guaranteed. Care-Tech products are concentrated, so a very little goes a long way, which makes them economical, too!

## CHAMBERS HAIR INSTITUTE
220 Congress Park Drive, Ste. 250
Delray Beach, FL 33445
800-237-1398; 407-276-4554 (in FL)

Founded by Dr. C. P. Chambers, D.O., the Chambers Hair Institute is dedicated to the "growing" interest in the field of "growing" hair via a transplant. Since 1969, Dr. Chambers has performed over 30,000 hair transplants and has achieved national recognition as a result of his skill and the new methods and technology that he has developed. Best known for the "Chambers Dovetail Closure" technique and the "Hats Off" technique, patients may leave his office directly after surgery without bandages. He's now operating clinics across the country, the author of several books, and a media talk-show authority. Readers will receive a free video and information kit upon request. Donations are accepted in lieu of any money for the video to the Upper Pinellas Association for Retarded Citizens. Send check directly to The Center Foundation, 2037 Gulf to Bay Blvd., Ste. A, Clearwater, FL 34625.

## COMPASSIONATE SHOPPER
Beauty Without Cruelty
175 West 12 Street
New York, NY 10011-8275

If you care enough to stop the cruelty to animals all in the name of beauty, subscribe to this newsletter published three times a year, listing companies that don't test their products on animals, along with information on the products themselves. Cost is $10 for students and seniors; $15 others.

**GENESIS WEST**
Fetal Cell Therapy
800-227-8823; 415-365-6692 (in CA, call collect)

Celebrities have traveled to European rejuvenation centers for years, claiming that injections of live cells help maintain their youthful appearances. Now, twenty minutes from San Diego, European-trained physicians, using live cells that are flown overnight from Germany, perform a nonsurgical biological procedure that supposedly does the same. Call for free booklet, "Live Cell Therapy & Novadermy."

**HMC**
**FINGERNAIL FUNGUS**
Box 458-J
Milltown, NJ 08850

Write for this step-by-step all natural method to rid yourself of the unsightly nail fungus growing among us. You'll be amazed at the results without costly and often dangerous medical alternatives. Money back guarantee. $10.

GREAT BUYS readers: price is only $8; save 20 percent.

**KIEHL'S PHARMACY**
212-677-3171

Kiehl's skin care products include cleansers, scrubs, toners, masques, and moisturizers. They are available in specialty stores and by mail (call the number above). Some of their "hot sellers" are: a scalp massage oil with herbal extracts that smells "pretty awful," and an offensively named "callous cream, but nevertheless, a Kiehl's mainstay." Product prices range from $8.95 for an "ultra facial moisturizer" to a "high altitude moisturizer." Prices aren't listed in any catalog since they encourage customers to call and discuss their needs.

They claim to often be guilty of even talking customers out of ordering things!

## KLUTCH FREE SAMPLE OFFER
**I. Putnam & Sons**
**P.O. Box 444**
**Big Flats, NY 14814**

A generous FREE sample is yours for the asking (limit one per family) of "Klutch" Denture Adhesive Powder.

## KRAMER LAB
**8778 SW Eighth Street**
**Miami, FL 33174**
**800-824-4894**

Fungi-nail is a topical antifungal compound used for treatment of fungal nail infections. It is easy to apply with fingernail polish application and is colorless and odorless. Use it over a prolonged period of time until nails show no evidence of fungus infection. However, it's recommended that you consult your physician about your condition before beginning treatment.

## LA 'n FAIR
**c/o Dallas Images, Inc.**
**1710 Westbridge Way**
**Garland, TX 75044**
**214-530-2917**
**B**

For the fanciest of French creams, expect to pay $600-plus for a full regimen of skin-care rituals. Forget it! With the women's kit from LA 'n FAIR, you pay a fraction of that and receive a whole lot more. Their extensive product line includes cleansers, toners, conditioners for men and women, a facelift kit that will help you look and feel younger, a body shaping kit, cellulite control gel, a loofa body scrub, cherry aloe drinks, lipsticks, shampoos, whipped moisturizers, and a delicious sun and ski conditioner, all with penetrating potency comparable to the most expensive European products in the marketplace today. A 90-day money-back guarantee is their assurance of complete satisfaction. Write for free brochure and price list.

Identify yourself as a *Great Buys* reader and receive a *free* gift with your first order over $100.

**LOTUS LIGHT/AUROMA INTERNATIONAL**
**LOTUS FULFILLMENT SERVICE**
**P.O. Box 2**
**Twin Lakes, WI 53181**
**414-862-2395**
**CK,MO**
**C**

Formerly Fox River Naturals, Lotus Light is still the place to go for just about everything in body care products as well as the bulk herbs and spices you might expect to find in the best-stocked whole-foods stores. They offer a wide variety of mineral bath products and bath soaps, different herbal formulas and dietary supplements. For orders up to $25 shipping is 15%; add 10% of the total after $25 for shipping.

*Great Buys* readers: 5 percent discount on orders over $75; 10 percent on orders over $125 for herbs, supplements, or natural body care products.

**LUMÉ**
**1717 Marsh Lane**
**Carrollton, TX 75006**
**214-418-1900**
**MC,V,CK,MO**

Tired of making those endless trips to the manicurist to get your nails done? Tired of getting "nailed" every time one nail breaks? Do your own thing with a LUMÉ nail care system and even in the middle of the night, you can do your own— and save big bucks. It's easy and averages only $5 to maintain. It lengthens and strengthens, prevents chipping, splitting and cracking, there's no excess buffing and nail care system contains no formaldehyde. Independent contractor LaDean Diercoff offers free demonstrations if you're in the area or will gladly answer any of your questions. Call or write for more information.

Special Gift: Free gift with purchase. Please identify yourself as a reader of *Great Buys*.

**NATURAL WHITE**
**P.O. Box 440**
**Cresskill, NJ 07626**
**800-528-0800**

A smile with pearly whites shouldn't be worth its weight in gold crowns. Now this revolutionary whitener system developed by a dentist can transform stained and discolored teeth into dazzling whites. This 3-part system works through an "oxygenation bleaching mechanism" and is perfectly safe for the teeth. (Not recommended, however, if you suffer from gum diseases or sensitive teeth.) Takes about three minutes to apply and *only* works on real teeth (not crowns or dentures, for example). About $50 per kit and should last a year. Write or call for ordering details.

## PERMA LAB
### P.O. Box 134C
### Millersburg, OH 44654

Loose dentures? You need "Perma-Soft II," the professional denture corrective reline material. With just one application, you can save on dental bills and stop gum shrinkage, and it lasts up to two years. Plus, you may enter the "Free Denture" sweepstakes. One out of every thousand who respond will receive a certificate good for a free set of dentures (upper and lower) from a licensed dentist, paid for by Perma Lab. Winners will be notified upon receipt of each 1,000 entries.

## SALLY BEAUTY SUPPLY
### Check the white pages for the location nearest you.

This is America's source for everything to make you beautiful. A full range of salon products (for home use) to rub, soak, tint, tease, massage, and soothe you from top to bottom. Licensed cosmetologists guide you to do the right thing! Thousands of items for your nails and toes, gallons of shampoos, conditioners, mousses and spritzes to choose from, color yourself beautiful as well as smart. Sally's is a do-it-yourself mecca with professional products often not seen on the retail shelves of your typical health and beauty aids counter. Hair and nail care products create an emporium of endless endings to harried hair-do's and frayed fingernails.

They've got your number. At the check-out register, simply tell them you're a senior shopper over 55 for your special discounts.

## SEQUENCE ADVANCED HAIR GROUP
**106 Grand Avenue (4th Floor)**
**Englewood, NJ 07631**
**201-567-5332**
**B**

Do you have "headaches" or problems with thinning hair, unmanagability or limited growth? Men and women of all ages plagued by such "headaches" have found solutions at the hands of the friendly staff at the Hair Group. Their solution to the hair replacement dilemma is called the Sequence Supplement which incorporates natural hair in the client's own for more style, thickness and body. The company offers a one-on-one free seminar. Not satisfied with the process? It's completely reversible! Call for more information and request free brochure explaining the process with sensational before and after photos of clients.

## WINGS PRODUCTS, INC.
**P.O. Box 680**
**East Hampton, NY 11937**

Wrinkle-free adhesive patches will cost you $5.50 (for 50), $11 (200), or $20 (400) and are worn during sleep to supposedly help frown lines turn around. Lots of smiling faces in their brochures support the fact that they work. Prices include shipping, but write for a current price first.

## WYNNEWOOD PHARMACY
**Wynnewood Shopping Center**
**Wynnewood, PA 19096**
**800-966-9999; (in PA) 215-642-9091 or 215-878-4999**
**CK,MC,AE**
**C,B,F,PQ**

Get a whiff at up to 70 percent off famous fragrances by NORELL, IVOIRE, BAL A VERSAILLES, NINA RICCI, PAUL SEBASTIAN, LYDIA O'LEARY, ROYAL COPENHAGEN, OMBRE ROSE and GIORGIO and bathe in luxurious perfumes and colognes. Make-over with BORGHESE, STENDHAL, DERMABLEND, ORLANE, and CHRISTIAN DIOR. This small but jam-packed full-service pharmacy provides you with one-touch dialing discounts of 20 to 60 percent on all your pharmaceutical needs, prescriptions, and health and beauty aids. Write for their free 32-page fragrance and cosmetic catalog for men and women called "Paris in Wynnewood."

Free gift with first purchase to readers of *Great Buys*.

# HEALTH AND FITNESS

**COMPLETE GUIDE TO EXERCISE VIDEOS**
**Video Exercise Catalog**
**Department G**
**5390 Main Street NE**
**Minneapolis, MN 55421**
**C**

Confused about which workout video to choose with so many on the market? A new free catalog not only lists 200 workout videocassettes but rates them as well. Those receiving "best" ratings are highlighted. Also included are audio tapes, video news, gift ideas, and workout accessories.

**CREATIVE HEALTH PRODUCTS**
**50 Saddle Ridge Road**
**Plymouth, MI 48179**
**800-742-4478; 313-996-5900**
**MC,V,AE,CK,MO**
**C**

Write for their free 12-page catalog and start (or continue) your fitness regimen on a firm footing. Save 30 percent and more on popular state-of-the-art makes and models of fitness equipment: stationary bicycles, treadmills, ergonometers, and rowing machines sporting such names as AVITA, TRACK MASTER, and TUNTURI. Track your heart rate with monitors from BLOSIG INSTRUMENTS, MONARK, or NISSEI and take a skinfold test to determine your percentage of body fat. This is a professional source and may be too sophisticated for your use, but the staff at Creative Health might direct you to another supplier.

## DANCIN' GRANNIES
**10 Bay Street, Suite 3**
**Westport, CT 06880**

Dance your way to better health and have fun every step of the way with the "Dancin' Grannies!" This 50-minute video of high-energy, low-impact exercises is set to music, easy to do, and requires no special equipment. Exercises are designed to increase endurance, flexibility, coordination, and range of motion and are specifically geared toward the older individual who wants to get in shape or stay in shape. It's $29.95, including shipping and handling.

## HEALTHTRAX FITNESS PRODUCTS
**747 Aquidneck Ave.**
**Middletown, RI 02840**
**800-521-9996; 401-849-2400**
**B**

Fitness fanatics cannot find any better source for state-of-the-art equipment and health-related products. Over 100 manufacturers are represented that provide the end user (be it a health club or for home use) with specialty boutique health equipment. Save 10 to 30 percent, with shipping usually within a week or less, on high-end treadmills (LIFE CYCLE, LIFE FITNESS, TRACK MASTER), ski and rowing machines, STAIR MASTER, multistations, pulse meters, free weights, body-fat analyzers, and blood-pressure cups. They even assist in the design and layout, flooring, and more for your fitness retreat. Get on their mailing list to receive a bimonthly newsletter and new equipment updates.

## FIFTY-PLUS RUNNERS' ASSOCIATION
**P.O. Box D**
**Stanford, CA 94305**
**415-723-9790**

Run for your life and also for science are the bywords of the members of this organization. On your mark, get set, go for it! Sponsored by the Center for Research in Disease Prevention at Stanford University, its goal is to gather names of active seniors and learn more about the effects of extended physical activity on older people. Of course, the members run for all those other reasons, too: keeping fit, losing weight, improving their cardiovascular system, and dealing with stress or tension. You can participate with over 1,600 other senior runners and research while you enjoy running for all the right reasons.

## GUIDES FOR GREATER ENJOYMENT OF AN ACTIVE LIFE
**American Physical Therapy Association**
**Public Relations**
**Alexandria, VA 22314**
**B**

Send a SASE to secure your free copy of this brochure from the American Physical Therapy Association on how to protect yourself from injury before beginning a program of activity, be it strenuous or not (like gardening). From warm-up exercises to sunscreens, these tips are worthwhile and free.

**HEALTHIER TOMORROW**
**P.O. Box 2143**
**Longmont, CO 80502-2143**
**800-777-3131**
**MC,V,CK**
**C**

Start today for a healthier tomorrow! A Sentron Health scale that calculates calcium, fat, protein, fiber, iron, salt, carbohydrates and calories in over 1,200 food items will have you well on your way ($179). To tone the body along the way, use the compact, easy-to-use Lifeline Sport Gym. Over 25 exercises are included for $49. After your workout, sink into a warm tub, being sure to use the Tubguard safety rail ($49). Thirty-day money back guarantee.

Readers of *Great Buys* will receive with purchase a free copy of the book "39 Forever."

**NORDICTRACK**
**141 Jonathan Blvd.**
**Chaska, MN 55318**
**800-328-5888; 800-433-9583 (in MN)**
**C**

Get on the right track to fitness and good health with NordicTrack, the most effective aerobic exercise machine available. It provides a complete cardiovascular workout while using all major muscle groups. Three models are offered to fit your budget as well as your fitness needs. All three provide independently adjustable resistance levels for upper and lower body exercise, and it's smooth, quiet and easy to use. Prices range from $399 to $1099, depending upon the model you choose. Their gift catalog has a variety of health-related products, including diet books, sweatshirts with logos, and a storage bag designed especially for

NordicTrack. Thirty day trial. Orders shipped within three days. Two year limited warranty.

**THE POESTENKILL HIKING STAFF MFG. COMPANY**
**P.O. Box 196-J**
**Poestenkill, NY 12140**
**518-279-3011**
**C**

Albert Fromberger has turned the discovery he made in the Catskills into a popular and profitable business. Can't guess what the discovery was? Well, if the name of the company doesn't give it away, maybe his success with celebrities like Joanne Woodward and Ronald and Nancy Reagan will give you a clue. While in the Catskills, Fromberger discovered six 19th century Alpine walking sticks, made popular during the Victorian era and now fast becoming popular again with outdoor and walking activities. For $15 to $40, he will handcraft your choice from the authentic 19th century walking/hiking sticks to functional replicas. Many people buy them just for looks, as they would antiques; still others buy them to go walking, hiking, snow-shoeing, ice-walking, as well as for other outdoor activities. They also sell the new, even more popular aluminum sticks. Walking sticks also make great gifts. Ask about discounts with the purchase of additional sticks.

**SELF CARE CATALOG**
**P.O. Box 130**
**Mandeville, LA 70470-0130**
**800-345-3371; 504-893-1195 (Customer Service)**
**C**

Take control of your own health with fitness equipment, back care, water tests, air purifiers, stress control, skin care, blood pressure monitors, massage tables (with CFC-free polyurethane foam), home medical tests and health books. Self Care has added a cervical pillow made of natural and renewable fibers. Paper for the filler in their packaging is shredded and recycled, and the catalog is being printed on recycled paper. Unconditional guarantee. Full refund or exchanges. Most orders shipped in 24 hours.

**WONDERBED MANUFACTURING CORPORATION**
**Grimes Bridge Road**
**P.O. Box 1551**
**Roswell, GA 30077**
**800-631-1746**
**CK,MC,V,AE**

According to Dr. William Mayo, co-founder of the Mayo Clinic, "It's a good night's sleep and not the apple-a-day that keeps the body fit." Good rest is the secret to good health. Studies report that the adult body cannot tolerate the many contorted sleeping positions we endure during a night's sleep. The Wonderbed was designed to provide the therapeutic support necessary to produce a comfortable sleep. It's built to keep the back muscles relaxed and the spinal column free from distortion. It's also electric, adjustable, has a hand remote control and comes with an optional massage unit. Fits all standard headboards, available in different firmnesses and comes with a 15-year warranty against defects in materials and workmanship. It's long been recommended for sufferers of swollen legs and feet, hiatal hernia patients, those with breathing difficulties (asthma, emphysema, et cetera) or anyone else deserving to awaken without that morning groan.

# HEALTH AND MEDICAL

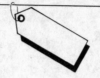

**AMERICAN ACADEMY OF ALLERGY &
IMMUNOLOGY
800-822-ASMA (800-822-2752)**

Call the toll-free Asthma and Allergy Information Line and
request the helpful hints brochure for the allergic patient—
and stop sniffling you can't get relief. They will send you a
list of allergists best able to meet your needs as well as their
credentials and the association's criteria for doctor accep-
tance. This way you'll know if their training is anything to
sneeze at.

**AMERICAN STAIR-GLIDE CORPORATION
4001 East 138 Street
P.O. Box 4001
Grandview, MO 64030
800-383-3100; 816-763-3100 (in MO)
816-763-4467**

Find stairs an impassable barrier, or at best, difficult and
painful to negotiate? If you are looking for ways to become
more independent and for accessibility and convenience, the
Stair-Glide and Stairway Lift make a definite contribution to
your way of life at home, as well as in churches, lodges and
other public buildings. Many models are available and an
international network of authorized dealers is in place to

help customers choose just the right lift. The American Stair-Glide Corporation offers a no obligation "accessibility survey" of your home or building. Call their toll-free number today for the dealer nearest you.

## AMERICAN WALKER
**797 Market Street**
**Oregon, WI 53575**
**800-828-6807; 608-835-9255 (in WI)**
**B**

Write for your free color brochure on the Walk-a-Cycles and accessories for some of the latest in walking aids. These cycles help you walk as well as allow you to maintain levels of aerobic fitness and good health. Sold factory direct, and a layaway plan is offered if requested.

## AMERICA'S PHARMACY SERVICE, INC.
**P.O. Box 10490**
**Des Moines, IA 50306**
**800-247-1003; 515-287-6872**
**MC,V,CK**
**C, PQ**

Shop by phone at one of America's largest mail-order pharmacies offering name-brand trade and generic prescription drugs that represent savings of 25 to 60 percent off the cost of your Rx bill. (Generic equivalents are chemically identical to brand-name products and are approved by the FDA.) Also available are vitamins and minerals, aspirin and cold capsules, sleeping aids, and creams and ointments. They even have hearing-aid batteries and the popular blood-pressure kits. Refunds and exchanges are made within 30 days. There is no charge for shipping via UPS or parcel post, although there is a $.75 handling fee. Check out their 32-page catalog for more information.

## ARTHRITIS: WHAT WORKS
**800-221-7945 ext. 577**
**212-674-5151 ext. 577**
**$22.95 + $2.95 (shipping)**
**CK,MC,V,AE**

Thousands of sufferers of arthritis were asked "What worked?" And the results are revealed in this very readable, practical, and, yes, workable book on the treatments— experimental, alternative, and traditional—that really help (or not). Joe Graedon, author of *The People's Pharmacy*, applauds this effort as the best book on arthritis today. Learn new avenues of therapy that are now being explored, like nutrition and diets that ease pain, innovative new drugs, and bold surgical procedures that are proving effective.

## BRAIN TUMOR INFORMATION SERVICE
**312-684-1400**

This national hotline is provided by the University of Chicago Medical Center for people who need information on tumors. Volunteer doctors talk with callers to answer questions and will frequently send additional medical information or request to see their medical records. Their aim is to make national resources available to anyone anywhere in the U.S.

## BRUCE MEDICAL SUPPLY
**411 Waverly Oaks Road**
**Waltham, MA 02154**
**800-225-8446 (orders); 617-894-6262 (in MA)**
**617-894-9519 (FAX)**
**C**

From America's leading medical supplier comes this 56-page, 4-color catalog showcasing savings on the practical as well as essential items contributing to healthier and happier lifestyles. General home health items for the kitchen, bathroom and bedroom; magnifying glasses without a prescription, blood glucose monitoring kits, diet scales, easy-to-grip light switches, tie-once shoelaces, zipper pulls and more. Other medical specialty items for which Bruce is well known include ostomy, laryngectomy/tracheostomy, diabetic, or incontinence supplies from catheters to undergarments, flanges to irrigation kits. Brand names include SQUIB, HOLLISTER, UNITED, 3M, FOSTERGRANT, JOHNSON & JOHNSON, DEPENDS, and MENTOR, to name a few. Satisfaction is guaranteed and there is a 60-day full refund or exchange policy. Next day and second day express delivery available.

**CHENEY**
**A Mediquip Healthcare Company**
**2445 South Calhoun Road**
**P.O. Box 188**
**New Berlew, WI 53151-0188**
**800-782-1222; 414-782-1100 (in WI)**
**C**

Call toll-free for the Cheney representative nearest you who can answer your questions regarding any of their products designed to help people help themselves. The Cheney Company has over 50 years of bringing convenience, technology, and freedom of movement to the disabled. A recent survey noted a 98 percent customer satisfaction in their high quality products and service. Stairlifts, wheelchair lifts and ride-a-stair are just some of the popular products used in thousands of homes by cardiac, arthritic, stroke, and post-operative patients, as well as senior citizens.

**CHIROLINK**
**800-366-8487**

Don't hurt. Call 24 hours a day, 7 days a week to find a chiropractor nearest you.

## COMPREHENSIVE VISION PLAN, INC.
123 North Wacker Drive
17th Floor
Chicago, IL 60606
800-373-0881

Enroll in this eye-catching plan to save you money (15–25 percent) at thousands of nationally respected optical centers across the country like Lenscrafters, Pearle, Sears, Montgomery Ward, J.C. Penney, and Royal Optical, to name a few. Just show them your discount membership card and save on both lenses and frames regardless of how complicated a prescription. Also includes contacts, eye care products and at some locations, eye exams. Family membership for one year is $25; two years is $40. With just one purchase of glasses, for example, with the savings you could easily recoup your membership fee. No claim forms and no deductibles . . . you just have to present your CVP discount savings card to be able on a clear day, to see forever.

Additional plans at additional costs are also available:

### Comprehensive Hearing Aid Plan

Hear ye! Hear ye! Save 10 percent on point-of-purchase discounts on all products and services throughout their network of audiological care facilities. Hearing aids, molds, tubes and batteries are offered at this discount without having to fill out cumbersome claim forms, deal with exclusions or pre-existing conditions—just show them your card.

### Comprehensive Pharmacy Program Plan

This national pharmaceutical network provides for its members 10 percent off name-brand, generic and maintenance drugs as well as 10 percent point-of-purchase discount for traditional drug store items (excluding alcohol, tobacco, newsstand items, sale and promotional items).

All *Great Buys* readers will receive a free gift with membership.

## CORPORATE ANGEL NETWORK (CAN)
## 914-328-1313

Long-time friends and recovered cancer patients Priscilla Blum and Jay Weinberg are the driving force behind this non-profit organization that flies cancer patients FREE to specialized medical treatment centers. (They will not fly to unacceptable or unorthodox treatment centers, however.) Over 400 companies participate by allowing patients to fill up the empty seats on their corporate jets and therefore avoid the hassle and strain of commercial travel.

## DIABETES COMPUTER
**Merlin Diabetes Management System**
**Bockringer Mannheim Diagnostics**
**800-858-8072**

About the size of a pocket calculator, this device can monitor blood sugar at home. After blood testing, the user logs the results and other data: date, time, insulin injection and such things as food intake, exercise, and state of health at the time. All of this helps the doctor interpret the results quicker and more accurately, ultimately regulating diet and medication faster.

## A GUIDE TO HEALTH & CONSUMER TOLL-FREE HOTLINES
Essential Information
P.O. Box 19405
Washington, DC 20036
$1

Jam-packed with essential toll-free resources that'll answer your most quintessential questions, this handy guide has got your number! Published by a Washington, DC, nonprofit group, it covers two basic categories—health and consumer concerns. Find out the source to donate your organs to for research (the Living Bank) or which agency to call if you feel you've been discriminated against (the Equal Employment Opportunity Commission) and more. Just send $1 for booklet to address above.

## HEALTH-HOTLINES
NLM Information Office
8600 Rockville Pike
Bethesda, MD 20894

FREE booklets on the many sources for medical help. Over 250 organizations that can help answer your health-related questions with their addresses and toll-free numbers, such as:

- 800-341-AIDS;
- 800-4-CANCER (Cancer Information Service);
- 800-343-4573 (American Diabetes Association);
- 800-662-HELP (National Drug Information Referral Line); and
- 800-336-4797 (National Health Information Center).

## INTERNATIONAL HEALTHCARE PRODUCTS, INC.
**3364 Commercial Avenue**
**Northbrook, IL 60062**
**800-423-7886; 312-634-2626 (in IL call collect)**
**312-890-4669 (FAX)**

If you suffer from pressure sores or need help in getting out of the bathtub, these two products are a godsend. Both economical and easy to use, the THERA-FLO gel floatation cushion offers unsurpassed pressure relief at $39 and fits all standard wheelchairs or day chairs. A viscous gel in the cushion conforms to body contours. You actually sit "in" rather than "on" this cushion. The other aid is a portable bath lift that fits all regular sized tubs and uses only water power to lower and lift a bather of any weight. It connects to the tub's faucet and can be packed for travel ($399; $419 with optional back rest). A 30-day return guarantee if not completely satisfied.

*Great Buys* readers will receive free shipping and handling on any order.

## LIFESTYLE RESOURCE
**921 Eastwind Drive**
**Suite 114**
**Westerville, OH 43081**
**800-872-5200**
**B**

If your lifestyle demands health-care resources, this company can provide them. Got a headache? Try their ice pillow. Need to unwind after a long day's drive? Consider the portable massager. Doctor yourself with the automatic blood pressure and pulse monitors. Hot flashes? Have they got a fan for you!

**LINGERIE FOR LESS**
11075 Erhard
Dallas, TX 75228
214-341-9575
CK

Write or call for brochure on this natural breast form developed by a physician who specialized in creating prostheses from synthetic gels. "Soft Touch Breast Form" is available at a fraction of what comparable prostheses cost, molded gel to conform to the body like a natural breast. State your bra size when ordering. One year unconditional guarantee is provided.

**LUPUS FOUNDATION OF AMERICA, INC.**
1717 Massachusetts Avenue NW
Suite 203
Washington, DC 20036
800-558-0121; 202-328-4550 (in DC)

Write for information about the disease lupus as well as local chapter contacts and physician referrals. Over 500,000 people in the U.S. suffer from lupus erythematosus (lupus), a chronic inflammatory disease affecting connective tissue. This foundation, founded in 1977, encourages public support and directly sponsors research to discover the causes and improved methods of treatment, along with providing educational programs and lots more.

**M & M HEALTH CARE APPAREL COMPANY**
1541 60 Street
Brooklyn, NY 11219
800-221-8929; 718-871-8188 (in NY call collect)
718-436-2067 (FAX)
MC,V
C

M & M is probably the largest fashion-by-mail collection exclusively designed for men and women who struggle to dress with ease. At last you will find back-closure dresses that are either wraparound, have snaps, or use Velcro®, daytime dresses, lingerie, lounge and sleepwear, slippers, therapeutic hose, socks to be worn over casts, accessories for wheelchairs, and more. Basic but functional clothing for comfort and care. Free shipping and unconditional satisfaction guaranteed.

**MADISON PHARMACY ASSOCIATES**
429 Gammon Place
P.O. Box 9641
Madison, WI 53715
800-558-7046

Madison Pharmacy has been bringing the most up to date and helpful information to women for many years. Although they specialize in PMS, their expertise covers many other areas relating to women's health problems and needs. Working in conjunction with doctors and nutritionists to bring you the most current information, their dedicated staff is able to acquire the latest research and sift through it sooner since they specialize in the women's health needs area. Call if you have concerns or questions.

## MEDESCORT
**800-255-7182; 215-791-3111**

Need a medical escort? Call this service that handles everything from packing for the trip to providing wheelchairs or any other medically related equipment. One call does it all—from the actual travel booking to providing transportation to the airport, bus terminal, dock or train station. Trained to handle medical emergencies and travel mix-ups, they only escort clients who can sit up during take-offs and landings (airline regulations) on domestic flights. International flights can handle stretcher-bound clients. MedEscort can provide a companion on short notice and they often carry special equipment such as glucose monitors for diabetics, elevated toilet seats for patients who have had hip surgery, and more.


## MEDICAL AIR SERVICES
**800-458-5259**

Call Mr. Marshall Shanbrom for one of the most overlooked but economical investments in medical protection you can make—emergency air transportation. Rest easy, knowing that in the event you need to be cross-country for medical treatment, you will be transported in a state-of-the-art, medically equipped private jet complete with medical personnel and a companion or spouse to accompany you. Medical Air Services will transport an organ should you require a transplant, the return of your mortal remains, transportation of a person of your choice if you should be hospitalized away from home, your return home, the return of a vehicle should it be left stranded, and more—all for a very low, low fee ($5 per month). One trip by ambulance alone could cost $60 or more just to go across town. Medical Air Services will fly you across America (including Canada, Mexico, the Caribbean, Hawaii, and Alaska) for FREE. Avoid the astronomical cost of emergency flights and advance cash payments if you need it and sign up for this program—and rest assured while you travel.

## MEDIC ART FOUNDATION INTERNATIONAL
P.O. Box 1009
Turlock, CA 95380
209-634-4917

The Medic Art Foundation provides confidential 'round-the-clock information related to its members' emergency medical conditions printed on a free bracelet or necklace that members wear once they've joined. For more information, contact the above.

## MED-I-PANT, INC.
P.O. Box 448
Champlain, NY 12919-0448

Priva is a new line of washable personal protection (incontinence care) products as a practical, economical alternative to costly disposable products. Formerly sold only to hospitals and institutions, these products are now available for the home-care market as well.

## MEDIVAN
### A Project of the Elderly Interest Fund, Inc.

This unique program of bringing retired medical personnel to the people who need it most was started in 1986 by a visionary social worker in Florida who spearheaded the liaison of retired doctors and the senior citizenry in need. They took a rebuilt recreational vehicle and outfitted it with a full range of diagnostic equipment: examining rooms, a counseling and treatment clinic, a pharmacy, EKG machines—even a hydraulic lift for those wheelchair bound, and reached out to those who do not see a physician regularly, for whatever reason (mobility, money, lack of transportation) and who meet the financial conditions. Giving hope, providing care and bringing love to this segment of the senior community is why this staff can restore health as well as save lives. This concept deserves repeating to all of this country's aged, especially since in the 1990s, it is predicted that the over-85 group will be the fastest growing segment of the population.

**"MYOFLEX" SAMPLE OFFER**
**Warren-Teed Labs**
**P.O. Box 2450**
**Columbus, OH 43215**

Get a free sample tube of Myoflex analgesic cream and see if it doesn't help relieve the pain of muscle or joint aches. Works deep without heat and is marketed to arthritis sufferers.

**NATIONAL CLEARINGHOUSE ON DRUG ABUSE**
**   INFORMATION**
**P.O. Box 1706**
**Rockville, MD 20850**

"Using Your Medicines Wisely: A Guide for the Elderly" is a FREE record-keeping booklet that will help keep track of medications. This way you can be sure of proper dosage.

## NATIONAL COUNCIL ON ALCOHOLISM
**12 West 21st Street**
**New York, NY 10010**
**800-NCA-CALL (800-622-2255); 212-206-6770 (in NY)**

Call toll-free for information if you or someone you know needs help with alcoholism or other drug addictions. Additionally, local resources are usually listed in the Yellow Pages under "alcohol." Alcoholics Anonymous (AA) has chapters everywhere; support groups include Al-Anon for adults affected by someone's drinking and Alateen for adolescents.

## NATIONAL DRUG ABUSE TREATMENT REFERRAL AND INFORMATION SERVICE
**800-COCAINE (800-272-2465)**
**B**

This national service can refer callers to the nearest in- or out-patient treatment center, self-help program or private practitioner, if you or someone you know suffers from substance abuse. Though not a crisis hot-line, they will intervene in emergencies. Free brochure upon request.

## NATIONAL INFORMATION CENTER ON DEAFNESS
**Gallaudet University**
**800 Florida Avenue NE**
**Washington, DC 20002**
**202-651-5051 (Voice); 202-651-5052 (TDD)**

National Information Center on Deafness is a centralized resource for information on all topics related to deafness and hearing loss. Their suggestion for *Great Buys for People over 50* readers is a series of publications concerning communication tips, management strategies, commonly asked questions, hearing aids, and alerting and communication devices.

Normally the cost of the series of publications is $5.50, but for *Great Buys* readers, NICD is making a special offer of $4.

## NATIONAL INSTITUTE ON ADULT DAY CARE
### Washington, DC

Adult day-care programs are accelerating across the country as a viable alternative for the elderly. These centers give seniors lots of opportunities for socializing, intellectual stimulation, and some even provide medical treatment, physical therapy or dental care. There are roughly 2,000 centers around the country, usually open Monday through Friday. Most of them serve hot lunches and offer round trip transportation, giving primary caretakers some time off. Check in your local community for a program most appropriate for your needs.

## NATIONAL JEWISH CENTER FOR IMMUNOLOGY AND RESPIRATORY MEDICINE
### Living Line Information Service
### 800-222-LUNG (800-222-5864); 303-388-4461 (in CO)
### B

The National Jewish Center specializes in treating and researching respiratory and immune system disorders. The Lung Line was established to educate patients and their families about respiratory health problems. Registered nurses answer questions Monday through Friday. Over 100 years of service, the center is recognized worldwide for providing respiratory-related medical treatment for all ages and religious faiths. Brochures are available for further understanding of chronic lung diseases (asthma, emphysema), allergies or immune disorders.


## NATIONAL PARKINSON FOUNDATION, INC.
**800-327-4545; 800-433-7022 (in FL)**
**305-548-4403 (FAX)**

Operating strictly by donations and certain pharmaceutical support, this foundation, with Bob Hope as honorary chairman, responds to inquiries about Parkinson's Disease through public information. They are the catalyst for raising funds for patient services and particularly research to find the cause and cure, not only of Parkinson's, but other allied neurological diseases as well. Add your name to the mailing list for their quarterly newsletter "Parkinson Report" and receive a handbook for patients and their families, plus a beautiful brochure titled, "Fighting Back: One Woman's Winning Battle."


## 101 QUESTIONS TO ASK YOUR HEART DOCTOR: AN INSIDER'S VIEW
**Tamarack House**
**Decatur, Georgia 30033**
**404-982-9758**

In an easy-to-read, conversational style, author Joy Hannah (her fictional name) shares her 20 years' experience as a nursing practitioner in the cardiac field in answering some of the most common and often-avoided questions you might have, such as: What really are the causes of heart disease? And what are a patient's options? More pointed questions to raise: How many of the particular procedures a week does the surgeon-in-question perform? Or, how high is his mortality rate? Will there be students helping? Is the doctor on drugs or addicted to alcohol? These tough questions and more are explored so you can determine, if, indeed, you're getting the best care possible.

Regular price: $14.95. *Great Buys* readers can order for $9.95.

## ORTHO-KINETICS
**800-446-4522**

In just 25 years, Ortho-Kinetics has become a world leader in mobility products. They offer a "no obligation" home demonstration on their state-of-the-art "Larks," a virtually trouble-free series of mobile three-wheelers that climb hills, go over curbs, take on rugged terrain, or take you to the mall to shop. (Note: a special container behind the seat on the Lark XL can accommodate two shopping bags, at least.) Options are endless and can literally put you in the driver's seat. Another product from Ortho-Kinetics is their cushion-lift chair which not only is comfortable and attractive but, with the press of a button, can bring you to your feet. An extra optional massage-like feature to the chair is the Ortho-ease Stress Reduction System which can be built into the chair providing soothing, rhythmic motions and soft, humming sounds.

## OSBORN MEDICAL SYSTEMS, LTD.
**P.O. Drawer 1478**
**Augusta, GA 30903**
**800-438-8592; 404-724-9017 (in GA)**
**800-356-4676 (in CAN)**
**MC,CK,MO**
**B**

It is estimated that over ten million men suffer from impotence. Though surgery is often a course of action, this company has developed a non-invasive system that has proven to be a very safe and effective product approved for medical use. ErecAid is available by prescription only, and compared to other treatments, is perhaps the most economical solution for impotence. Since impotence is now recognized as a physical problem, many insurance and Medicare carriers will cover its purchase. Ask your physician if he is familiar with the product. If not, show him the brochure (he can request additional data and evidence) and see if you might not be a candidate for its successful use (some medical conditions like certain blood disorders are contraindicated).

**PHAR-MOR**
**Check the yellow pages for location nearest you.**

Shop Phar-Mor where *their* buying power gives *you* far more buying power. This leader in the deep discount drug store business offers a state-of-the-art store where you can save 20–50 percent. Save yourself from the headaches of full retail prices on everything: health and beauty aids, housewares, non-perishable food items, supplies for the lawn and garden, pets, office supplies, and equipment, books, magazines, tapes, cards and an inventory that's Phar-Mor extensive to list here. Seniors are first reminded to shop and compare prescription prices (since an AARP study in August 1989 found as much as a 50 percent difference between pharmacies). Look for a pharmacy with the ability to track your medications so as to always be aware of any potentially harmful drug interactions. Always follow the pharmacist's advice in taking your prescription as ordered.

These and other tips are available FREE from Joe Graedon, author of the *People's Pharmacy* books. Write to "Ten Tips to Improve Your Rx-IQ," P.O. Box 400, Youngstown, OH 44501-0040.

## PRESCRIPTION AIR
**11837 Judd Court**
**Suite 104**
**Dallas, TX 75043**
**214-690-6404**

You can soon be sitting in the lap of luxury and comfort in your Medi-Lift Premium full-power lift and recliner chair system. With a touch of the hand-held wand, you can raise, lower or recline. Each system comes with a sturdy metal lift mechanism on a high-grade (two-year waranteed) velour fabric with a one-year warranty on parts and in-house labor. Constructed with a solid hardwood frame with deep, wide seats, the system is only $500 cash sales price, in gray only. Prescription Air also offers an asthma treatment neutralizer that is AC/DC battery-packed for traveling that can operate on a cigarette lighter adapter.

## REGIONAL RESPIRATORY SERVICES CORP.
**Davis Mobile Oxygen Maker**
**West Highway 54**
**Pratt, KS 67124**
**800-835-2705; 800-362-2385 (in KS)**

Now you can take long car trips with no fear or inconvenience and make/use oxygen in your vehicle as you travel. At last, you can pick up and go, traveling with ease; your days of semi-confinement are over. Hundreds of heart-felt thanks are recorded in their company's literature and yours can be, too. The oxygen maker component is self-contained and can be used wherever there is a 110 volt outlet. Regional Respiratory leases and services the OMC on a monthly basis and will accept whatever is approved by your insurance company under certain conditions. To find out if you qualify, write or call the toll-free number for more information.

**RIC CLARK**
**9530 Langdon Avenue**
**Sepulveda, CA 91343**
**818-892-6636**

Did you hear us right? A half-price offer that's genuine? We have Ric Clark's promise that his prices are about half those charged by dealers. These are not cheap "made-for-mail-order" hearing aids, but of the same excellent quality you would expect from the best dealer in town. You want to save, but you certainly don't want an inferior hearing aid. Full 30-day refund is offered.

Readers of *Great Buys*: If you order now, you will receive a month's supply of batteries free.

**RITE-WAY HEARING AID COMPANY**
**P.O. Box 59451**
**Chicago, IL 60659**
**312-539-6620**
**CK (with terms)**
**B,PQ**

The Rite-Way is one of the best ways to save on hearing aids. Right away, they're 50 percent off, with batteries 25 percent off and repairs about 25 percent less than at your local repair station. Brands include ROYALTONE, DANAVOX and more and come with a 30-day trial, one-year unconditional guarantee and a six-month warranty on repairs. An impression kit for custom ear molds will be sent upon request. Select from behind-the-ear, all-in-the-ear, eyeglasses and body aids. Write for free brochure and/or call for price quote.

## SEARS HEALTH CARE CATALOG
**800-255-3000**
**C**

Call for your free copy of "America's largest catalog assortment of hospital-quality merchandise." Relax in a whirlpool spa or relieve tired, aching feet in Dr. Scholl's footbaths, maintain independence with durable bedside commodes as well as other unique bathing accessories. Enjoy a soothing back massage with a variety of products designed to ease back pain and tension, and relieve those allergy symptoms with humidifier/clean-air machines. Keep tabs on blood pressure between doctor's visits. You'll find lightweight leisure clothing with easy opening smocks and snappy velcro® closures, oxfords for comfortable walking, underwear and nightwear designed with wide armholes, extra shoulder room, longer hems and straps that don't slip down, therapeutic support hose, post-mastectomy needs, trusses and body supports, and incontinent undergarments. Also, wheelchairs and accessories, walkers, canes and tri-wheelers. Other helpful items that may just change the way you live are: a dressing assistance kit with button loops and 23″ long shoe horn, placemat and coaster set with latex coating on both sides to prevent slipping, a mealtime kit with vacuum feeding cup, curved rail food bumper, plastic inner lip plate to keep food on the plate, and a phone caddy that can be hooked to a wheelchair or walker. Satisfaction guaranteed or your money back.

## SIGNATURE DENTAL PLAN
**800-346-0310**

Take the bite out of exorbitant and rising dental costs. This plan has got you covered for at least 30 percent less and even offers FREE select preventive services like x-rays and oral exams. Preexisting conditions included and there are no deductibles. Signature Dental Plan was conceived to help consumers save money on virtually all of their dental needs. Their nationwide network of dentists and specialists participate because it helps expand their practices. All dentists are carefully screened for the highest standards of excellence in health care, facilities, and cleanliness. Individual memberships begin at $48 per year; $60 for husband and wife; $72 for a family, including all children and grandparents living in your home. Periodontal (gums), endodontics (root canals), prosthodontics (dentures), and oral surgery (extractions) are available, besides general restorative dentistry, i.e., fillings, crowns, bridges.

**SNORING BROCHURE**
**NEW YORK EYE AND EAR INFIRMARY**
**Department GH**
**2nd Avenue at 14th Street**
**New York, NY 10003**

Write for the "Snoring: Not Funny, Not Hopeless" brochure. Information regarding what causes snoring and the ways it can be helped is yours FREE. Send a SASE.

**THERABATH**
**c/o Medical Electronics Company**
**123 North Second Street**
**Stillwater, MN 55083**
**800-321-6387; 612-430-1200 (in MN call collect)**

Soak your aching feet or hands in a heated paraffin tub called the Therabath and experience relief from arthritis pain, joint stiffness, muscle spasms and inflammation. Though used in salons as a beauty treatment to soften hands or feet, it's cheaper to order through a medical supply dealer at a cost of approximately $152. Therabath has been recommended by physical therapists and doctors for over 25 years. Call this family-owned manufacturer for the dealer nearest you.

## TRD (TONGUE RETAINING DEVICE)
**c/o Baylor College of Medicine's Sleep Disorder Clinic**
**713-798-5333**

Chicago psychiatrist Dr. Charles Samelson has invented this plastic mouthpiece to prevent snoring. It is custom-fitted by dentists by prescription and costs from $400 to $1200, depending upon the dentist's fee. Not all dentists are trained to fit the device yet, but call for more information and possible referral to a dentist in your area.

## UPJOHN HEALTHCARE SERVICES
**(800) 462-9556**

The folks at Upjohn, a leading provider in home health care, have just what the doctor ordered. Offering a wide range of services—including some that used to require a hospital setting—Upjohn HealthCare Services is a comfortable, less costly alternative to institutional care. With more than 225 offices in the United States and Canada, Upjohn provides part- or full-time caregivers for any home care need. From routine custodial or housekeeping tasks to full-service skilled nursing care, Upjohn's bonded, insured caregivers provide professional service. Comprehensive services include INDEPENDENT LIVING SERVICES, a program to help mother and baby leave the hospital sooner and make a smooth transition back to home and family; AFTERCARE, which provides nurses and home health aides with specialized skills to help clients and their families cope with psychiatric illness at home. If you do not have a long-term insurance plan, it may be worth your while to explore—especially those that will cover home care.

FREE to readers of *Great Buys*: "A Guide to Home Health Care," by Alan E. Nourse, M.D.

**UPSHER-SMITH LABORATORIES, INC.**
**Attn: Lubrin Sample Offer**
**P.O. Box 4420**
**Maple Plains, MN 55348**
**800-328-3344**

Today's society places great emphasis on health. As our population ages, we become more attuned to changes that occur within us. Vaginal dryness is a natural occurrence with many causes, and an estimated forty million women are affected by this problem at one time or another. Lubrin inserts are a convenient solution to the problem, providing lubrication for vaginal dryness. Lubrin is water soluble, colorless, stainless and odorless. Call toll-free if you have any questions. Be sure to ask your doctor's opinion. For free sample, write to the address above.

**WHEATON MEDICAL TECHNOLOGIES**
**800-654-5455**

Can't remember when you took your last medication? Prescript TimeCap records the time and day of the week when you opened the container. It displays the information until you open the container again. An alarm will beep when your dose is due. Easy to open. Call for more information and prices.

# Health and Medical Free Offers

**AMERICAN HEART ASSOCIATION**
**205 East 42nd Street**
**New York, NY 10017**

A whole host of heart-fact items (including charts, puzzles and more) to help prevent heart attacks can be had by writing the American Heart Association.

**BRISTOL-MYERS COMPANY**
**Consumer Information Department**
**345 Park Avenue**
**New York, NY 10022**

A $2.00 value FREE when you write for your 191-page book of basic household information on products, prescription drugs, appliances, personal care items, and more.

**JOHNSON & JOHNSON**
**Attn: Consumer Services**
**501 George Street**
**New Brunswick, NY 08903**

A FREE wall chart of first aid facts is yours for the asking. And what a lifesaver it can be.

**METROPOLITAN LIFE INSURANCE COMPANY**
**One Madison Avenue**
**New York, NY 10010**

Write for their free list of educational health and safety items, such as their wonderfully graphic "First Aid Chart."

**PFIZER PHARMACEUTICALS**
**P.O. Box 3852**
**Grand Central Station, NY 10163**

Write for the free handbook "Help Yourself to Good Health," compiled by the National Institute on Aging.

See also the section titled "Organizations" for additional medical associations.

# Women's Health Care Facilities

**BRIGHAM YOUNG WOMEN'S HOSPITAL**
**Boston, MA**
**617-732-7139**

For cardiology.

**BONE HEALTH PROGRAM**
**St. Louis, MO**
**314-454-7775**

For diseases of the bone.

**DIAMOND HEADACHE CLINIC**
**Chicago, IL**
**312-878-5558**

For chronic headache syndrome.

**EATING DISORDERS PROGRAM**
**612-626-6188**

For eating disorders with or without chemical dependency.

**HAZELDEN**
Minneapolis, MN
612-257-4010

For chemical dependency.


**M.D. ANDERSON CANCER CENTER**
Houston, TX
713-792-3245

For treatment of breast cancer.


**UNIVERSITY OF ALABAMA AT BIRMINGHAM**
Multipurpose Arthritis Center
205-934-3881

For early diagnosis and treatment of joint damage.

# HEALTH AND VITAMINS

**FREEDA VITAMINS**
**36 East 41 Street**
**New York, NY 10017**
**212-685-4980**
**MC,V,CK,COD**
**C,PQ**

Vitamins are easy to swallow when they're 30 to 50 percent off regular retail price. Scan Freeda's 48-page catalog and start to feel peppier just looking at mega-vitamins, multivitamins, amino acids, nutrients . . . just about every kind of health supplement on the market today. There is no minimum order and unopened merchandise can be exchanged for something of equal value. Remittance required with first order to establish credit.

Special to readers: 25 percent off already discounted prices.

**L & H VITAMINS**
37-10 Crescent Street
Long Island, NY 11101
800-221-1152; 212-937-7400 (in NY)
MC,V,CK
C

L & H . . . Lively and healthy is what you can be with vitamins at discounts of 20 to 40 percent. Name-brand and hard-to-find health products are always sold from their catalog at well below standard retail prices. They promise to ship the very same day your order is received. Just call the toll-free number for speedy service. Don't forget to ask the operator for the "BEST BUY OF THE DAY." Staying healthy has never been easier. A new catalog is issued quarterly. There is no minimum order and returns are accepted within 30 days.

**LAFAYETTE PHARMACEUTICAL**
4200 South Hulen Street
Fort Worth, TX 76109
817-763-8011; 817-731-9389

Confused about dietary and fiber supplements? We all know we "need roughage" and doctors recommend a high-fiber diet, but how best to get it? Psyllium is the newest word in mega-fiber and one dose of Konsyl fiber supplements provide six grams of psyllium. Also, Konsyl contains no dextrose (sugar), artificial sweetener or flavoring and is 100 percent natural. You'll receive a sample shaker cup, a recipe booklet with suggestions for mixing with fruit juices and a $1 off store coupon. If you do not see Konsyl on the shelf at your pharmacy, ask the pharmacist.

## STUR-DEE HEALTH PRODUCTS
**Austin Boulevard**
**Island Park, NY 11558**
**800-645-2638 (Orders only); 516-889-6400**
**MC,V,CK,COD**
**C**

Stur-Dee pioneered the nutritional consciousness that has been raised to coffee-table conversation of late. Twenty-five years ago, Stur-Dee launched the movement of "health nuts" that exploded in the 1980s with nutritional labeling, vitamin therapy and an all-around devotion to a healthy lifestyle. Today, seniors can order Stur-Dee's own brand of drugstore products—vitamins, minerals, and cosmetics, formulated to their specifications. Many of these products are natural and contain no sugar, artificial color, or starch. Prices on house vitamins, minerals, cosmetics, healing agents and aloe vera products average a sturdy 15 to 30 percent lower than most national brands. Gifts often accompany orders.


## SUNBURST BIORGANICS
**838 Merrick Road**
**Baldwin, NY 11510**
**516-623-8478**
**MC,V,CK,COD**
**C**

Combat dietary deficiencies with all-natural supplements—such as with the preferred form of vitamin C, Spirulena (a protein food praised by dieters and joggers). Pep up your pets by getting them to "pop" pet vitamins. At discounts of up to 70 percent, brands include SUNBURST, FUTURE BIOTICS, and HERBAL TEAS. (We don't want to B complex, but check out their catalog and C for yourself!) All orders processed in 24 hours. No postage except for $1 shipping charge when shipped within the continental U.S. Full refund given within 30 days if not completely satisfied.

**VITAMIN SPECIALTIES COMPANY**
8200 Ogontz Avenue
Wyncote, PA 19095
800-666-5683
MC,V,CK
C

If you're prone to vitamin deficiencies, this company will have you back on your feet in no time with discounts of 40 to 60 percent on vitamins, dietary supplements, over-the-counter drugs and cosmetics. You'll not only feel better, you'll look better. All products are manufactured under the VITAMIN SPECIALTIES brand and about half are 100 percent natural. Unopened merchandise may be returned within 30 days for a full refund or credit. No shipping costs on orders over $15.

*Great Buys* readers are entitled to an extra 10 percent on orders over $20, as well as free shipping!

# HOME AND OFFICE

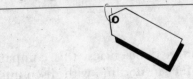

**ABC VACUUM WAREHOUSE**
6720 Burnet Road
Austin, TX 78757
512-459-7643
MC,V,AE,D,CK,MO,COD
B,F

Readers 55 and over get 50 percent savings on top-of-the-line vacuums. It's as simple as A-B-C. Don't be a sucker and get taken by those fast-talking door-to-door salesmen. This company's so honest, they even print the phone number of the local Better Business Bureau on their flyers. Big volume purchasing and buying from distributors who are over-stocked or going out of business means they pay less and so do you. Two-year warranties. Returns accepted within 15 days for a full refund. Even central vacuum systems can be shipped to your builder. Since 1977, owner Ralph Baccus has been laying out the red carpet for thousands of satisfied customers who've bought RAINBOW, KIRBY, ROYAL, RICCAR, FILTER QUEEN, ORECK and other top-of-the-line vacs from him.

*Great Buys* readers get FREE shipping on all orders.

**AGATHA'S COZY CORNER**
Dept. 90355
Woodbury Plaza
Portsmouth, NH 03801
603-543-8800
V,D,CK
C

Freeze to death no longer! Discover the ultimate in luxury for the cold-natured—the plush, dreamy comfort of flannel sheets. You won't have to be buried under layers of heavy comforters to be warm anymore. And this is a great way to save on heating bills, while feeling rich and special. Agatha's sheets are not the flimsy pilled kind, but luxuriously soft, thick, real 100 percent cotton-flannel. No polyester allowed! Also available are heavenly down comforters and other items. Agatha will send you a color catalog with every purchase and the story behind everything she sells. It's free.

**ALBERT S. SMYTH CO., INC.**
29 Greenmeadow Drive
Timonium, MD 21093
800-638-3333
CK,MC,V,AE
C

Since 1914, Albert Smyth has been dishing it out, from here to china (crystal, silver, gifts, too). Only famous makers are served—LENOX, MINTON, WEDGWOOD, ROYAL DOULTON—at 20 to 60 percent off retail. Fine jewelry also discounted 25 to 50 percent. Their extensive color catalog is appetizing and guaranteed to keep you full of savings. A 30-day full-refund policy is issued along with a prompt shipping schedule.

## ALLIANCE TO SAVE ENERGY
**P.O. Box 96785**
**Washington, DC 20090-6785**

For $15, you can get a GE compact 15-watt bulb which provides the same light as a 60-watt incandescent bulb and also a brochure with energy-saving tips for the entire household. Save money (around $55), save energy (it's about 75 percent more efficient), and save time (it lasts about 9,000 hours or six years). Also available through your local utility company.

## AMERICAN BLIND FACTORY
**28237 Orchard Lake Road #105**
**Farmington Hills, MI 48018**
**800-351-1150; 313-553-6200 (in MI)**
**MC,V,AE,D,CK,MO**
**B,PQ**

Custom blinds in mini or micro aluminum, verticals, pleated shades, and wood blends in 1″ and 2″ widths are their claim to fame. Save up to 50 percent but measure carefully (free brochure will tell you how), as custom cuts are nonreturnable. If your blinds are not shipped in 5 days, they are FREE.

## AMERICAN DISCOUNT WALLCOVERINGS
**1411 Fifth Avenue**
**Pittsburgh, PA 15219**
**800-777-2737; 800-245-1768**
**MC,V,CK,MO**

Cover the town green with envy once they see your windows and walls. Save from 20 to 60 percent off the best brands in decorator window and wall coverings. From blinds to custom bedspreads and draperies, hang out with names like IMPERIAL, RALPH LAUREN, SCHUMACHER, WALLTEX, WESTGATE, BALI,

LEVOLOR, and DELMAR. For price quotes by mail, please send a SASE.

**ALUMINUM GREENHOUSES, INC.**
**14605 Lorain Avenue**
**P.O. Box 11087**
**Cleveland, OH 44111**
**216-551-3377**
**MC,V,D**
**C $2 (Refundable)**

Cut it out! Stop wishing and let nature bring sunshine into your life all year! Fragrances and cascades of exotic colors are yours in an Everlite (that is, the world's first aluminum greenhouse). At modest cost, choose from hundreds of standard, fully prefabricated models designed for easy owner assembly. Fully insulated models available. This company has been in business since 1952. Send $2 for catalog, refunded on your first order.

**BARNES & BARNES**
**190 Commerce Ave.**
**P.O. Box 1177**
**Southern Pines, NC 28387**
**800-334-8174**
**919-692-3381 (in NC)**
**B,PQ**

No need to weave any yarns about Barnes & Barnes. When it leaves their door, you can expect furniture delivered at 40 to 50 percent less than retail (including freight). Their connections net you AMERICAN OF MARTINSVILLE, FAIRINGTON, HIGHLAND HOUSE, TEMPLE, and others of equal worth. Fill up your hearth with a dearth of namebrand living-room, dining-room, bedroom, and patio furniture and expect birth in 8–12 weeks or longer. A fabric swatch will be sent for verification before order is confirmed. A 50 percent deposit is required with order; balance upon delivery. Returns are accepted minus freight charges.

Mention you read about them in *Great Buys* and receive a special 2 percent discount off your order.

**BEARDEN BROTHERS CARPET AND TEXTILE CORPORATION**
**3200 A Dug Gap Road**
**Upper Level, Department 208**
**Dalton, GA 30720**
**800-433-0074; 404-277-3265 (in GA)**
**404-277-1745 (FAX)**
**B**

Save 40 to 85 percent from this carpet source, which has previously serviced carpet dealers, chain stores, hotels, and movie sets. Now open to the public, each carpet and textile product comes with name-brand warranties and is first quality only (no flaws). Names like BIGELOW, CORONET, DAN RIVER, EVANS & BLACK, GALAXY, J.P. STEVENS, LEES, MOHAWK, and PHILADELPHIA are laid out and waiting to be stepped on.

**BENINGTON'S**
**1271 Manheim Pike**
**Lancaster, PA 17601**
**800-252-5060**
**PQ**

No need for a Ph.D. to understand savings of 35 to 75 percent on any make of wallpaper, fabric, and border available. Same-day processing of your order. All it takes is knowing which manufacturer and pattern number you want and a toll-free call. And that's all, folks!

## BETTY CROCKER CATALOG
General Mills, Inc.
P.O. Box 5000
Minneapolis, MN 55440-5000
612-347-0202 (customer service hotline)
C

You can save up to 50 percent (or more) off retail prices and up to 77 percent on ONEIDA COMMUNITY stainless flatware by collecting BETTY CROCKER points on over two hundred General Mills' products. Clip and save these points on the packages of such products as BISQUICK, CHEERIOS, and HAMBURGER HELPER. Select the items you want from this catalog and send your order along with your BETTY CROCKER points to save big bucks. Butter up your gift or wish list with PFALTZGRAFF, ROYAL DOULTON, or any number of glorious kitchen gadgets, utensils, and other at-home partying accessories. Even kids' kitchens can be outfitted.


## BLACKWELDER'S
U.S. Hwy 21 North
Statesville, NC 28677
800-438-0201; 704-872-8921 (in NC)
CK,MC,V,COD
C, $7.50; Portfolio $2 (refundable)

Since 1938, this fine family tradition has led the pack in furniture to go. A continuous blend of quality, service, and price has helped Blackwelder's establish itself as one of the premier North Carolina purveyors. Their 60-page 4-color catalog has doubled in size and offers the largest collection of namebrand furniture in catalog form today. The portfolio offers over 300 different MARTINSVILLE COLLECTION English and American 17th- and 18th-century reproductions in solid cherry, oak, or pine with four different finishes. Handmade and appearing much more expensive, at last, an affordable look that spells high class.

Attention readers: Not only will you receive the $2 portfolio free upon request, but you'll receive 10 percent off any MARTINSVILLE COLLECTION purchase. You must identify yourself, however, as a *Great Buys* reader.

## BRAIDED RUGMAKER
**369 Roosevelt Avenue**
**Pawtucket, RI 02860**
**401-723-6734**
**MC,V,CK,MO**

The Braided Rugmaker does just that—custom-braided rugs in many different constructions. Savings on comparable rugs anywhere from 50 to 70 percent. Send color swatch and size information when ordering, along with a $10 deposit (deductible from order). They'll send back a price quote, including braid sample and diagram. A 50 percent deposit is then required with order; balance upon delivery. Save the COD fee by paying in full in advance. No return on custom orders allowed unless defective or damaged in shipment. Allow 8 weeks for delivery.

*Great Buys* readers: Receive FREE 2 × 3-foot rug when purchasing any room-size rug measuring 5 × 8 feet or larger.

## CHERRY HILL FURNITURE, CARPET & INTERIORS
**FurnitureLand Station**
**P.O. Box 7405**
**High Point, NC 27264**
**800-328-0933; 919-882-0933 (in NC)**
**CK,MO**
**B**

Hand-picked by this second-generation furniture family, Cherry Hill sells seasoned lines too plum to mention. Since 1933, you can shop by phone for furniture, rugs, and carpets and save 40 to 50 percent, plus the sales tax outside North Carolina. Expect shipment in 12–16 weeks, depending on manufacturer (and there are hundreds to pick from). Returns accepted only with authorization from the company.

**COLONIAL GARDEN KITCHENS**
**P.O. Box 66**
**Hanover, PA 17333-0066**
**800-752-5552**
**C**

An appetizing catalog fit for a feast can help great cooks save time and money. Gadgets and gifts for home and hearth run the gamut from gourmet to practical. Stop stooping with a dustpan-broom set for $12.90; open jars, glue tubes, or bottles with a jar and bottle opener for $9.95; turn any surface into an ironing board for $15.95; cover your entire bath or shower with a nonslip mat for $16.85 to $18.95; separate cholesterol-laden fats from gravies and soups with a heart-healthy dispenser, $7.95; and a whole lot more!

**A COOK'S WARES**
**3270 37th Street Extension**
**Beaver Falls, PA 15010-1263**
**412-846-9490**
**MC,V,AE,CK,MO**
**C $1.50**

Take the cook's tour and detour to the kitchen and cookware items available here at up to 60 percent off. Two master cooks have hand-picked and detailed each cookware utensil selected for their 46-page catalog. Many hard-to-find items, too. Cookware, bakeware, cutlery, and food-preparation items by LE CREUSET, KITCHEN AID, CUISINART, SPRING COPPER, and gadgets galore. Also mouth-watering condiments, dessert sauces, and chocolates from GHIRADELLI are enough to make my silver palate whistle.

## COUNTRY CURTAINS AT THE RED LION INN
Stockbridge, MA 02162-0955
800-456-0321 (Orders); 800-937-1237 (Customer Service)
413-243-1067 (FAX)
MC,V,CK,MO
C

Even if you're a city gal, Country Curtains will fill the bill for all your decorating projects. Each order receives individual attention from a company that started business in 1956 with only one curtain style. The first of many retail stores at antique-filled Red Lion Country Inn (Stockbridge) welcomes visitors for breakfast, lunch, dinner and overnight stays. (For reservations, call 413-298-5545). An insert in the catalog gives directions for measuring and hanging your curtains. Shipping is primarily by UPS, but Express Service is available at three times the regular shipping charge.

## DECORETTE
123 S. Tennessee
McKinney, TX 75069
214-542-3528 (in Dallas); (800) 486-BLINDS
MC,V,D,CK
B

Decorate with the Decorette from top to bottom. Up to 80 percent off name brands (manufacturer's list prices): mini blinds (1″, 1-⅜″ and 2″) and micro blinds, PVC and fabric verticals, 1- and 2-inch wood blinds, pleated shades, HUNTER DOUGLAS duettes. Decorative fabrics and name brands, custom draperies and bedspreads, too. One-stop window and wall dressing to the nines can literally save you from the ground up. Call for up-to-the-minute prices.

## DEUER MANUFACTURING, INC.
**2985 Springboro West**
**Dayton, OH 45439**

A way to protect your interests, your belongings and your life is to install a home security system. But, watch out, it can cost you an arm and a leg. Check your local home improvement or hardware stores (like Home Depot, etc.) for a U-Bolt-It Lock if you want security for less. It's perfect for apartments and homes, easy to install and requires no keys, so who could ask for anything more?


## DIRECT WALLPAPER DISTRIBUTORS
**370 Hall Street**
**Phoenixville, PA 19460**
**800-336-WALL; 800-332-9255 (in PA)**
**MC,V,CK**
**B,PQ**

Direct and to the point. Save 40 to 70 percent on the best brands in wallpaper, period. Shop around and then call with book name and pattern number to get factory-direct shipment. UPS next-day service available. A do-it-yourself booklet is FREE; swatch book is not (that's $5.50, refundable with order).


## ELKES CARPET OUTLET, INC.
**1585 Bethel Drive**
**High Point, NC 27260**
**919-887-5054**

These Elkes are such "deers" for offering such low prices, especially on their seconds, discontinueds, and contract carpeting. They stand behind all their great buys on carpets, vinyl, and parquet. Call with manufacturer's name, color, and pattern number and they're apt to connect you with a deal on CORONET, DOWNS/CARPET, PHILADELPHIA, WORLD, or ARMSTRONG. A restocking charge varies between mills if after delivery you decide to return. Shipping is extra.

**FABRICS BY PHONE**
P.O. Box 309
Walnut Bottom, PA 17266
800-233-7012
MC,V,CK,MO
B and samples/$3

Fabrics by Phone has been a long-time favorite source of home decorating (and decorator) buffs who want a bargain off the cuff. Most major manufacturers (ROBERT ALLEN, SCHUMACHER, FABRICUT, WAVERLY, and WESTGATE) are represented and are available at up to 50 percent off. Send SASE if you want a price quote by mail; if not, call for a *free* one. Minimum order is one yard on goods not in stock.

**FACTORY DIRECT TABLE PAD COMPANY**
1036 North Capitol
Suite C-210
Indianapolis, IN 46204-1007
800-428-4567; 317-631-2577 (in IN)
MC,V,AE,CK
F

Did you know that up to 60 percent of the price of a custom-fit table pad goes to the measurer? Factory Direct Table Pad Company lets you do the measuring (in five minutes or less!). Cut out the middleman and realize a drastic price reduction. They even guarantee a proper fit—every time. Factory Direct makes pads like they were made 50 years ago, maintaining a tradition of excellence. All pads are hand-tailored, have washable leatherette tops, cotton or velour backing, are spill-resistant and fold easily for convenient storage. Mat and color selection mailed to assist you in choosing just the right style for your table. Flyer with material and color selection card sent upon request. Satisfaction is guaranteed.

**FULLER BRUSH COMPANY**
**P.O. Box 1020**
**Rural Hale, NC 27098-1020**
**800-522-0499; 919-744-8047 (in NC)**
**MC,V,AE**
**C**

Been brushed off lately? Not if you've used the Fuller Brush line for all your household chores. The Home Catalog experts at Fuller Brush have done everything conceivable to make life easier for you. Products you might never dream of: the Magic Cart, a broom closet on wheels; ten-year light bulbs; back-saving, long-handled broom and dustpan; precision physicians' scales; Spray 'N Sparkle eyeglass cleaners; a deluxe safety grab bar for the tub; tortoise-shell combs and oak boar bristle brushes; a useful magnifying mirror, and much, much more! And it's all backed by a 100 percent satisfaction guarantee, with Federal Express service available. You'll receive a $25 gift certificate with orders of $250 or more.

**THE FURNITURE STUDIO**
**3401 West Airport Freeway**
**Irving, TX 76053**
**800-899-SOFA (800-899-7632); 214-255-7799**
**MC,V,AE,CK**
**B**

Even your best friend won't tell you you're sitting on a "copycat" version of a very expensive couch. Just cut out a picture from a magazine, and this company can duplicate most upholstered pieces for up to half the price. Why pay

for fancy names with pricey tags? Get the look for less. Send
SASE for brochure.

**GRAND FINALE**
**P.O. Box 620049**
**Dallas, TX 75262-0049**
**800-637-7714; 214-243-6200 (in TX)**
**C $2 (refundable with purchase)**

What a grand beginning to ending your home furnishings/
fashion/gift-giving dilemma. From hand-carved wooden fe-
lines to Belgian rugs, you can order wall-to-wall bargains at
40 to 70 percent off. Save big on sleeper sofas or earthenware,
sleep cheap on designer sheets and fashions. Silk arrangements, outfitting your table top, silk blouses to top off an
evening out . . . the name's the same, the only difference is
the price.

**GREEN RIVER GALLERY/BOSTON CORNERS**
**Route 2, Box 130**
**Millerton, NY 12546**
**518-789-3311**

Texas Longhorns in New York? You bet! Ride 'em right to
Green River. They're the ones who breed Longhorns, but
in addition to publishing and selling Western art in original
and limited editions, their specialty is rustic-looking log cabin
kits (you can buy the blueprints or they'll help you design
your own). All this at prices that are 20 to 40 percent less
than conventional prices. No minimum order, no restocking
charge on returns, and exchanges or refunds are honored
up to 60 days after delivery. Materials warranted for one
year.

**HARRIS LEVY, INC.**
**278 Grand Street**
**New York, NY 10002**
**212-226-3102**
**MC,V,AE,CK**
**PQ**

Harris Levy throws in the towel, as well as the sheets, comforters and other bedroom and bath items at 25 to 50 percent off. Major brand names include WAMSUTTA, J.P. STEVENS, MARTEX, SPRINGMAID, FIELDCREST, DAN RIVER and CANNON. They carry over 60 different styles of sheets and a large selection of country-style sheets and towels, so be specific when ordering by mail or by phone. Their custom order department can fill special requests for table linens, draperies, and shower curtains, including monogramming. Returns handled on an individual basis within 30 days if the item is returned in its original condition. Store credit is usually given. Orders take two to three weeks.

**HC SPECIALTIES**
**Dept. GHNW 050**
**P.O. Box 1116**
**Radio City Station**
**New York, NY 10101**
**CK,MO**

Have you been robbed of valuable counter space by those unsightly, messy, tangled electrical cords? Now, you can hold wires off counter tops and floors easily, neatly, and inexpensively with Cord-A-Way, a simple, space-saving device (only 3″ in diameter) made of strong molded plastic. Use Cord-A-Way for lamps, toasters, radios, blenders, TV's, telephones, or any appliance having a small electrical cord. It comes in your choice of white, clear or brown. Note: each set of six can be ordered in one color only and is just $10.95, plus $2 shipping and handling, for a total of $12.95 per set. On a separate piece of paper, indicate the color preferred, PRINT your name and address (including zip code) and be sure to include the Department code. Mail your order with check or money order to above address. Allow 30 days for delivery.

**IMOCO, INC.**
**3225 Premier Drive**
**P.O. Box 152052**
**Irving, TX 75015**
**800-247-5505 (orders only); U.S. and U.S. territories**
**214-580-1122**
**C $2**

Imoco is the place to go for housewares and electronics, period. Renowned for selling CORNINGWARE at ridiculously low prices, popular 45-piece sets like Peach Floral, Shadow Iris, and Country Cornflower were only $69.95—compared to $126. See-through VISIONS, only $49.95 plus postage. Extra-heavy stainless steel cookware set (19 pieces) that retails for $251.13 was just $129.95. SYLVANIA and MAGNAVOX electronics were discounted 30 to 50 percent; 4-piece SAMSONITE luggage was $99.95; SHARP carousel microwave was $179.95; ECHO "Baker's Secret" bakeware's no secret—a 29-piece set was $39.95. There's a full refund if merchandise is returned (with authorization) within 30 days, and they'll replace defective items. Shipping is immediate; cost is $9.95 anywhere in the United States or United States Territories; allow two to six weeks for shipment.

Catalog is FREE by identifying yourself as a reader of *Great Buys*.

**JOAN COOK HOUSEWARES**
3200 SE 14th Avenue
P.O. Box 21628
Ft. Lauderdale, FL 33316-1628
800-327-3799; 305-761-1600 (in Ft. Lauderdale)
305-522-0641 (FAX)
MC,V,AE (over $20), CK (under $20)
C

Morning, or night, through sleet or snow, your orders are filled seven days a week without fail. Items to make you sing, such as "Summertime and the living is easy." Take note: a POLLENEX filter to attach to your kitchen faucet that'll make gallons of homemade bottled water for pennies, or an auto-mop that does the job of three tools for damp or dry-mopping or waxing, an ironing board that is kept in a drawer, a folding shopping cart, a light bulb that lasts 20 years, non-slip rug liners, safety gates so your grandkids stay out of trouble, and more.

**L.A. DESIGN CONCEPTS**
1-800-926-SHOP

This national buying service allows shoppers access to the items found in *House Beautiful* or *Metropolitan Home* that are often not seen in mainstream furniture galleries. Frank Kesheshian will escort you through L.A.'s Pacific Design Center for $15.00 an hour or will track down your request order at 15 percent above wholesale. Call for price quote and more information.

**L & D PRESS**
88 Vincent Avenue
Lynbrook, NY 11563
516-593-5058
CK
B,F

If you don't want to save money, it's none of our business, but if you do, L & D Press can provide the following items at discounts of up to 50 percent: business cards, envelopes, letterhead, announcements, stock forms, invoices, et cetera . . . the list goes on. (And over 20 years in business is very im-press-ive, too.) Luxurious damask-smooth stationery, specially priced only twice a year, in your choice of color and imprint style (100 Princess sheets and matching envelopes or 80 Monarch sheets and matching envelopes only $10.95 retail $22). Business cards in a variety of print styles from $16.95 to $29.95 per 1,000 should be everybody's calling.

**LEHMAN'S HARDWARE AND APPLIANCES, INC.**
P.O. Box 41
Kidrun, OH 44636
216-857-5441 (Orders/Customer Service)
216-857-5785 (FAX)
MC,V,D,CK,MO
C $2

Step back in time. Take a stroll down memory lane in Lehman's Non-Electric "Good Neighbor" Heritage Catalog, past one-of-a-kind items like a 50-year-old radio in its original box, an antique toy wagon that serves as a sled, blacksmith tools 150 years old, even a pot-bellied stove with a patent date of 1889. Since their business began and continues with the Amish, many of their products are non-electric appliances, hand tools, and hand-cranked housewares. Whether your pleasure is cooking, canning, or woodworking, it's all here. Along with a diverse selection of hardware and appliances, they pride themselves in fast shipping, postpaid delivery and consistently low prices.

## LOCATORS INCORPORATED
800-367-9690; 501-371-0858 (in AK)
MC,V,CK,MO
PQ

Missing a plate from your eight-piece dinnerware setting of WEDGWOOD? Can't bear to pour into a chipped WATERFORD waterglass? Embarrassed by your mismatched silver? Weep no more, m'lady, for Locators may be just the missing link. They literally have thousands of items of china, crystal, and silver bought in mint condition from estate sales, jewelry, and gift stores or from individuals. Give them a call. Orders shipped in 72 hours.

## MANUFACTURER'S SUPPLY
P.O. Box 157
Dorcester, WI 54425-0157
800-826-8563
MC,V,CK,MO
C

Manufacturer's Supply is *the* do-it-yourself-and-save mecca for the handyman and -woman. If your nonhuman machinery breaks down (like a lawn mower), this is the 160-page sourcebook to savings of up to 50 percent. Parts to make 'em new again, for lots of tools and stuff, are this company's claim to fame.

## THE MAYTAG COMPANY
Home Service Department
Newton, IA 50208

From the folks that rarely have to make house calls, write for their FREE book that talks dirty: on how to clean all kinds of different fibers and more. Also, their Home Service

Department offers a marvelous "Chart on Removing Spots & Stains." Great to post right near your washer and dryer (but it had better be a Maytag, eh?).

## NEVER PAY RETAIL/SENIORCRAFT
**9011 Carpenter Freeway**
**Dallas, TX 75247**
**800-521-3274; (214) 638-1977 (in Dallas)**
**B,PQ**

One-of-a-kind samples from name-brand manufacturers and artisans at 40 to 70 percent off. Never pay retail again when buying furniture and accessories. A "Never Pay Retail Shop-by-Mail Decorator Kit" has been designed to make shopping for custom items a breeze, including fabric swatches in your choice of color schemes. Also available is a new manufacturing resource for the senior market that makes custom furniture especially designed for ease and comfort. SENIOR-CRAFT sofas and chairs are built for ease in getting in and out of, as well as with firmer backs and seats, while tables are built to accommodate different heights for wheelchairs.

Special to readers: The "Never Pay Retail Decorator Kit" retails for $99; your price is $39 (refundable with purchases over $200), exclusive of freight.

## NEWLINE PRODUCTS
**200 West 14th Street**
**Wilmington, DE 19801**

Have trouble opening those pesky milk cartons? Well, never again, with the Pouring Pal. It snaps over the top of the container, is easy to use, and stops those messy drips and leaks. Dishwasher safe, it comes in pint-, quart-, and half-gallon sizes. Either size is $2.99 plus $.95 shipping and handling; or order two and save, at $4.95 plus $1.25 shipping and handling.

## PEERLESS WALLPAPER
700 Connor Road
Pittsburgh, PA 15228
800-999-0898
MC,V,AE,D,CK,MO
PQ

Save 30 to 50 percent right off the wall from Peerless Wallpaper. Just call with the book name and pattern number to get your free price quote. Also available are matching fabrics and accessories to complement your new walls.

## PINTCHIK HOMEWORKS
2106 Bath Avenue
Brooklyn, NY 11214
800-847-4199; 718-996-5580 (in NY)
PQ

Call for a free blinds-ordering kit with color card and measuring instructions to begin shopping for blinds and wallcoverings at 40 to 75 percent off manufacturers' list price. BALI mini's and micro's are custom-made in seven days. Also available: LEVELOR, DUETTE, LOUVERDRAPE, VERO-SOL, JOHANNA, GRABER and HUNTER/DOUGLAS—custom-crafted wood, pleated, mini, micro and vertical blinds. Free UPS on custom orders in 48 states with readymades as low as $10 in 65 sizes (white or vanilla).

## POST WALLCOVERING DISTRIBUTORS, INC.
**P.O. Box 7026**
**Bloomfield, MI 48013**
**800-521-0650**
**MC,V,CK,MO**

Post is the most for savings of up to 70 percent for name-brand wallpaper, borders, murals, and coordinating fabrics. If it's in a wallcovering book, they can get it for you for less. Deliveries post haste, in seven to ten days.

## RAFAEL
**291 Grand Street**
**New York, NY 10002**
**212-966-1928**
**MC,V,CK**

You might want to lie down when you hear Rafael's discount prices on bedding and accessories. They offer the latest in patterns and colors on namebrand bedroom and bath decor like SPRINGMAID, BILL BLASS, and MARTEX—all at 20 to 50 percent off regular prices. And you can sleep easy, because your order will arrive in three to four weeks, with no minimum purchase required.

Rafael will offer an additional 10 percent off to readers, in addition to its already low prices, with the mention of *Great Buys*.

## RAINBOW HOT TUBS AND SPA, INC.
**5921 North High Street**
**Worthington, OH 43085**
**614-888-8881**
**MC,V,CK,COD**
**C $5**

You won't need to search for a pot of gold at the end of this Rainbow, for what you will find here is a wide spectrum of hot tubs and spas, up to 60 percent off. Somewhere over this rainbow you'll find spas, saunas, steamers, solariums, and even tanning beds with brand names like FOUNTAIN VALLEY, GALAXY, LANDIA, SKYTECH and CURTIS FRP.

**RENOVATOR'S SUPPLY**
**Millers Falls, MA 01349**
**800-346-6370; 413-659-2241**
**MC,V,CK**
**C $3**

If you're restoring a Victorian home or grew up in the Victorian age, this catalog is a must. A memorable hardware collection of brass doorknobs, porcelain faucets, weathervanes, copper lanterns, and drawer pulls, plus the world's largest selection of switch plates. Over 1,500 hard-to-find renovator's items and at savings up to 70 percent.

**ROSS-SIMONS**
**136 Lambert Lind Highway Route 5**
**Warwick, RI 02886**
**800-521-ROSS (800-521-7677) (Customer Service);**
**800-556-7376;**
**800-553-7370; 401-463-3100 (in RI)**
**401-463-8599 (FAX)**
**MC,V,AE,D,DC**
**C**

Since 1952, Ross-Simons has been the source of all things beautiful. Fine jewelry, china, silver, and gifts fill each page of their four-color catalog. Save up to 40 percent on name-brand and custom-crafted items, but don't pass up the collection plates. Names like MIKASA, ROYAL COPENHAGEN, ROYAL WORCESTER-SPODE, WEDGWOOD, and LENNOX to dress up any table, complemented by crystal stemware from BACCARAT, WATERFORD, GORHAM, DANSK, VILLEROY and BOCH, and FITZ and FLOYD. Silver and stainless, of course, in place settings that will whet anyone's appetite, especially if they're hungry for quality.

**R. P. FALCONER CORPORATION**
3130 Marquita
Fort Worth, TX 76116
800-541-3507
MC,V,CK

Light up your life with the Falcon Eye, the automatic light that turns on when approached, inside or out, when a person is 30 feet away, and then turns off after the detection zone is vacated. If you can change a light bulb, you can install the Falcon Eye. It's $49.95 (less $10 senior citizen discount). Include $4.95 shipping and handling. Total: $44.90.

**RUBIN & GREEN INTERIOR DESIGN STUDIO**
290 Grand Street
New York, NY 10002
212-226-0313
PQ

If it's good enough for the New York's Pierre Hotel on Fifth Avenue, it's good enough for me. Fancy, shmancy, yes, but also at 50 percent off makes them one of the best deals around. Wholesale fabrics and custom interior design work is available to the public as well as to the trade. They'll replicate any window treatment or furniture photo/idea you want, size and scale it to fit your home . . . the only difference is the price, half of what a shop on Madison Avenue would charge for the same or comparable item.

**S & S MILLS**
P.O. Box 1568
Dalton, GA 30722
800-241-4013
C (with samples included)

Be snug as a bug with a rug from this carpet manufacturer. Deep in the heart of the carpet capital of the world, S & S Mills stands alone. Comparable to ARMSTRONG and other better brands, S & S manufactures wall-to-wall savings of at least 50 percent. Call toll-free for your free carpet swatches and delivery within seven to ten days. Experienced service representatives can answer all your questions and you can expect every style of carpet whether it's DUPONT ANTRON, STAINMASTER, OLEFIN. Average homeowners can save $3,000 to $6,000, but even a small roomful can net you big bucks.

**SICO ROOM MAKERS**
5000 Belt Line Road, #250
Addison, TX 75240
214-960-1315
214-920-1320 (FAX)
B

The Sico® Life-Flex bed is just one of the heavenly additions offered to seniors for a great night's sleep. Its contouring arch slat foundation and state-of-the-art adjustable latex core mattress offers ideal support and comfort, a removable mattress cover lined with natural fibers to regulate body temperature and two quiet ⅓ horsepower motors. It's a total sleep system designed to conform to your shape and weight as well as meeting the contours of your body. Also, Sico®'s famous wallbeds and cabinet systems for that "Murphy bed" of the 90's.

*Great Buys* readers get $100 off regularly priced twin extra-long Sico® Life-Flex adjustable bed or any Sico® wall-bed system.

## SINGER SEWING CENTER OF COLLEGE STATION
1669 Texas Avenue
College Station, TX 77840
800-338-5672
PQ

Sew at 33 percent off retail by calling this center for savings on sewing machines. Selling their wares since 1976, the Singer Sewing Center has at least given College Station something to boast about other than A & M and the Aggies. Call or write for a price quote on SINGER models, as well as ELNA, NECCHI, and PFAFF. Send SASE for price quote. Layaway available.

## SLIPCOVERS OF AMERICA
P.O. Box 590
Bethlehem, PA 18016-0590
215-868-7788
C

Custom-looking slipcovers and other readymade coverups can create the decorator look at a fraction of the price of upholstery. You'll even save up to 30 percent over the same kind of slipcovers found in another major catalog we reviewed. Easy-to-measure instructions assure you a perfectly snug fit, and coordinating accents are available through their free color catalog.

**SUBURBAN SEW 'N SWEEP, INC.**
8814 Ogden Avenue
Brookfield, IL 60513
800-642-4056; 312-485-2834 (in IL)
MC,V,D,CK,MO
B

Known around town as "The Sewing Machine Outlet." When you receive their free brochure, you'll say more than "Sew what!" Savings range as high as 50 percent on major brands such as SINGER, NEW HOME, VIKING, and WHITE. Call for free brochure and price quote. (Send SASE if you want a quote by mail.)

**TELEMART**
8804 North 23rd Avenue
Phoenix, AZ 85021
800-426-6659
MC,V,AE,CK,COD
F

Save 30 to 60 percent on computer hardware, software and peripherals for home or office or home/office. Brands such as EPSON, TOSHIBA, LOTUS, BROTHER and others were made for talking. Shipping and handling $7 under 10 pounds; $10 over 10 pounds and orders shipped within 48 hours. All manufacturer warranties apply.

*Great Buys* readers can save 50 percent on joysticks or Universal System fans with any purchase.

---

# The Telephone

A phone is a friend, especially to older people who live alone. A phone should be low enough that it can be reached from the floor in an emergency. Some special services are provided by phone companies, such as a button to wear around your neck permanently; when pushed, it will activate a 24-hour emergency-service switchboard whose operator will send the help you need. Louder bells and devices to amplify sound, as well as larger, more legible numbers, "memory" capability, and cordless phones could also be useful to the senior caller. Contact your local phone company to see what's available in your area.

---

**TREND-LINES**
**375 Beacham Street**
**P.O. Box 6447**
**Chelsea, MA 02150-0999**
**800-767-9999 (Order Hotline); 800-877-7899 (Customer**
**Service) 800-884-8951 (Technical Questions)**
**MC,V,D,CK**
**C (call 800-366-6966 for free catalog)**

If you're a chip off the old block (professional or amateur), you'll want to join woodworking devotees who band together in their unanimous support of this woodworking catalog source. It's 68 pages of more power and hand tools under one roof than projects permit. Nevertheless, one call and you can snare a cordless vacuum sander for $9.95; a RYOBI radial arm saw, which retailed at $540, for $299.95; a PORTER CABLE saw boss that retailed at $170 is $129.95; planers, joiners, project plans, books, tools, woodbits, dowels, drills,

---

## Used Typewriters

Call the IBM office in your area and ask about their
IBM HANDICAPPED PURCHASING PROGRAM, whereby,
with a doctor's note stating typing would be therapeutic, you could secure a used typewriter at a very
low price.

---

and bits—even a gimlet that won't make you drunk. Woodn't
that be a new trend!

**U.S. GENERAL SERVICES ADMINISTRATION
202-557-8646**

Call Washington, D.C., to get the number for the office
nearest you and add your name to their mailing list for
surplus or seized goods. Everything from cars, boats, houses,
you name it. Confiscated items are then auctioned off at a
fraction of the original cost. Also, other good deals can be
had by calling your local VA office for their list of foreclosures
as well as checking with Housing and Urban Development
(HUD) for their listings. Even the IRS has property that has
been seized for delinquent property taxes. All sales are "as
is," but you do have the right to inspect prior to the auction.

**WAREHOUSE CARPETS, INC.
P.O. Box 3233
Dalton, GA 30721
800-526-2229; 404-226-2229 (in GA)
CK
PQ**

Price quotes by phone if you give them the manufacturer,
style, and color to net you 15 to 45 percent on carpeting,
including vinyl and padding. Best buys are on MOHAWK

because they concentrate on that brand, but also available
are ALEXANDER, SALEM, CORONET, and MASLAND. They offer
Karastan rugs along with the broadloom, and, like other
wholesalers, a 50 percent deposit is required with your order;
balance due before carpet leaves the warehouse. Shipping is
freight collect. Restocking charges are 5 percent and up,
depending on the mill. Typical delivery is two weeks, but no
cancellations are allowed after carpeting has been cut.

**WEISSRUGS**
**The Area Rug Store**
**2621 Murray Avenue**
**Pittsburgh, PA 15217**
**800-422-7848**
**PQ**

Don't let them pull the rug from under you. Selected carpet
mills and area rugs are up to 50 percent off retail and sport
such names as KARASTAN, CABIN CRAFTS, ELIFERIE, MASLAND,
HELIOS, and CAPEL. All prices quoted include freight.

**WELLS INTERIORS, INC.**
**7171 Amador Plaza Drive**
**Dublin, CA 94568**
**800-547-8982**
**C,PQ**

A lowest-price guarantee assures you you'll be getting rock-
bottom prices on namebrand window treatments and accessories. Every imaginable blind or vertical by phone (LEVOLOR,
RIVIERA, HUNTERDOUGLAS, LOUVERDRAPE, DELMAR, DUETTES,
KIRSCH hardware), with a Wells warranty. It's your window
to the world of savings.

# HOUSING AND ALTERNATIVE HOUSING

As seniors approach and enter their retirement years, housing becomes a very significant part of planning for a secure and happy future. In today's market, the choices are varied and alternatives exist for almost every pocketbook. The dream of a comfortable, affordable home for the next thirty years or more is still a very real possibility, but careful planning and consideration of all the options is essential.

Many will elect to stay with their previous family home or move into an adjoining wing or house on the property of children or relatives. Others will choose to relocate to a new area and into a smaller, more compact or affordable home, in areas where the possibility of socializing with other seniors exists, such as one of the many retirement communities across the country. Another option is the retirement hotel, a recent addition to the senior housing market and certainly an attractive one to some. There are many housing opportunities out there. We have listed a few to whet your appetite and give you a taste of the myriad of possibilities—from medically oriented neighborhood communities to lush mobile parks.

**NATIONAL DIAL-OGUE ON SENIOR HOUSING**
**800-321-3788**
Call for your free booklet "Options for Senior Housing" and read first-hand the myriad of possibilities.

**AARP HOUSING**
**Consumer Affairs**
**1909 K Street NW**
**Washington, DC 20049**
**B**

The AARP, in its continuing effort to bring the retired person valuable information and services, has joined with the Federal Trade Commission to offer comprehensive assistance in the all-important decisions to be made about housing. A variety of tips and information is available in booklet form: everything from making your present home fit your needs easily, to adaptable ideas about their alternative housing project called ECHO (Elder Cottage Housing Opportunities). Write for more information.

**CAROLINA MEADOWS**
**P.O. Box 3484**
**Whippoorwill Lane**
**Chapel Hill, NC 27515**
**800-458-6756; 919-968-9423 (in NC)**
**C**

Carolina Meadows may conjure up a beautiful mental picture for you, but the reality is even better in the quiet, wooded serenity of Chapel Hill, North Carolina. The location is the beginning of the many amenities offered by this A-1 rated retirement community. Spacious apartments and villas; a Club Center with a dining room, lounges, and a library; a golf course; an emergency call system; and a variety of other recreational activities are all part of the lifestyle at Carolina Meadows. They offer a very attractive 100 percent equity refund plan and on-site health care with the completion of the Health Center, and are still expanding in many areas and adding new features for their residents. Optional services such as housekeeping, personal care assistance and medical care are available, too, but paid for only as needed. Tours of models can be arranged by calling the toll-free number.

**CENTURY COMMUNITIES**
**P.O. Box 7079**
**Winter Haven, FL 33883-7079**
**800-444-1581; 813-533-3533 (in FL)**
**C**

With names of adult communities such as Crystal Lake Club, Country Meadows, Plantation Landing, Saddlebrook Club, et cetera how could one go wrong? Florida's outstanding Century Communities feature the finest in affordable manufactured homes. Whether you are searching for ideal retirement living, a second home for the winter or a year-round investment, Century Communities will make your search a worthwhile adventure. All have active clubhouses, heated pools, tennis and much more. So, head south, young man, to sunny Florida and find the perfect haven for rest, relaxation, and retirement. A pre-retirement "special purchase plan" to allow you a headstart is also available.

## CHAMBREL AT CLUB HILL
**1245 Colonel Drive**
**Garland, TX 75043**
**(214) 278-8533**

Count on Chambrel for affordable senior living and where your dollars go the extra mile toward an all-inclusive, comfortable, and secure lifestyle. One of several in the Oxford Senior Living Communities, where basic prices include one meal daily, housekeeping every other week, weekly laundry, free medical alert, cable TV, utilities (except phone), transportation to appointments and shopping, fully equipped kitchens, a postal center, barber and beauty shops, a wellness-exercise-fitness center, clubhouse, greenhouse, arts and crafts studio, library—it's "come on'a my house, my house, come on!" Developments in Texas (Woodlands), Ohio (Akron), Georgia (Roswell), Virginia (Williamsburg), and Florida (Longwood and Ocala). For more information, contact the corporate headquarters, Oxford Retirement Services, Inc., 7316 Wisconsin Ave., Bethesda, MD 20814 (301-654-2100).

## CLASSIC RESIDENCE
**Hyatt Hotels, Inc.**
**Corporate Office**
**Madison Plaza**
**200 West Madison Street**
**Chicago, IL 60606**
**312-750-1234**
**C**

Looking for a high-class high-rise retirement alternative? Hyatt now offers an acceptable bridge to loftier living with many of the amenities of a full-service hotel such as a restaurant, concierge, security, a health club, lounge, beauty salon, and library and meeting rooms. Monthly rates include the cost of rent, 25 meals, and continental breakfasts. Two-bedroom suites range in size from 840 to 1500 square feet.

Hyatt's aim is to provide "independent living" for active seniors who are looking for an elegant style of self-contained retirement living. Facilities opened to date are in Reno, Nevada; Dallas, Texas; Teaneck, New Jersey; Chevy Chase, Maryland; Chicago, Illinois; and Monterrey, California.

**COLONNADES COUNTRY HOMES**
**1501 West Pipkin Road**
**Lakeland, FL 33811**
**800-342-4647; 813-647-1981 (in FL)**
**C**

At Colonnades Country Homes, you will find a peaceful, comfortable lifestyle centered in a country setting, complete with a beautiful lake and surrounded by lush gardens and flowers. Whether it's sunning by the pool or bingo in the recreational complex, or even the chance to try your hand at shuffleboard, golf or tennis, you will find everything you want in this retirement community that boasts energy efficient, value-oriented, site-built housing. All homes are built with quality construction and low maintenance in mind, and introductory prices start at $40,000, including homesite. Call or write for more information.

**COUNTRY CLUB ESTATES/WINDMILL/MOUNTAIN**
**SHADOWS**
**c/o Andy Anderson Realty**
**1723 South Highway 92**
**Sierra Vista, AZ 85635**
**800-759-2639; 602-458-6100 (in AZ)**
**C**

Three breathtaking communities have land sites that are still affordable for building your dream home on. Sierra Vista is the major population center in southwestern Arizona, seventy miles southeast of Tucson. Plenty of sunshine headed your way, though the activities alone will keep your disposition cool. Offerings in the community include lunch get-togethers, dances, bazaars, exercise, and arts and crafts. This was also the location of the first Senior Olympics in Arizona and the home of *The Senior Echos*, a seniors' newspaper.

**COUNTRY CLUB VILLAGE**
**Hot Springs National Park**
**3125 Malvern Road**
**Hot Springs, AR 71901**
**501-624-6435**
**C**

Near Oaklawn Racing Park in Hot Springs, Country Club Village offers one or two bedroom apartments or cozy cottages with most bills paid and in some cases, meals are even provided. A newly built AMI Hospital is just across the street. So, call or write today for more information. Response to this community has been overwhelming, so special offers and housing go fast.

**DEL WEBB'S SUN CITY**
Corporate Offices
P.O. Box 29040
Department 5001
Phoenix, AZ 85038-8746
800-433-5932

**DEL WEBB'S SUN CITY—SUMMERLIN**
9119 Gardenview Drive
P.O. Box 82040
Las Vegas, NV 89180-2024
800-843-4848
B

Like Del Webb's original Sun City in Phoenix, Summerlin offers a complete living package for pre-retirement or retirement individuals. The special people who come here experience a unique, attractive lifestyle that includes swimming, racquetball, shuffleboard, jogging, golf, tennis, lapidary, silver craft, woodworking and weaving, not to mention the lure of nearby Las Vegas! Residents of Sun City enjoy a year-round array of activities, in addition to the full assortment of restaurants, shows and casinos that are a part of the Las Vegas scene. Home prices start at $82,000.

**DIRECTORY OF INDEPENDENT LIVING PROGRAMS (ILRU)**
3400 Bissonnet
Suite 101
Houston, TX 77005
713-666-6244

Order your directory for $8.50 (including postage and handling) and have at your fingertips listings of almost 400 independent living centers and other programs geared to independent living services across the U.S. During the year, you will receive free updates and periodic newsletters. This is an annual publication.

## DUNAGAN ASSOCIATES INSURANCE/REAL ESTATE
**212 West Stevens**
**Carlsbad, NM 99220**
**800-345-4665; 505-885-2138 (in NM)**
**B**

Dunagan Associates is the oldest real estate firm in Carlsbad, New Mexico, serving its clients since 1925, with rentals as well as new construction. In addition to their good prices, Carlsbad offers the older adult many things no other city does. Besides the obvious Carlsbad Caverns, it also boasts a year-round mild temperature, two beautiful lakes perfect for boating, fishing and water skiing, and it's only two hours to Ruidosa and the heart of ski country. Call or write for more information concerning real estate and the attractive lifestyle in Carlsbad.

## ECHO HOUSING
## ELDERLY COTTAGE HOUSING
**Sponsored by AARP**

Now, it's easier for grown or growing families to join with their elderly parents under the same roof or nearby and still keep the peace. Thanks to ECHO (Elderly Cottage Housing), it is now possible for older adults to live near family and avoid the expense and upkeep of a separate property. Most ECHO homes range in size from 300 to 900 square feet and come equipped with special features that make life easier for its residents to move about. If you are interested in this wave of the future, contact the AARP about ECHO Housing.

## FHA Reverse Mortgages

Contact your nearest HUD (Housing and Urban Development) field office for information on the FHA-insured reverse mortgages, designed to allow you (though you must be at least 62 and either own your home free and clear or have minimal mortgage debt) to convert your home equity into a monthly income check or line of credit.

**THE FORUM AT PARK LANE**
**7845 Park Lane**
**Dallas, TX 75225**
**214-369-9902**
**B**

Although the Forum is one of the "top of the line" retirement community developments in the country, their thoughtful, cost-sensitive approach appeals to anyone planning a sound financial strategy for the retirement years. Because it is a rental community, there is flexibility, not to mention the fact that there are no up-front fees. Even though you'll be living "Forum-style," you will get the maximum for the minimum—a wise investment in anyone's book. Personal tours can be scheduled at any one of their 34 communities throughout the U.S. Call or write for additional locations.

---

**GUIDE TO INDEPENDENT LIVING**
**800-283-7800**
Call the National Arthritis Foundation Hotline to
order this very helpful book. Identify yourself as a
reader of *Great Buys* and you may order for only $7.

---

**GULFSTREAM HARBOR**
**4505 South Goldenrod Road**
**Orlando, FL 32822**
**800-321-2152; 407-282-6340 (in FL)**
**B**

Disneyworld and the Factory Outlet Malls are not the only
attractions in Orlando. These beautiful budget-minded
homes at Gulfstream Harbor have guaranteed lot rentals
priced from $29,995 for the St. Croix models (2 bedrooms/
2 baths) to $54,995 for the Nassau (also 2 bedrooms/2 baths
with cathedral ceilings, panoramic bay windows, wet bar,
sunken garden tubs, walk-in closets). In their state-of-the-
art clubhouse, the activities for just one month will keep you
swimming upstream.

**HEIGHTS**
**220 Whispering Hills North**
**Hot Springs, AR 71901**
**501-525-1599**
**B**

Hot Springs has long been a sought-after and popular
attraction for outdoor sports enthusiasts and mountain lovers
alike. But if you seek something a little more on the relaxed

side, you won't find a prettier setting for golf, boating, cultural events, and the Springs themselves, than the Heights special garden retirement homes. All units are on one level with carport and outside-locked storage, two bedrooms/two baths, with modern kitchens, and are close to hospitals, shopping, and banking. Besides, you'll have a magnificent view of the mountains and you'll always be looking up. Call or write for more information.

**HIGHLAND FAIRWAYS**
**Country Club Community**
**2101 West Griffin Road**
**Lakeland, FL 33809**
**800-462-4840; 813-858-1441 (in FL)**
**C**

By now, no one has to tell you about the advantages and perks of living in Florida, particularly central Florida. Located a little north of Lakeland, Highland Fairways is a beautiful, modern, affordable retirement community within a "stone's throw" of such places as Epcot Center, Sea World and Busch Gardens, not to mention the fact that the new Lakeland Mall is right at your back door. Still not convinced? Well, if the beautiful 18-hole golf course winding through the country club community doesn't do it, nothing will. That is, unless you take a closer look at the price of the home (starting at $50,000) and model plans that are available for you to study. Isn't it time you found out what all the fuss is about? Call or write for more information and make sure your retirement plans include sunny, warm, Lakeland, Florida.

Note: All Chambers of Commerce have information regarding their city and housing opportunities. Call the toll-free directory assistance (800-555-1212) for the number of the Chamber of Commerce in the city you have in mind, such as Sedona, Arizona; Key West, Florida; Treasure Island, Washington; Kittering, Maine; you're but a call away.

## HOT SPRINGS, ARKANSAS, RETIREMENT DEVELOPMENT
**P.O. Box 1500**
**Hot Springs, AR 71902**
**800-326-1878; 501-321-1878 (in AR)**
**B**

In beautiful Hot Springs, you will be treated to four mild seasons, beautiful lakes and mountains, low taxes and reasonable health care. All that, not to mention one of their most popular "draws," horse racing in the spring. Hot Springs has several attractive accommodations and living possibilities, complete with recreational options: exceptional golf courses, country clubs and a variety of places to share with family once you get settled and feel like having visitors. You can let the Hot Springs Board of Realtors assist you with your long-term plans, or just write to the above address or call for more information regarding vacation and special activities and events. Be sure to ask about historic "Bathhouse Row," considered by many to be equal to a European type spa vacation.

**HSH ASSOCIATES**
**800-874-2837**
Get the lowdown on mortgage rates without leaving home. This company charges $18 and provides you with a list of lending institutions in your area and their mortgage rates if you're itching to close a deal on a new house, condo, or co-op.

**HOT SPRINGS VILLAGE**
**HOT SPRINGS VILLAGE, AK 71909**
**800-228-7328; 800-334-3760 (in AK)**

From sunup to sundown, you'll enjoy the amenities of Hot Springs Village in the heart of the Quachita Mountains. Established in 1970, this affordable but first-class recreational community boasts four 18-hole golf courses and 11 lighted tennis courts. Add two country clubs, six lakes, a health spa, parks, a racetrack nearby—well, get the picture? Part of the Cooper Development, they'll even invite you for a complimentary condo weekend if you'll agree to take the 3-hour tour.

**KEYS-GATE AT THE VILLAGES OF HOMESTEAD**
**888 Southeast Kingman Road**
**Homestead, FL 33035**
**800-338-7374; 800-633-5397 (in CAN); 305-247-3838**
  **(in FL)**
**305-247-0284 (FAX)**
**C**

This award-winning active adult leisure community of Keys-Gate is setting the pace for affordable senior housing. Located between Biscayne National Park and Everglades National

Park, just thirty minutes south of Miami at the gateway to the Florida Keys, Keys-Gate is sure to become the standard for retirement value and style. Prices on their modern and well-built villas, single-family homes, and condos start from the low $40s; this planned community will ultimately encompass over 1,000 acres and have over 6,200 units. The sales office houses a totally automated, unique film presentation about the community. Write or call for more information.

**LEE PLANTATION**
**10950 Old South Way**
**Ft. Myers, FL 33908**
**800-228-5561; 813-454-0022 (in FL)**
**B**

Lee Plantation is a premier mobile country-club community located just minutes from the Fort Myers beach in sunny southern Florida. Whether it's swimming or shell hunting on the sandy white beaches of the Gulf, you can enjoy the convenient host of fun activities located within the exciting country club community. You'll find all you need for a comfortable, home away from home, year-long or lifelong vacation and living experience. Lee Plantation's high standard manufactured homes provide a spacious, comfortable, stylish setting you'll grow to call home. Prices start in the $80s. Write or call for more information and a brochure.

**MIDLAND/ODESSA HEALTH & RETIREMENT**
**ENDEAVOR (MOHRE)**
**P.O. Box 5592**
**Midland, TX 79704-5592**
**915-561-5331**
**B**

Situated halfway between El Paso and Dallas/Fort Worth, MOHRE has everything you could possibly want in a warm, friendly Texas environment to assure you a most pleasant

---

**NATIONAL DIRECTORY OF RETIREMENT
  FACILITIES**
**Oryx Press**
**2214 North Central at Encanto**
**Phoenix, AZ 85004-1483**
Put this book on your list of *musts* if you want
information on retirement facilities. Included are the
contact person, the facility type, and the capacity for
over 12,000 residential alternatives for today's senior.
Priced at $100+, check and see if your local library
has a copy.

---

retirement experience. The Midland/Odessa area is perfectly
situated to all spots of interest outside the city and boasts its
own share of fun activities, as well as a year-round average
temperature of 64 degrees. Particular points of interest
include America's only authentic replica of Shakespeare's
Globe Theater, four museums, the ballet, and a world class
symphony and chorale. Write or call for more information
and y'all consider the friendly cities of Midland/Odessa for
your retirement oasis.


**OAK RUN**
**P.O. Box 5824**
**Ocala, FL 32678**
**800-874-0898; 800-342-9626 (in FL)**
**C**

Whatever you're looking for in a retirement community,
Oak Run's got it: beautiful homes, apartments, and villas
ranging from the $40s to the $90s, and a variety of indoor/
outdoor activities offered within their 1,385 acre facility; you
will have everything you need. And when you want to leave

the community and discover the rest of the Sunshine State, you'll find Oak Run to be near some of Florida's most exciting attractions, all within a 30 to 300 mile radius. The Orchard Club is their ten-acre recreation complex featuring tennis, swimming, shuffleboard, billiards . . . you name it, they've got it.


**OAKWOOD RESORT APARTMENTS**
**2222 Corinth Avenue**
**Los Angeles, CA 90064**
**800-421-6654**
**B**

You can stay at some of the world's most affordable resorts and experience some of the most exciting cities for a month or more at a fraction of the price of a one-week cruise. For example, enjoy Oakwood Resort Apartments in cities like Los Angeles and Washington, DC—all equipped with everything you need to make your stay a home away from home. All come completely furnished. Be sure to ask about special discounts. Winter is a particularly good time to take advantage of their great senior deals.


**OCEAN DUNES RESORT AND VILLA**
**P.O. Box 2035**
**Myrtle Beach, SC 29577**
**800-845-0635; 803-449-7441 (in SC)**
**B**

Hailed as one of Myrtle Beach's most complete vacation and golf resorts, this oceanfront resort offers a day on its newest golf course, designed by Jack Nicklaus at Pawley's Plantation, or you can use the day to explore nearby shops, restaurants, or, of course, just relax on the beach. Whatever you decide, Ocean Dunes and Sand Dunes Resorts offer you a distinctive taste of Myrtle Beach. You can call it your home away from home or your special getaway. Whichever it is, you'll be sure to remember it. A haven for senior adults for some time, individual hotels and resorts at Myrtle Beach offer senior discounts. Be sure to ask.

## THE OSBORN RETIREMENT COMMUNITY
**101 Theall Road**
**Rye, NY 10580**
**914-967-4100**
**B**

Miriam Osborn's legacy, the Osborn, has been serving retired individuals, mainly women, since 1908. But thanks to a recent New York State Supreme Court ruling, now men, women, and couples can enjoy this beautiful Georgian structure, reminiscent of an old Gold Coast resort hotel. In addition to 24 hour on-site medical care and nursing facilities, the Osborn also offers a variety of activities and entertainment, not to mention fine dining. The resort hotel has 160 private rooms and two-room suites to choose from and a courteous staff to assist you in every way. Call or write for more information.

## PENNBROOKE: TROPICANA COMMUNITY
**500 West State Road**
**Leesburg, FL 32748**
**800-367-6286; 904-326-5600 (in FL)**
**B**

Pennbrooke is an award-winning resort/manufactured-home community offering activities and a leisurely lifestyle for the mature adult. Its year-round homes and winter cottages begin at prices as low as $30,000 and contain everything you would ever need to enjoy the life of Riley. Don't miss the beautiful golf course, tennis courts and clubhouse, in addition to nearby Atlantic Ocean (90 minutes to the east) and the

Gulf of Mexico (60 minutes to the west). Write or call for more information.

## PRESBYTERIAN VILLAGE NORTH
**8600 Skyline Drive**
**Dallas, TX 75243**
**214-349-3960**
**214-341-3846 (FAX)**

This nonprofit corporation operates as part of the Presbyterian Healthcare System and is one of the few retirement communities closely aligned with a hospital and health care network. Open since 1980 for seniors 62 and over, this village on 63 acres creates the ambience of a neighborhood complete with custom homes, patio homes, and apartments. Three service levels (independent living, personal care, and health units) offer a continuum of care based on the residents' changing needs and offers the convenience and service of a pharmacy, clinic, security, transportation, meals, and social activities. Your invitation to excellence is but a phone call away.

## RESOLUTION TRUST CORPORATION
**550 17TH Street, NW**
**Washington, DC 20429**
**202-898-8750**

Write to the Assets and Real Estate Management Division to secure lists of available real estate, which might provide a home (or second home) at 50 percent or more off their mortgage value.

## SAVANNA CLUB
8630 South U.S. 1
Port St. Lucie, FL 34952
800-325-0006; 800-468-6289
B

Tailored to fit the best years of your life, the Savanna Club is one of Florida's manufactured home golf communities just south of Fort Pierce. Join the many newcomers who've discovered if the New York Mets can play there, they can, too. Golf, walk the beaches of the Atlantic, fish in the St. Lucie and Indian rivers and shop. The beautiful 5,000 plus acre State Reserve adjoins this very affordable adult community where at least one member of the family has to be 55. Base prices start around $40,000 plus homesite. Write for free brochures.

## SUN 'N LAKE
4101 Sun 'N Lake Blvd.
Sebring, FL 33877
800-824-0501; 813-382-3111 (in FL call collect)
B

Built around one of the top 50 golf courses in the state, Sun 'N Lake is rooted on 2,000 acres of beautiful central Florida soil, and is convenient and accessible. More than 3,000 residents are already proud to call the sunny, green lake community home and you can, too. The helpful sales staff is prepared to share more information on the warm and beautiful lifestyle of Sun 'N Lake. They can explain in detail why you should have Sun 'N Lake as a second home site or a retirement destination. Year-round seasonal temperatures and a variety of indoor/outdoor activities are just the beginning. Homes and villas range from $40,000 to $400,000.

**SUN STATE HOMES**
4110 South Florida Avenue
Lakeland, FL 33813
800-537-2935; 813-646-0557 (in FL)
B

Sun State Homes is ranked among the top 500 home builders in the United States. That's pretty good for a business that started with only $1,000 eighteen years ago. Today, while still building homes with a Caribbean influence, Sun State is also involved in projects like the one at Waterview, an adult villa community. You can now get quality and style and receive all the amenities, convenience, and services you'd expect from an adult community. And your Sun State Home, if you choose Waterview, will start in the $50s. Lakeland, Florida, and Sun State Homes could add up to just the right equation for your perfect retirement.

**WFC, INC.**
**West Florida Communities, Inc.**
**P.O. Box 7626**
**Winter Haven, FL 33883-7626**
**800-331-8605; 800-722-6601; 813-956-5777 (in FL)**
**C**

West Florida Communities offers two planned retirement complexes, Sandalwood and Sweetwater, complete with every amenity imaginable. Florida's famed sunshine, fun, and affordability provides the groundwork for these two developments.

# ORGANIZATIONS

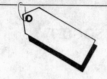

**AARP**
**AARP FULFILLMENT SERVICE**
**1909 K Street NW**
**Washington, DC 20049**

This premier organization for retired persons has so many benefits and such a wide array of services designed to help seniors, it's no wonder it's the largest private, nonprofit, nonpartisan organization in the world (and probably has the most reasonable membership fee—only $5 per year!) A guide is available (of course!) that sets forth all the different ways they can go to bat on your behalf. Write for it today.

**ALZHEIMER'S ASSOCIATION**
**70 East Lake Street**
**Suite 600**
**Chicago, IL 60601-5997**
**800-621-0379; 800-572-6037 (in IL); 312-853-3060**
  **(in Chicago)**
**B**

Since 1980, this non-profit organization has led the fight against Alzheimer's and currently has almost 200 local chapters and 1,000 family support groups across the country. Write for brochures about the disease, services you may need, local chapters and reprints to help guide you in the care of patients. Its slogan, "Someone to Stand By You," means a lot to families having to deal with this dreaded disease.

**AMERICAN CANCER SOCIETY**
**1599 Clifton Road NE**
**Atlanta, GA 30329**
**800-ACS-2345 (800-227-2345)**
**B**

One call does it all. At last, with the millions of questions about cancer, there's now one place to call for some answers, whether it's the most appropriate detection guidelines or the latest treatments. Pamphlets are free, informative, and perhaps even life-saving, such as: "How to Stay Quit Over the Holidays" and "Taking Control—10 Steps to a Healthier Life and Reduced Cancer Risk."

**AMERICAN COUNCIL OF THE BLIND**
**1010 Vermont Avenue NW**
**Suite 1100**
**Washington, DC 20005**
**202-393-3666**

A clearinghouse listing companies and organizations that, through catalogs, sell useful products for the blind and visually impaired. Write to the Council to learn of such companies as the LS&S Group who sell talking watches, TV radios, voice-activated telephones, and The Capability Collection Ways & Means who sell over 1,000 products related to housekeeping, sewing, yard, and garden care.

**AMERICAN DIABETES ASSOCIATION**
**National Service Center**
**1600 Duke Street**
**Alexandria, VA 22314**
**800-ADA-DISC (232-3472)**

Published by the American Diabetes Association, *Diabetes '91*, the newsletter for people with diabetes, is brimming with information on managing diabetes, exercise, nutritional recipes, and the latest breakthroughs and newest technology.

*Great Buys* readers will be the recipients of a one-year subscription (four issues) to *Diabetes '91* upon request.

**AMERICAN DIETETIC ASSOCIATION**
**216 West Jackson Blvd.**
**Suite 800**
**Chicago, IL 60606-6995**
**312-899-0400**

"Staying Healthy—A Guide for Elder Americans" is number one in a series of nutrition informational messages brought to you by the American Dietetic Association. Did you know that the less active you are, the more likely you are to break a bone, OR that fading taste buds may be revived by zinc, OR that mineral oil used as a laxative removes important vitamins from the body?

**AMERICAN FOUNDATION FOR THE BLIND**
**15 West 16 Street**
**New York, NY 10011**
**B**

Write for their brochure describing additional publications specifically related to the blind and visually impaired (single copy is free; bulk orders are processed with shipping and handling charges), from mobility issues to getting help for the disabled child.

## AMERICAN KIDNEY FUND
**6110 Executive Blvd.**
**Rockville, MD 20852**
**800-638-8299; 800-492-8361 (in MD); 301-881-3052**

The American Kidney Fund is a non-profit, national, voluntary health organization that provides direct financial assistance to thousands of sufferers of kidney disease. Besides direct funding, it also provides services through its community services, public and professional education, kidney donor development, and research programs.

## AMERICAN LIVER FOUNDATION
**998 Pompton Avenue**
**Cedar Grove, NJ 07009-9990**
**201-857-2626**

The American Liver Foundation is the only national voluntary health organization dedicated to fighting all liver diseases through research, education and support groups. Knowledge could prevent more than half of all liver ailments. More than 25 million Americans are afflicted with liver and gall bladder diseases; 27,000 die of cirrhosis. To secure information on how to cope with the medical, financial and emotional problems associated with liver diseases, contact the American Liver Foundation.

## ARTHRITIS FOUNDATION
**P.O. Box 96012**
**Washington, DC 20090-6012**

Join the Arthritis Foundation for a tax deductible contribution of $15 or more and receive their bi-monthly magazine *Arthritis Today* free. Well over one million people read it as it is one of the most comprehensive and reliable sources of information about the research, care, and treatment of the disease that affects 37 million people in the U.S.

## BAYLOR 55 PLUS
**800-522-9567**

If you're lucky enough to live in the Dallas/Fort Worth Metroplex, you get something great—for nothing. A free membership entitles you to informative seminars, travel programs, priority tickets to the theater and more. It's part of the Baylor Health Care System. Other hospital networks are beginning to pay attention to the 55 plus community, so call your local hospital to see if they have jumped on the bandwagon, too.

## BETTER HEARING INSTITUTE/HEARING HELPLINE
**P.O. Box 1840**
**Washington, DC 20013**
**800-EAR-WELL (327-9355); 703-642-0580; 703-750-9302**

For information about hearing impairment, causes of hearing loss, and how most people with this problem can be helped, contact the Better Hearing Institute. Included will be a two-minute self-hearing test, the results of which can indicate whether an actual hearing test is needed. A list of registered audiologists in your area will also be provided. Many celebrities like Bob Hope, Arnold Palmer, Nanette Fabray, and Florence Henderson have overcome their own hearing losses and encourage others to get help as they have.

## C.A.R.P.
## CANADIAN ASSOCIATION OF RETIRED PERSONS
**27 Queen Street East**
**Suite 304**
**Toronto, ONT M5C 2M6 Canada**
**416-363-8748**

For a $10 membership (including spouse), this is THE non-profit association for those 50 or older (you need not be retired). A multitude of opportunities for improving the quality of the mature citizen's life is offered: discounts on various services such as travel, insurance, medical, and financial advice, representing mature citizens in matters affecting their rights, general well-being, and welfare.

## DEPARTMENT OF HEALTH AND HUMAN SERVICES
## HEALTHY OLDER PEOPLE HOTLINE
**800-336-4797; 202-429-9091 (in DC)**

This comprehensive health/promotion program is a partnership between federal, state, and local governments, professional organizations, voluntary groups, businesses, and the media. Sponsored by the Department of Health and Human Services, the Healthy Older People's program provides educational materials and technical assistance. If you are involved in a group and would like a variety of support items such as broadcast materials, posters, guidebooks, and information on preventive health services, call for more information and program assistance.

## EPILEPSY FOUNDATION OF AMERICA
**4351 Garden City Drive**
**Suite 406**
**Landover, MD 20785**
**800-EFA-1000 (800-332-1000)**

The Epilepsy Foundation has a number of informative booklets at a very nominal cost ($.10 to $1.50). Some of their titles include "Epilepsy, Medicine and Dental Care,"

"Answers to Your Questions about Epilepsy," "Seizure Recognition and First Aid." Call the toll-free number for information. Their trained staff can answer your questions and direct you to local affiliates.

## GRAY PATCH NETWORK
311 S. Juniper Street
Philadelphia, PA 19107
215-545-6555

For $15 a year, subscribe to the *Gray Panther Newsletter* and be informed on issues directly affecting life and health services for the elderly and disabled. This politically savvy problem-solving group is also involved in legislation, second careers, and other relevant senior activities.

## HALT
1319 F. Street, N.W., Ste. 300
Washington, DC 20004

Join this nonprofit, nonpartisan organization with the other 160,000 Americans for Legal Reform. With as little as $15 a year, you will receive information and facts to help protect you from the legal system and help support legal reforms. HALT is working to simplify legal procedures so you can handle many of your legal affairs without a lawyer. They are working to allow paralegals and other nonlawyers to handle simple legal matters. You'll even receive a 104-page manual on how to *fire* your lawyer and get your money back! There's really no way to hold unscrupulous and incompetent lawyers accountable for their actions save suing them, and there's not too many lawyers willing to sue another lawyer, so they often get off scot-free.

**IBM CORPORATION**
**P.O. Box 2150**
**Atlanta, GA 30055**
**800-IBM-2133 (800-326-2133); 404-238-4806 (in GA)**

IBM has designed a program to make selected IBM computer products available at special prices to persons with disabilities. For most people, technology makes things easier; for the disabled, technology makes things possible. IBM's National Support Center for Persons with Disabilities was created to help disabled professionals and others on how computers can enhance their work and life-style. The PC can be the window to the world for the blind and other visually impaired. It offers new hope, as well, to the deaf, voiceless, slow learners, mentally retarded, people with brain injuries and perhaps most dramatically, to those with severe mobility restrictions. People who have control only of an eyelid or a toe, for example, can now communicate with little or no assistance using IBM's special equipment. Today, there are systems that talk, listen, teach, communicate, and translate. Equipment includes speech synthesizers, voice recognition devices, keyboard emulators, talking terminals, Braille computer printers and attachments. These tools are available for use in the workplace, at home or in schools, where a modem can link its formerly isolated user up to a whole new world. Request the list of participating national, regional, and community service organizations who will help in the selection, ordering and installation of these devices.

**INTERNATIONAL PEN FRIENDS**
**Box 290065**
**Brooklyn, NY 11229-0001**
**SASE**

Fun and friendship from across the seas can be yours through International Pen Friends, whose doors are open to young and old, male and female, married and single. The youngest member is only 8 years old and the oldest was born in 1893! C7 service is designed for the person over 60 (a list of 14 names will be supplied). Membership is for one year, and during that period your name will be passed on to 14 persons in your own age group. Each subscriber may be assured that from among IPF's 250,000 members, they will be provided with many new, exciting, and interesting contacts just as quickly as the enrollment form can be filled out and returned. Be sure to send SASE with request for information.

*Great Buys* readers are entitled to $1 off the service fee, but you must identify yourself as a senior shopper.

**NARCUP**
**Box 391**
**Madison, WI 53701**
**608-238-4286**
**B**

For $12 first-year dues, membership is open to any retired resident or spouse who was (or is) a member of a credit union and anyone (and spouse) who is a credit union member and at least age 50 (you don't have to be retired). In fact, NARCUP's services help plan and manage your retirement and resources. Here's what you get for the low membership dues: *Prime Times* magazine and newsletter, retirement planning and management, free access to consumer complaint services, travel discounts, as well as discounts on prescriptions, eyewear, and MedicAlert. Write for free brochure. Allow three to four weeks for delivery of membership package.

## NATIONAL ASSOCIATION OF PRIVATE GERIATRIC CARE MANAGERS (NAPGCM)
**Box 6920**
**Yorkville Finance Station**
**New York, NY 10128**

NAPGCM is an association of private practitioners whose purpose is the development, advancement and promotion of humane and dignified social, psychological, and health care for the elderly and their families. The locations, availability, and range of services offered by this group are set forth in the *Directory of Geriatric Care Managers*. Services may include assessment, counseling, home care, crisis intervention, placement, education and information, and referral. A copy of the directory may be obtained at no cost by writing to the address above.

## NATIONAL COUNCIL OF SENIOR CITIZENS
**925 15th Street NW**
**Washington, DC 20005**
**202-347-8800**

A $12/year annual membership to the National Council of Senior Citizens will net you the monthly *Citizen News*. That's just one of the benefits of this organization, which works toward keeping readers abreast of the pertinent issues related to senior housing, Social Security, energy policies, and more.

## NATIONAL COUNCIL ON THE AGING, INC.
**600 Maryland Avenue SW**
**Washington, DC 20024**

The National Council on the Aging is one of the major forces lobbying in Washington, helping to shape policy for the elderly. Annual individual membership is $60; organizations $125; lifetime membership $1000. Members receive discounts to conferences and bi-monthly publications.

## NATIONAL INSTITUTE ON AGING
P.O. Box 8057
Gaithersburg, MD 20898-8057
301-495-3455

Publications from this organization include "A Resource for Older People," a brief overview of medical self-care for seniors, and "Age Pages," which describes health subjects such as arthritis, food, crime, foot care, and more. Free upon request.

## OLDER WOMEN'S LEAGUE
730 11th Street NW
Washington, DC 20001
202-783-6686

The Older Women's League is primarily concerned with issues affecting older widowed or divorced women, such as the cumbersome Social Security system, equal employment, access to health care insurance, pension equity, and other problematic concerns facing older women. Founded in 1980, there are over 125 chapters nationwide, with a membership fee of $10.

## SENIORNET
University of San Francisco
San Francisco, CA 94117-1080
415-666-6505

This nonprofit organization's membership fee of $25 connects you to a communications network of other seniors who are computer literate. It has trained thousands of older people to become computer-wise, plus it provides a newsletter, access to the national onlines, and a primer for computer novices called *Computers for Kids over 60*. For more information on how to get in touch via the computer generation, call or write to SeniorNet.

**UNITED CEREBRAL PALSY OF NEW YORK CITY**
**120 East 23rd Street**
**New York, NY 10010**
**212-979-9700**

The flagship publication of United Cerebral Palsy of New York City's Governmental Action Office is entitled *Issues,* and is available upon request. The edition we received focused on employment initiatives for people with disabilities and featured an interview with Robert Dole, U.S. Senator (R-KS), along with articles on computer training, supported employment, and business hiring.

**WORLD WILDLIFE FUND**
**1250 24th Street NW**
**Washington, DC 20037**
**202-293-4800**

"Without firing a shot, we may kill one-fifth of all species of life on this planet in the next 20 years." Do we have your attention yet? Rain forests that provide food and shelter to at least one-half the world's species of wildlife are being bulldozed and burned off at an alarming rate, but what can one person do? World Wildlife Fund now directs more than 500 scientifically based projects, and contributions can help with gorilla conservation in Rwanda, panda research and habitat protection in China, and rescue of the Arabian oryx, the peregrine falcon, and the golden tamarin monkey in Brazil. Membership levels begin at $10, and for a gift of $15, a special gift offer is being made to send a free, members only tote bag.

# OUTLET TOWNS

## Introduction

The concentration of manufacturers' outlets within certain towns or areas has made saving money almost effortless and absolutely fun. Call the chambers of commerce in each town for an area's shopping-tour organizers, or call major bus companies who conduct tours to areas like Reading, PA, or Burlington, NC. Grab a few friends, car pool, hop a bus, Amtrak, or fly-drive to these towns where a dollar saved will make your day. Combine bargain hunting with a fun-filled weekend excursion. There are over 200 factory outlet centers throughout the U.S., where nonshoppers can sightsee or walk the beaches while the shopper goes in for the hunt. You can save 20 to 80 percent, but heed this warning: hazardous to your feet. Wear comfortable shoes. Most businesses accept checks and major credit cards.

**Boaz, Alabama:**
**Off Hwy. 431**
**20 miles east of Gadsden and 70 miles north of Birmingham**
**Open M–S 9–9; Sunday 12:30–5:30.**

Join the busloads of hungry bargain seekers who converge daily at this northeast Alabama town previously known as the "used car capital" of the world. Though not situated in a touristy area, Boaz boasts 50 factory-owned outlets and more than 30 off-price stores. Boaz ranks in the top three U.S. outlet centers. Vanity Fair's 35,000 square foot outlet often lets shoppers browse in shifts if it becomes too crowded. Reading China and Glass is over 50,000 square feet and revealed record breaking sales. It's also crystal clear why Boaz is so popular. These manufacturers also have outlets: L'EGGS, HANES, BALI, BASS, MUSHROOMS, L.L. BEAN, LEVI STRAUSS, ONEIDA, AMITY LEATHER, MANHATTAN, NIKE, HEALTH-TEX, CORNING, IZOD, SWANK, VAN HEUSEN, POLO, REVEREWARE, BLACK & DECKER, CARTERS, JOCKEY INTERNATIONAL, CAMPUS, GITANO, JACK WINTER, NETTLE CREEK, BENETTON, EVAN PICONE, AMERICAN TOURISTER.

**Orlando, Florida:**
**BELZ FACTORY OUTLET MALL**
**International Drive & Oak Ridge Road**
**M–S 10–9; Sunday 10–6**

One of the founders of the Outlet Mall movement, Belz boasts malls in Memphis, Tampa, St. Louis, and Pigeon Forge, TN. Home for such stellar outlet and off-price performers as MAIDENFORM, BARBIZON LINGERIE, VAN HEUSEN, AILEEN, BASS, CONVERSE, MIKASA, PFALTZGRAFF, ANNE KLEIN, CALVIN KLEIN, HARVE BERNARD and more.

Also, Orlando is home to two Quality Outlet Centers nearby and offers VILLEROY & BOCH, CAMPUS, JONATHAN LOGAN, LINENS 'N THINGS, STONE MOUNTAIN HANDBAGS, AMERICAN TOURISTER, CORNING GLASS, ROYAL DOULTON and others. Located next to the Belz Outlet Mall.

**Freeport, Maine:** The Maine attraction is, was, has been, and may always be, L.L. BEAN, the veritable merchant who continues to sell clothing and equipment for the great outdoors and attracts millions of visitors annually. Open 24 hours a day, 365 days a year, now it's no longer the "only" drawing card in town. Today, Freeport boasts COLE-HAAN, J.G. HOOK, DANSK, JONES NEW YORK, RALPH LAUREN, FRYE, HATHAWAY, WHITE STAG, ANNE KLEIN, FILO, JOAN & DAVID

SHOES, BOGNER, CHARLES OF THE RITZ, SWANK, CALVIN KLEIN, REEBOK, LESLIE FAY, POLLY FLINDERS, BUXTON, LONDON FOG, NIKE, GUESS? JEANS, JOHNSTON & MURPHY, plus scores of local artisans, antiques, hand-crafted and one-of-a-kind novelties, good food, Maine lobsters and more.

For a FREE directory of shops, stops and activities, write to Freeport Merchants Association, Box 452, Freeport, ME 04032.

**Kittery, Maine:** On Rt. 1, 50 miles from Boston or Portland, Kittery is giving Freeport a run for your money. Still the smaller of the two, its strength is building with such power outlets as ROYAL DOULTON, BASS SHOE, OSHKOSH B'GOSH, LIZ CLAIBORNE, J.H. COLLECTIBLES, HANES, SERGIO VALENTE, ONEIDA, WATERFORD, LE SPORTSAC, TOWLE SILVER MFG. CO., HATHAWAY SHIRT, VAN HEUSEN, AILEEN and others.

**Flemington, New Jersey:** Located about 60 miles from Philadelphia or New York City, a visit to this town is a throwback to the good old days. Many of the outlets are housed in restored homes among buildings listed in the historic register. Take the day to meander between old battlefields and bargain outlets. Favorites include HAMILTON CLOCK, ADIDAS, VILLEROY AND BOCH, ROYAL DOULTON, FLEMINGTON FUR, QUODDY FOOTWEAR, BILL BLASS, RALPH LAUREN and VILLAGER.

**Secaucus, New Jersey:** Take the NJ Turnpike to Rt. 3, Meadowlands Parkway exit. Park. And walk. And walk 'til you drop. From one industrial doorway to the next, you will never want for another thing (except a foot massage). ARGENTI, JOAN & DAVID, BASS SHOE, CALVIN KLEIN, KENAR, PUMA, ICELANDIC, CAROLE HOCKMAN, BALLY, ALEXANDER JULIAN, GITANO, and more, are part of this vast commercial warehouse wonderland.

**Lake George, New York:**
**FRENCH MOUNTAIN COMMONS**
**Box 3095-16**
**RFD #3**
**Lake George, NY 12845**
**518-792-1483**

Located in the heart of the Adirondacks, French Mountain
Commons is smack dab in the middle of the "Million Dollar
Half Mile" in Lake George and is home to over fifty factory
outlet stores and still growing (some even are too famous to
name publicly). Six outlets have been generous enough to
offer SENIOR SHOPPERS another 10 percent off their
already low prices. They are:

- SKYR—Ladies' and Men's better sportswear and skiwear
- MAINLY BAGS—"Big on handbags and small on
  prices"
- LITTLE RED SHOE HOUSE—Famous brand-name
  shoes at discount prices
- ONEIDA FACTORY STORE—Factory direct savings
  on famous ONEIDA silver products
- FIELDCREST-CANNON—40 to 60 percent savings on
  bed and bath products
- ALL SEASONS FACTORY OUTLET—Savings up to
  60 percent on sportswear, outerwear and accessories

Other notables on the Route 9 corridor worthy of note
include the Adirondack Factory Outlet Center, the Log Jam
Factory Stores, and Lake George Plaza Outlet Center. Out-
lets not to miss are HARVE BERNARD, LONDON FOG, MAIDEN-
FORM, HANES, DANSK, GILLIGAN & O'MALLEY and CARTER'S
CHILDRENSWEAR.

**Burlington, North Carolina:** This outlet capital of the
south is similar to Reading in that there are several major
outlet centers and many little inlets of outlets in between.
Burlington lies in the middle of the Piedmont plateau,
surrounded by rich farmland and rolling hills. You'll see

tobacco farms and peanut harvesters as you drive from town to town. Lots of fine and affordable eateries to nibble and nosh on—even some downright obscene desserts to down (remember there are one-size-fits-all outfits and plenty with elasticized waistbands). Piedmont Outlet Crescent is 20 minutes from Greensboro, 45 minutes from Winston-Salem and 30 minutes from the Raleigh/Durham/Chapel Hill area. There are numerous bus tours and a free train that carries shoppers within the area. Outlets for everything: appliances, fashions, accessories, cosmetics, giftware, crystal and glass, shoes, sporting goods, food, interior decor, luggage, and domestics with names like POLO, RALPH LAUREN, ADOLFO, BALI, ANNE KLEIN, MIKASA, LECREUSET, MANHATTAN, CAMPUS, EVAN-PICONE, LIZ CLAIBORNE, and CARTER'S CHILDRENSWEAR. Who said, "too much of a good thing can be . . . ?" The more the merrier in my book!

**Reading, Pennsylvania:** The outlet capital of the world, "Pretzel Town" as it is called by the locals in honor of one of the traditional industries in the area, is situated within easy travel distance of major eastern cities: Philadelphia (58 miles), New York (138 miles), and Pittsburgh (280 miles). The major highways transverse the Reading area and make it quite accessible. There are multi-center campgrounds open seven days a week, such as The Big Mill, just four blocks from the LUDEN's Candy Factory, housing the DELTA HOSIERY MILLS, the Shirt Factory and SKYR Sportswear. The Great Factory Store Outlet Mall houses a 10,000 square foot outlet for misses' clothing at 30 to 70 percent off, the Fashion Works Outlet for EVAN PICONE and JACK WINTER, a large and half-size outlet. Across from the Big Mill, don't miss Hiesters Lane Outlet Center and the Designer's Outlet, Talbot Knitting Mills, Burlington Coat, the Reading Outlet Center (LONDONSTOWN, CARTERS, MUNSINGWEAR, OSHKOSH B'GOSH, SHIP 'N SHORE, and more), and the famed VANITY FAIR Outlet Complex.

## THE OFF-PRICE CHAINS
**8117 Preston Road, Suite 100**
**Dallas, TX 75225**

Send $5 for a complete listing of the top off-price stores across America, where you can shop for name-brand merchandise for less.


## THE FACTORY OUTLET GUIDE
**8117 Preston Road, Suite 100**
**Dallas, TX 75225**

Send a check for $8.95 for a complete listing of outlet towns and factory stores across the country.

# PETS

## Animals for the Handicapped

Animals trained specifically to aid the elderly and/or
handicapped may be obtained from the following:

Canine Companions for Independence
P.O. Box 446
Santa Rosa, CA 95402

Handi-Dogs, Inc.
P.O. Box 12563
Tucson, AZ 85732

Support Dogs for the Handicapped
6901 Harrisburg Pike
Orient, OH 43146

**ANIMAL VETERINARY PRODUCTS, INC. (AVP)**
**P.O. Box 1326**
**Galesburg, IL 61401**
**800-962-1211**
**CK,MC,V,AE**
**C**

Since it's a dog-eat-dog world out there, you can make it more humane by paying less for all your pet care products. From everyday cosmic catnip to a poodle hair dryer, your pet will be pampered to perfection. The catalog contains a pet-lover's paradise: feeders, furniture, scoopers, pooper and piddle pads, clippers, chewies, chokes, vitamins, litter pans, scratching pads—the works.

**BEEF RAWHIDE**
**161 Riverdale Avenue**
**Yonkers, NY 10701**
**914-969-1537**
**MC,V**
**B,PQ**

Have Fido chew on this for a change—curls, rib rolls, chew sticks, pretzels, donuts and, of course, some 100 percent all-beef rawhide, basted with a freeze-dried liver coating for enhanced flavor and added nutritional value, or compressed rawhide chips in red and white—all at factory direct prices. Write for free brochure/price list. No handling charge for orders over $20.

**KENNEL VET CORP.**
**P.O. Box 835**
**Bellmore, NY 11710**
**516-783-5400**
**MC,V,AE,D,CK,COD**
**C**

Now you can keep your pet healthy, well-groomed, and happy with a full range of supplies for your dogs, cats, and other small animals from Kennel Vet. A full line of vaccines, sprays, ointments, and grooming aids keep your pet feeling and looking its finest at prices sure to make you feel good, too. Tools for professional care include grooming tables, stand dryers, clippers, trimmers, and nail groomers. Learn more about caring for your pet from their extensive selection of pet care books. Orders $50 or more receive an additional 10 percent discount and customers outside New York don't pay sales tax. Orders shipped UPS.

Offer to *Great Buys* readers: free catalog, brochures, and free samples.

**NORTHERN WHOLESALE VETERINARY SUPPLY**
**5570 Frontage Road North**
**Onalaska, WI 54650**
**800-356-5852; 800-362-8025 (in WI) orders only**
**402-731-9600 (Customer Service)**
**CK,MC,V,COD**
**C (specify large or small animal catalog)**

Meet your canine connection, the pet vet at Northern Wholesale, where questions about Fido or Fluffy can be answered by a pro. And when it comes to problems like fleas, worms, or anything else, your prayers are answered by Northern Wholesale's vast collection of complete animal health and beauty care products. Over 6,000 items displayed in their free 112-page catalog, and all brands are discounted 15 percent.

## PAWS WITH A CAUSE
**Home of Ears for the Deaf, Inc.**
**1235 100th Street, SE**
**Byron Center, MI 49315**

Applause for Paws with a Cause goes without saying. In fact, there should be a standing ovation, for these dogs are the lifeline to the blind, the hearing impaired, and the physically challenged. You can spot a hearing and service dog by the orange collar and leash. Owners carry ID cards, and both dog and master have equal access to all public places. The cost to train each animal is around $4,500, underwritten mostly by the United Way and service organizations like Kiwanis, Rotary, etc. Donations are always welcomed, since there is no cost to the recipient.

## RACERS RECYCLED
**P.O. Box 270107**
**Houston, TX 77277-0107**
**Attention: Janet Huey**

Adopt a retiring greyhound dog and bring a loving pet into your life. This national all-volunteer organization provides a national adoption referral network to match greyhounds and graying Americans. Greyhounds, very clean and quiet with placid temperaments, make terrific pets. Send SASE to put your name in for adoption.

**PERFORM**
**800-858-3500**
**MC,V,AE**

The Carnation Company has finally gone to the dogs. And cats, too. Delivering right to your door, Perform provides high performance pet food (canned and dry) that will outperform any of the other premium and prescription pet foods on the market. Comparable in price to SCIENCE DIET and IAMS, forget ever having to lug those bulky and heavy bags again. And, too, you'll never have to make that emergency run in the rain when you run out of Fido's food. Lite and Senior formulas available.

**PURINA "PETS FOR PEOPLE"**
**Checkerboard Square**
**St. Louis, MO 63164**
**314-982-1000**

Purina believes friends come in all shapes and sizes. For the past several years, they have conducted a program called "Pets for People" in cooperation with over 100 shelters nationwide. If you want to adopt a cat or a dog, just go to a shelter in your area and inquire about the program. They'll simply ask you to fill out an application, and if an animal is available, it's yours. They do request that you have the animal spayed or neutered, and all adoptions are final. The rest is up to you. The animals are free, but the love they'll give you is worth all the money in the world. And don't forget to call your local SPCA or Humane Society for their low-cost animals-for-adoption.

# SPAS

There are over 200 spas in the U.S. catering to a diverse group of customers intent on weight loss, rejuvenation, stress reduction, or just a pampered getaway. Traditionally for women, men are popping up alone or with a mate, and they concur that the spa vacation is the best investment for fun and feeling great.

The criteria established for review and inclusion as a recommended spa was the following:

- price
- moderate exercise regimen
- sensible and healthy food plan
- beauty regimens and other pampering services
- on-site medical personnel and access to a physician
- informative lifestyle, health, and nutrition programs
- emphasis on comraderie
- dedicated professionals on staff

**THE KERR HOUSE**
**17777 Beaver Street**
**Grand Rapids, OH 43522**
**419-832-1733**
**MC,V,AE,CK**

This Victorian landmark now houses a premier vintage/contemporary spa environment. An intimate, caring mistress of spas, Laurie Hostetler (a senior herself) greets you upon arrival and orchestrates your every move. Breakfast in bed, yoga in the loft, epicurean low-cal dining with fine crystal and chamber music at dinner, expert advice about creaky bones from Dr. Bob, and let's not forget your daily pampering regime—all part of the total price for a totally new and revived you. Call for Special Senior Weeks packages.

## LAKE AUSTIN RESORT
1705 Quinlan Park Road
Austin, TX 78732
800-847-5637; 800-252-9324 (in TX); 512-266-2444
MC,V,AE,CK

Sister spa to the Bermuda Inn in Lancaster, California, this rustic Texas Hill Country resort is anything but chic . . . but it is cheap. And it gets results. Comfortable surroundings and loving care are heaped upon you top to bottom. Exercise classes are first class; water aerobics, too. Mollie Wing, facialist, and her 80-year-old-plus mother/assistant have the best hands in the world.

## THE OAKS AT OJAI
122 East Ojai Avenue
Ojai, CA 93023
805-646-5573
MC,V,CK

## THE PALMS AT PALM SPRINGS
572 North Indian Avenue
Palm Springs, CA 92262
619-325-1111
MC,V,AE,CK

Spa empressario Sheila Cluff has the market cornered in California. Both facilities capture the essence of a spa vacation and lifestyle change. Special summer reduced rates make the Oaks' value almost priceless. (The more you stay, the more you save, too.) A great California escape that allows you to participate as much as you like (or none at all) and still receive maximum benefits of the well-managed and monitored fitness classes, water sports, beauty treatments, and night-time lectures.

**THE PLANTATION SPA**
**51-550 Kam Highway**
**Ka'a'awa (Oahu) Hawaii 96730**
**808-237-8685; 808-955-3727**
**MC,V,CK**

Escape the city lights of Honolulu and experience the magic of an exotic retreat complete with ocean, waterfalls, tropical birds and paradise-found. Contemplate more than the hula —and have yourself a return-to-nature splendor on the beaches, where you'll learn the art of natural cooking and the crafts of the island. Side trips to areas of cultural attractions are a must.

**RANCHO LA PUERTO IN TECATA, BAJA**
**    CALIFORNIA, MEXICO**
**c/o 3085 Reynard Way**
**San Diego, CA 92103**
**800-443-7565; 800-422-7565 (in CA); 619-294-8504**
**No credit cards**

South of the Border, down Mexico way, you can join the one hundred or so other guests for an exhilarating spa experience. Casual, comfortable and caring, with exquisite home-grown meals (breakfast and lunch are buffet style) and the wealth of wraparound activities in between classes, walking the beautiful vineyard trails, beauty treatments, or snoozing in the hammocks. For women only, except during special couples' week.

## REGENCY HEALTH RESORT & SPA
2000 South Ocean Drive
Suite P
Hallandale, FL 33009
305-454-2220
No credit cards

You must be over 50 to participate in this bargain-packed luxurious experience. Catering to the mature guest, Regency provides select beauty treatments like massages, sauna and whirlpool as part of the package. Shuffleboard, dancing and live entertainment at night, as well as card and bingo games are popular activities to enjoy while one benefits from the spa's commitment to help you lose weight and firm up.

## SAFETY HARBOR SPA & FITNESS CENTER
105 North Bayshore Drive
Safety Harbor, FL 34695
800-237-0155; 813-726-1161 (in FL)
MC,V,AE,CK

Just an hour's ride from Epcot Center, or a quick jaunt from Tampa's International Airport, you can experience an out-of-this-world haven for spa afficionados. Lifestyle changes are second nature to guests who return year after year during the winter months. Lots of outdoor diversions and excursions (Busch Gardens, for one), plus the carefree regime at affordable rates make this a safe bet.

## THE SPA AT BALLY'S PARK PLACE CASINO HOTEL
**Park Place and the Boardwalk**
**Atlantic City, NJ 08401-6709**
**800-772-7777; 609-340-4600**
**All credit cards**

Losing weight and winning at poker is my idea of a jackpot spa vacation. If you've got something to lose, why not sweat it out on the Boardwalk in Bally's $20 million spa facility. Walk the beaches or sink or swim in their multi-level, plush, lush, tropical indoor pool, complete with an underwater sound system. Plunge into a whirlpool or their Finnish sauna and inhalation room. Controlled (or out of control) meals available, plus plenty of pampering possibilities.

## THE SPA AT FRENCH LICK SPRINGS
**French Lick, IN 47432**
**800-457-4042; 800-742-4095 (in IN)**
**MC,V,AE,CK**

The Spa at French Lick Springs Golf & Tennis Resort offers a winter week's special of $449/double occupancy, that includes your room and meals, two fitness classes a day and a mineral bath, plus daily massage. The large hotel facility has indoor and outdoor tennis courts, two golf courses, indoor/outdoor pools, a bowling alley, skeet and trap shooting, miniature golf, surrey rides, horseback riding and more, in case you're bored.

**SUN SPA**
**3101 South Ocean Drive**
**Hollywood, FL 33019**
**800-327-4122; 305-944-9666 (in Dade County)**
**305-921-5800 (in Broward county)**
**No credit cards**

Fun in the sun for the senior spa goers can turn some into heavenly bodies that are full of vim and vigor. Plenty of spa activities and menus (if you want to lose), bingo and bridge, mini-trips on their mini-bus, even a magnifying mirror in each room to apply makeup before making your entrance into dinner and meetings with plenty of new friends.

# SPORTING GOODS

**ALLYN AIR SEAT COMPANY**
**18 Millstream Road**
**Woodstock, NY 12498**
**914-679-2051**
**CK,COD**
**B(SASE)**

The "kiss of comfort" for "fanny fatigue" is coming your
way from Allyn Air Seat Company. Bicycle and motorcycle
seat cushions for the long haul are worth their weight in
comfort. And at Allyn's, they are 25 percent off if you buy
a dozen or more (50 percent for *Great Buys for People over 50*
readers). The air-filled cover for a bicycle seat is only $12
(including shipping) and for cycles and car seats, the price
is $35. These air cushions are also available for trucks, planes
and wheelchairs! Deliveries immediately upon receipt of
order.

**AMERICAN MARINE ELECTRONICS & SUPPLY, INC.**
**5700 Oleander Drive**
**Wilmington, NC 28403**
**800-243-0264**
**MC,V,MO,CK**
**C**

Stop fishing around elsewhere and reel in 40 percent savings on fishing and boating accessories. Salute American's FREE catalog, offering chart recorders, depth sounders, compasses, autopilots, CB radios, as well as equipment for deep-sea fishing. Besides their shop in NC, visit also in Pompano Beach, Florida, at 900 East Atlanta Blvd. Minimum order by mail is $25.

**AUSTAD'S**
**4500 E. 10th St.**
**P.O. Box 1428**
**Sioux Falls, SD 57196-1428**
**800-759-4653 (orders 24 hours a day)**
**800-444-1234 (7 A.M.–7 P.M. CST)**
**MC,V,AE,D,CK,MO**
**C**

If you've been en-golfed with the urge to hit a little white ball, boogie on down and putt in an order here. Since 1963, Austad's has been supplying the fairways with quality golf gear (SPALDING, MACGREGOR, WILSON, DUNLOP, NIKE, BAG BOY, and other top-flight manufacturers) at prices sliced as much as 40 percent off retail. With their outstanding selection highlighted in their FREE full-color catalog, Austad's won't put a divot in your green. Choose bags, clubs, carts, shoes, training aids, sportswear, accessories, and gifts. Many items are made exclusively for Austad's. Orders shipped within 48 hours, by UPS, so you can start chipping away within a week or two. If golf is your handicap, tee off here. Or to request a catalog, call 800-759-4653, extension PR90, 24 hours a day.

**BASS PRO SHOPS**
**P.O. Box 4046**
**Springfield, MO 65808**
**800-227-7776; 417-883-4960 (in AL, HI)**
**CK,MC,V**
**C $2**

You'll fall for this catalog hook, line, and sinker. Their bait is tempting—savings up to 50 percent off on an ocean-size selection of boats, rods, reels, lines, hooks, clothing—everything but the catch. Holy mackerel, that's your contribution.

**BIKE NASHBAR**
**411 Simon Road**
**P.O. Box 3449**
**Youngstown, OH 44512**
**800-627-4227**
**MC,V,D,CK**
**C $1**

Wheel on over for up to 60 percent discount on the finest in biking equipment. Racing and recreational bikes, touring bikes and street bikes—they're all here, including major brands like CITADEL, SHIMANO, VITUS, COLNAGO, CINELLI, and BIKE NASHBAR. Don't be caught out on the road without those necessary accessories like bike pumps, water bottles, shoulder holders, helmets, shoes, and mirrors, all at bargain prices. Is your own bike less than roadworthy? Order replacement parts such as chains, brake levers, cranksets and flywheels. Tires, fenders, seats, and tool kits are also available, along with sporty racing gear. Orders shipped fast with 100 percent satisfaction guaranteed.

**BILL LACKEY COMPANY**
P.O. Box 35109
Dallas, TX 75235
214-526-5211

A washable peel-and-stick identification (called the Lackey Identification Tag) can be applied to your walking or running shoes indicating your name and other pertinent information (like medical data, your telephone number, who to call in an emergency). The size of a postage stamp, you'll get up to 4 lines and 20 letters per line. Price is $5.95 for four tags.

**CABELA'S**
812 13th Ave.
Sidney, NE 69160
800-237-4444 (orders); 800-237-8888 (customer service)
CK,MC,V
C

You can count on Cabela's for down-home discounts on outdoor gear and wear for the rugged individualist. Save 10 to 75 percent off retail prices through their multicatalog offerings. Fishing, hunting, and camping gear, plus their own brand of noteworthy down jackets that should keep you protected from the harsh realities of the full retail world. Jump in with both feet and get on their mailing list.

**CARLSEN IMPORT SHOES**
524 Broadway
New York, NY 10012
212-431-5940
CK
C

Foot the bill for less with running footgear from Carlsen Import Shoes. Track shoes are their specialty with brands like PUMA, PONY, PATRICK, BROOKS, SPALDING, AUTRY, and

ADIDAS. Check out sports equipment like bags, balls, and track suits in their catalog and order at discounts that range from 15 to 30 percent off. Only unused items are returnable. All orders prepaid and shipped in 48 hours.


**FISH 'N' SHACK**
**P.O. Box 1080**
**Camdenton, MO 65020**
**314-346-4044**
**MC,V,CK,MO**
**C**

It's either sink or swim toward the savings of up to 50 percent below retail (and more on the house brand). Lampoon a bargain on every item in this 132-page catalog with about every product imaginable for freshwater fishing and boating. This ocean-array of inventory includes reels, rods, tackle boxes, fishing lines, bait, fly tying, and more. How-to videos even teach you the art of the catch. Though the name's deceiving (half the inventory's devoted to hunting, camping, and other outdoor gear), the savings nevertheless are no fish tales.


**GANDER MOUNTAIN, INC.**
**P.O. Box 6**
**Wilmot, WI 53192**
**800-554-9410**
**MC,V,D,CK,MO**
**C**

Take a gander at this gigantic 144-page color catalog of fishing and hunting gear and save up to 35 percent across the pike. Equipment and gear that is equally enticing, from BUSHNELL to COLEMAN, to DVA black-powder rifles or MI-

CHAELS holsters. Expert service and selection adds to their overall appeal for the outdoor fishing and hunting enthusiast.

## GOLDBERG'S MARINE DISTRIBUTORS
**201 Meadow Road**
**Edison, NJ 08818**
**800-B-O-A-T-I-N-G**
**MC,V,AE,D,CK,MO**
**C,PQ**

Since 1946, the Goldbergs have been rocking the boat with savings of up to 60 percent on everything to put you afloat. From anchors to the kitchen (galley) sink—buoy, oh buoy, have they got the stuff! Life vests, marine radios, boating shoes, dinghies, but sorry, no guarantees you'll catch a thing. Price quotes by mail with SASE. Minimum order is $10.

## GOLF HAUS
**700 North Pennsylvania**
**Lansing, MI 48906**
**517-482-8842**
**MC,V,CK,MO**
**C**

Save yourself a long drive as well as some green—order clubs at 40 to 60 percent off retail from Golf Haus. Choose from 15 to 20 brands including these normally found on the leader board: SPALDING, DUNLOP, WILSON, TITLEIST, LYNX, and PING. Minimum order: $50. No CODs. Orders shipped prepaid in the continental U.S.

*Great Buys* readers: Free knit head covers with purchase of a full set of clubs.

## GOLFSMITH
**Custom Golf Clubs, Inc.**
10206 N. Interregional
Austin, TX 78753
800-456-3344 (U.S. and Canada); 512-456-3344
C

From their humble beginnings in 1969, Carl and Frank Paul have parlayed a few hundred dollars into a $30 million plus custom golf club company. Their catalogs make any golfer green with envy. With over two hundred employees to help you and 450,000 active accounts, they are the world's largest supplier of custom clubs, repair components, and accessories. If you want to tighten your grip on prices, plan on saving 10 to 30 percent off retail prices. Minimum order is $10. Their club-making component and supplies catalog is 180 pages; their accessory merchandise catalog is 100 pages.

## HOLABIRD SPORTS DISCOUNTERS
9004 Yellow Brick Road
Rossville Industrial Park
Baltimore, MD 21237
301-687-6400
301-687-7311 (FAX)
MC,V,AE,CK
B

"Birds of a feather" all flock to Holabird's and save up to 35 percent on major brand name sporting goods: REEBOK, PRINCE, AMF, HEAD, SPALDING, YAMAHA, DUNLOP . . . Cheep! Cheep! You will find all the accessories and equipment you need for squash, racquetball, tennis, golf, running, et cetera. Orders shipped in two days but for a refund, you must return unused merchandise in seven days.

**L. L. BEAN**
Freeport, ME 04033
800-221-4221 (orders); 800-341-4341 (customer service)
MC,V,AE,CK
C

The source of all things sporty from this shopaholic's all-night dream come true. Both economically and ecologically sound, L. L. Bean offers stress-free, toll-free, almost free-fun sporting goods, exercise and camping gear, and apparel. They offer skis and all the paraphernalia to keep you chic, sleek, and cozy on the slopes. There's also Swiss army knives, tents, boots, and treadmills, even walking pedometers, all fit to be tried. Specialty catalogs available upon request include Hunting, Home and Camping, Fall or Spring Women's Outdoors, Winter Sporting, Fly Fishing, Spring Sporting. Gift certificates, too. Free shipping, though you can request Federal Express rush delivery for $8.00. Toll-free shopping 24 hours a day, 7 days a week.

**MEGA TENNIS PRODUCTS**
800-228-2373
MC,V,CK,COD
C,PQ

Tighten those purse strings with savings on the strings here. Tennis racquets and racquet-stringing machines are their specialty, along with accessories for the court: grips, socks, wristbands, headbands, ball-hoppers, ball-machines, most state-of-the-art tennis gear. Stringing your own racquet will save you even more. $3 service charge on orders under $30.

**ORION TELESCOPE CENTER**
**P.O. Box 1158**
**Santa Cruz, CA 95061**
**800-447-1001**
**MC,V,CK,MO**
**C**

Be the first on your block to see the moon and save up to 40 percent on a telescope. Through this 56-page catalog, star performers include every astronomical and terrestrial telescope imaginable—from CELESTRON, MENDE, EDMUND, PENTAX, and, of course, ORION, to name a few. Star gaze at other equipment, too: tripods, binoculars, lenses, filters, eyepieces, and other tools to chart your course.

**"THE POKE BOAT"**
**Phoenix Products**
**207 North Broadway**
**Berea, KY 40403**
**800-354-0190; 606-986-2336 (in CAN)**
**B**

Factory direct boats that float are low-cost and durable. This no-frills approach with word-of-mouth advertising and simple black and white brochures can deliver a boat at 50 percent savings. Being a small, family-owned and -operated business, there's no room for fancy front offices and extravagant overhead that you, the customer, ultimately pay for. Yes, they can make a superior boat that sells for under $700. Write for their brochures and see-the-sea for yourself.

## ROAD RUNNER SPORTS
11211 Sorrento Valley Road
Suite K
San Diego, CA 92121
800-551-5558; 619-455-0558 (in CA)
C

Running circles around their nearest competitors, Road Runner guarantees the lowest prices on some of the top names (like FOOT JOY) in running, business, dress and golf shoes. Line up in SAUCONY, NIKE, ADIDAS, AVIA, NEW BALANCE, or ETONIC. Save big bucks (but sorry, no buck shoes were in stock). Shipment in 24 hours. Over 20,000 shoes in stock.


## THE SKI LOFT
2203 N. Ballard
Wylie, TX 75098
800-899-LOFT (5638); 214-442-5842 (Dallas area)
MC,V,AE,CK

Ski down the slopes and save 40 to 60 percent. Wonderful winterwear, skiwear, and accessories for the entire family in a full size range available in names too famous to mention. Equipment, too: skis, boots, and poles for less. Call for price quote on everything you'll need to at least make the downhill journey an uplifting experience. Ask for James or Ann for special *Great Buys* offer.

# SPORTS

**THE ASPEN SKIING COMPANY**
**The Inn at Aspen**
**800-952-1515; 800-826-4998 (in CO)**

You can participate, along with your fellow skiers who are over 50, in the Fit for Life/50 Plus program. This program (endorsed by the President's Council on Physical Fitness) is held on special weeks in January, February, and March and includes seminars on nutrition, stress management, and fitness, along with parties and races. Whether you're a downhill or cross-country skier, you're sure to improve with age.

**BROMLEY SENIOR SKIERS CLUB**
**Vermont Ski Areas Association**
**Box 368**
**Montpelier, VT 95602**

Open to any skier over the magic age of 65, the Bromley Senior Skiers Association is headquartered in Bromley, Vermont. Along with half-price season lift passes, members also get discounts on lessons and preferred parking.

## INSTITUTE FOR SUCCESS OVER 60
**605 East Main Street**
**Aspen, CO 81611**
**303-925-1900**

A recent market study at Aspen-Snowmass shows that 27 percent of its skiers are 50 + . Despite its name, this program is designed for anyone over 50, and even though it already sports a low, low price, there's an even greater discount for anyone over 70. This week-long ski-instruction program at Aspen is aimed at beginners and intermediate-level skiers who want to improve their skills. Along with instruction on the slopes, the program also offers ski videos and analysis; seminars on nutrition, stress management, and fitness; races and parties; lodging and meals at the Inn at Aspen. Who could ask for anything more? For information, write or call the Institute.

## JOAN & LEE WULFF FISHING SCHOOL
**Lew Beach, NY 12758**
**914-439-4060**

Learn the art of fly-fishing with the Wulffs in New York's beautiful Catskill Mountains. They offer classes during eight weekends from late April through June. Classes cost $400 and include equipment, but not lodging or food. Note: You'll learn how to fish, but you won't catch anything on this trip. Write or call for more information.

## NATIONAL SENIOR SPORTS ASSOCIATION
**10560 Main Street #205**
**Fairfax, VA 22030**
**703-385-7540**

For Americans over 50 who enjoy travel, sports, new friendships, fellowship, and more, membership in this organization provides benefits that include NSSA tournaments and recreational events, sports holidays abroad, monthly newsletter, discounts on rental cars, credit cards, air travel assistance and more. Allow four to six weeks for membership processing.

*Great Buys* readers receive 10 percent off on a one-year membership.

## OVER THE HILL GANG, INTERNATIONAL
**13791 East Rice Place**
**Aurora, CO 80015**
**303-699-6404**

From Chicago to Albuquerque to New York City—the Over the Hill Gang has almost 2,000 members, all over the age of 50 and each entitled to discounts on ski packages. In addition to opportunities in the U.S., the Over the Hill Gang sponsors at least one trip abroad each year. Other sports keep members together and active in the offseason, with organized trips for sailing, hiking, snorkeling, and golfing. Individual memberships are $25 ($15 additional for a spouse). Write for more information.

## 70+ CLUB
**104 East Side Drive**
**Ballston Lake, NY 12019**
**518-399-5458**

More than 200 ski areas, mostly in the East, give discounts to the more than 4,500 members of the 70+ Club. For a low membership fee of $5, members receive a colorful arm patch for their ski jacket, a newsletter, and a list of discounts. The only requirement for membership is that you must be over 70. (And be willing to be an inspiration on the slopes for people in their 40s and 50s who think they're getting too old to ski!)

## SMUGGLER'S NOTCH
**Smuggler's Notch, VT 05464**
**802-644-8851**

The village at Smuggler's Notch feels it's not enough that they offer $1 off the normal season pass rates for every year a senior is "old," they also offer seniors 65 and older half-price skiing every day, including holidays. And not only does the season pass include such benefits as 50 percent off all group lessons and 50 percent off bed and breakfast at the Highlander Motel or Red Fox Alpine Lodge, but the village also offers one of the most beautiful ski areas in Vermont. FREE skiing for Vermonters 70 years of age or older is an offer not to be spurned.

## STRATTON CORPORATION
**Stratton Mountain, VT 05155**
**802-297-2200**

At this ski resort heaven, senior skiers (62–69) pay $35 for membership dues (spouse pays half price, if eligible) and pay half price for daily lift tickets or season pass. Super Seniors (over 70) pay $35 for membership dues (eligible spouses, too) and receive a FREE Stratton season pass. There's a customer relations desk in the base lodge to handle seniors who need a membership card or updating.

## TELEMARK INN AND LLAMA TREKS
**Steve Crone**
**RFD 2, Box 800**
**Bethel, MN 04217**
**207-836-2703**

Llama trekking is great for adults because "it turns them into children," or so says Steve Crone, owner of the posh Telemark Inn. He also states that they do a lot of family travel and promises "comfortable wilderness trips." Full-course meals are offered and the llamas do all the work, while you walk along and take in the majestic sights. Trips run two to six days and cost $100 a day for adults, $60 for children. For more information, write to Steve at the Telemark Inn.

## "TRAVELING GOLFER"
## 1469 Bellevue, No. 804
## Burlingame, CA, 94010

Write for your free sample newsletter from veteran travel and golf writer Lee Tyler. If you're a golfer, you may want to know the bargain courses, as well as the exotic green paradises waiting for you to play. Annual subscription is $12.

## U.S. MASTERS SWIMMING NATIONAL OFFICE
## 2 Peters Avenue
## Rutland, MA 01543

Get into the swim of things and jump into the water at over 450 local Master Swim Clubs throughout the country (more are forming every day). Masters Swimming is an organized program of swimming for adults—from lap swimming to international competition. Though anyone 19 or older can join, members in their 90s still haven't sunk. Swim for your life; it is one of the best and safest exercises available for older citizens. Write for more details.

**WILD OLD BUNCH**
**Rush Speden**
**4131 Cumorah Drive**
**Salt Lake City, UT 84117**
**801-278-2283**

No rules, no lessons, no regular meetings—sound like your kind of club? Keep reading. This informal group, based in Alta, Utah, has 50 to 100 retired members from around the country who gather in Alta for skiing and to take advantage of big discounts.

# TRAVEL—AIR

A good pilot always keeps his checklist handy and so should you if you're a smart *Great Buys* shopper. Some of the things to check into:

- Even though you tell your travel agent that you're a *Great Buys* shopper, ask for the *lowest* available fare. Sometimes the restraints put on senior fares are restrictive.
- If you don't travel often, don't be bamboozled into a "yearly pass" or special offer. Make sure you pay for only what you will use.
- Check into fly-drive packages. Often airfare is combined with a hotel and rental car company and can result in package deals priced as much as 50 percent less than your airfare alone.
- Always book your trip as early as possible for the very best fare.
- Don't get to the ticket counter and discover you've left behind that membership card that must be presented to receive your special fare.
- Don't pack medications in the luggage you check. Even though it's not as convenient, at least carry a small supply with you on board.
- Always carry your destination phone number and address with you. Remember that it's easy to get confused and forget that number in strange, unfamiliar territory.

# Special Meals on Airlines

With some notice (usually 6–12 hours in advance of departure) you can get a special meal that's healthier or different from the fare usually served. Most popular substitutions include:

- vegetarian with whole-grain bread, fruits, and vegetables
- low-fat, low sodium
- low cholesterol
- hypoglycemic
- bland
- lighter choices

Call the selected airline or your travel agent for special requests and information.

## AIR CANADA
**800-422-6232**

Check out Air Canada's Freedom Flyer program if you're 62 or older. You may visit up to 12 cities in the United States or Canada with a companion (of any age) at reduced fares. There is a 14-day advance purchase, but changes or cancellations may be made for a fee of $59. You can even earn frequent-flyer credit with the tickets!

## Weather Hotline (900-370-8728)

This 24-hour weather hotline gives touch-tone callers the time, temperature, and 4-day forecast, 10-day outlook, and travel conditions for more than 600 cities worldwide. Plus updates on tropical storms and travel advisories. For cities in the U.S., dial, then punch in the city's area code. For foreign weather, dial, then punch in the first three letters of the city's name. Cost is $.75 for the first minute; $.50 for each additional minute. Texas callers: substitute "575" for "370" for your first three (3) numbers after dialing 1-900.

## ALASKA AIRLINES
## 800-426-0333

If the majestic beauty of Alaska is calling you, present your ID showing you're over 62 to receive a 10 percent discount on almost all of their flights in and out of the state. Offseason, the savings are even greater!

## ALOHA AIRLINES
## 800-367-5250

Okay, you're in Hawaii. You're over 65. Beat the normal fare of $39.95 by letting Aloha know your age and island-hop at a savings of $10. Can't beat that with a hula!

## AMERICAN AIRLINES
## 800-433-7300

The magic age on American is 62 years young. Passengers who meet that qualification travel for 10 percent off the lowest available fare at any time, or they can access savings through their coupon books. A book of four coupons was $420 ($105 per coupon) and a book of eight was $704 ($88 per coupon). One coupon will take you up to 2,000 miles; any further will require two. Travel any day of the week in the continental U.S. with 14 days advance purchase.

## AMERICA WEST
## 800-247-5692

Want to save 10 to 50 percent off coach fare? Call America West. They offer two different plans to choose from: (1) The Senior Discount Pack is a coupon book with 4 or 8 one-way tickets good wherever they fly in the continental United States (one ticket can be to Honolulu). (2) Their Senior Fare. Be sure to call and check, as the days you can travel are limited.

## BRITISH AIRWAYS
## Privileged Traveler Program
## P.O. Box 13130
## Stratford, CT 06461-8830
## 800-AIRWAYS (800-247-9297)

For the mature traveler (over 60), this card provides the waiver of all penalties for pre-trip cancellation or change in airfare reservation, up to 30 percent off normal advance purchase airfare; 10 percent off on all other British Airways airfares between the U.S. and England; special check-in procedures; additional discounts on airport limos, Cunard cruises and more. Allow four to six weeks for processing and delivery of your card.

## CANADIAN AIRLINES INTERNATIONAL
**800-426-7000**

You can receive a special discount if you're over 62 on domestic flights in Canada. Just book 14 days in advance and be sure to bring your ID. No restrictions on days or times.

## CONTINENTAL AIRLINES FREEDOM PASSPORT
**P.O. Box 526505**
**Miami, FL 33152-6506**
**800-441-1135**
**B**

If you are 62 or will be within a year, call for information on Continental's Freedom Passport to enjoy unlimited travel for a year and save thousands at the same time! Choose from 80 destinations in the U.S. (coach or first class) for one low price. You'll get one roundtrip coach to Europe, the South Pacific, Central America, and Hawaii, plus three round trips to your choice of Mexico, the Caribbean, 80 destinations in mainland U.S., Canada, or the Virgin Islands. A 90-day guarantee. Call toll free for brochure and more information.

## DELTA AIRLINES
**Ticket-by-Mail Department**
**201 Alhambra Circle**
**Ponce de Leon Building**
**Coral Gables, FL 33134-9937**
**800-221-1212**

"Young at Heart" fares at Delta will bring savings of 10 percent to you and a traveling companion. No club to join and no membership fees, just straight across the board discounts. Use your "Young at Heart" fares to such international cities as: London, Shannon, Dublin, Frankfurt, Stuttgart, Munich, Seoul, Tokyo, and Taipei. If you are at least 62, a book of eight coupons was $640, or $80 each way. A book of four coupons was $384, or $96 each way. Fly to any Delta or Delta connecting city in the continental U.S. or Puerto Rico and return on two coupons. Or fly to Hawaii or Alaska by using four coupons. Delta loves to fly and it shows—and you can, too!

## EL AL
**800-532-5786**

If you're over 60, it could be worthwhile to check out El Al's Golden Age Fare and save, save, save. You can even stay for up to two months in Israel and make a stopover in Europe. Fourteen days' advance purchase is required, and there is a fee for changing return reservations. Call for more information.

## FINNAIR
**800-777-5553**

Fly from New York or Los Angeles to Helsinki and save if you're over 65 and are flying on short (3 days') notice. Spouses permitted at the same fare. A stopover elsewhere in Europe is allowed.

## KLM/EUROPE BY DESIGN
**800-777-1668**

Europe by Design gives you the opportunity to design your own individual itinerary and explore Europe as only an insider can. Use the Vacation Planner, in which you'll find descriptions of their 15 most popular cities, including travel options (air, rail, car). And a choice of Unexpected Pleasures gives you the opportunity to detour to those often overlooked diversions: horseback riding through a city park, rituals of a Copenhagen spa, or the Van Gogh Celebration. If you prefer to have your vacation planned by KLM, just call for more details.

**MEXICANA AIRLINES**
**412 East Commerce**
**San Antonio, TX 75205**
**800-531-7921**

Let Mexicana fly you at a savings of 10 percent off their lowest fares to one or more of their thirty destinations. Blackout periods (times you cannot use this discount) range from March 16 to March 29 and December 15 to January 10, along with the months of July and August in some areas; otherwise, you can use your 10 percent discount at any other time.

**MIDWAY AIRLINES**
**5959 South Cicero**
**Chicago, IL 60638**
**800-621-5700**

It finally pays great dividends for you to straighten up and fly right. Seniors over 62 (and companions) get 10 percent off any ticket, anywhere, anytime on Midway Airlines. Proof of age is required. Wheelchair service at the airport and at check-in is available. Special meals can be ordered 72 hours prior to departure.

## MIDWEST EXPRESS AIRLINES
**800-334-1149**

Proof of age (65) and you're an automatic member of their Golden Travel Club and Frequent Flyer Program. Each time you travel, you'll save 10 percent. Though limited to select cities, with their hub being Milwaukee, you'll be mighty impressed with their total "first class" express, including meals that rival five-star restaurants. Can you imagine a chocolate chip cookie that's baked on board and served hot at 30,000 feet? or a French wine to accompany your steak and lobster? The *Wall Street Journal* or *USA Today* is complimentary to read and relax on board. Fly the aircraft that *Frequent Flyer Magazine* rated tops in comfort and roominess.

## NORTHWEST AIRLINES
**World Perks for Seniors**
**P.O. Box 1735**
**Minneapolis, MN 55440-1735**
**800-225-2525 (reservations); 800-666-2299 (enrollment)**

Northwest Airlines has just begun its World Perks Program, offering seniors (over 62) the opportunity to save on airfare, hotels, cruises, car rentals, restaurants and more. Just write to the address above or call the toll-free number and request an enrollment card. With it, you'll be eligible to receive up to 25 percent off airfare to select destinations, along with special discount certificates, in addition to a savings of up to 30 percent off on hotels and resorts—all for a one-time enrollment fee . . . the world awaits. Northwest also has the popular coupon program with a four-coupon book selling for $384 and eight-coupon book for $640. There are some blackout dates and some restrictions apply; travelers should double check with Northwest at the toll-free number or call their travel agent.

**NOW VOYAGER**
**212-431-1616 (Mon. to Fri. 11 A.M.–5 P.M.,**
 **Sat. 12:30 P.M.–4 P.M.)**
**212-431-1616 (6 P.M.–11 A.M. (for current destinations,**
 **prices, lengths of stay, and last-minute super reduced**
 **fares)**
**CK,MC,V,AE (additional fee for credit card use)**

Register for a year for $50 and unlimited travel (round trip
if needed) to various destinations for up to 75 percent off
on all major airlines as a courier. Europe, South America,
Caribbean, Los Angeles, the Far East, Mexico, and more are
on courier routes. Freight companies exchange your baggage
space for a package they need to ship, limiting you to only
one carry-on bag. Cancellations on international flights not
refundable; but you can cancel with 2 weeks' notice domestic
flights, with certain restrictions. You can book up to 2 months
in advance, but there's only one person per flight. For more
recorded information, call the number above.

**PAN AMERICAN WORLD AIRWAYS**
**P.O. Box 592055-A.M.F.**
**Miami, FL 33159**
**800-221-1111**

Pan Am can fly you just about anywhere you want to go. So,
what are you waiting for? They offer a 10 percent discount
if you're 62 or older, as well as a Value Pass for one year.
For just one low price, you are entitled to one trip to Europe,
a trip to Latin America/Mexico/Hawaii and two domestic
flights. Call or write for more information.

## SOUTHWEST AIRLINES
P.O. Box 37611
Dallas, TX 75235
214-263-1717

Southwest Airlines started recognizing seniors a number of years ago, possibly the first airline to do so. Believing age to be nothing more than a state of mind, they want to treat you like a kid and let you fly for peanuts on their low fun fares to any of the cities in Texas, as well as other cities they serve—Monday through Thursday from 9:00 A.M. to 3:00 P.M. or anytime Saturday. All you have to do is be 65 years of age or older. Call or write for more information.

## TWA/TAKEOFF PASS
800-221-2000

What a deal! Automatically deduct 10 percent from fares if you're over 62, and you may take along a companion for the same fare (regardless of age). Or, you may select the Travel Pack and purchase four coupons for $379 on domestic flights, or choose international flights (off peak travel periods), $449 and (peak travel periods) for $649.

## UNITED AIRLINES
Silver Wings Plus
P.O. Box 92591
Los Angeles, CA 90009-9912
800-628-2868

"United we fly . . ." further, for less! For a $50 enrollment fee, United Airlines can save you money on air travel. You even get $50 back in the form of discount certificates. Want to include a companion? Well, add $100 (regardless of their age) and do just that. Get your Silver Wings Plus at age 62 and really take off (10 percent that is) on fares in the U.S.,

Canada, Mexico, Singapore, Thailand, Korea, and the Philippines. Save 25 to 50 percent at specified hotels, resorts and rent-a-cars like Westin and Hertz. Good news and great savings arrive quarterly, thanks to *Silver Wings Plus Travel*, a beautiful full color magazine with details about special tours and travel bargains.

## US AIR
**800-428-4322**

In addition to the regular 10 percent discount like other airlines, US Air provides something special with their coupon books. For the 62-year-old or older passenger, four coupons can be purchased for $420 and an eight-coupon book for $704. Each coupon is good for a one way ticket. If you're over 100 years old, you travel free! There are some travel restrictions and blackout periods, as with any special offer.

# TRAVEL—AUTO CLUBS, CARS, AND MOTOR

In addition to their regular helpful road services, most auto clubs offer travel benefits, including discounts on car rentals, lodging, and travel planning kits.

**ALA AUTO AND TRAVEL CLUB**
888 Worcester Street
Wellesley, MA 02181
617-237-5200

**ALLSTATE MOTOR CLUB**
34 Allstate Plaza
Northbrook, IL 60062
800-323-6282

**AMOCO MOTOR CLUB**
P.O. Box 9048
Des Moines, IA 50369
800-334-3300

**CHEVRON TRAVEL CLUB**
P.O. Box P
Concord, CA 94524
415-827-6000

**EXXON TRAVEL CLUB**
P.O. Box 3633
Houston, TX 77253
713-680-5723

**MONTGOMERY WARD MOTOR CLUB**
2020 Dempster Street
Evanston, IL 60202
800-621-5151

**NATIONAL AUTOMOBILE CLUB**
3600 Wilshire Boulevard
Los Angeles, CA 90010
213-386-6591

**SHELL MOTORIST
  CLUB PLUS**
P.O. Box 2463
One Shell Plaza
Houston, TX 77001
713-241-6161

**UNITED STATES AUTO
  CLUB**
P.O. Box 660460
Dallas, TX 75266
800-348-2761

**TEXACO STAR CLUB**
P.O. Box 224669
Dallas, TX 75222
214-258-2060

**AARP MOTORING PLAN**
Amoco Motor Club
P.O. Box 9041
Des Moines, IA 50369-0002
800-START-UP (800-782-7887)

800-START-UP is a number you won't want to forget as a member of the AARP Motoring Club. One quick call to this number will bring you all the help you need for your ailing car, with no additional calls required, no call backs, and no out-of-pocket expenses. This emergency telephone system is available on a nationwide basis. Also, planned trips will be routed for you on large, easy-to-read maps upon request, and you may use this service as often as you wish. In addition, Holiday Inn guest certificates can be combined with your AARP 10 percent discount, making your savings as high as 20 percent. You'll also have Emergency Check Cashing privileges, $250 Hospital Emergency Room Bond, $500 Trip Guarantee and Guaranteed Arrest Bond certification. It's easy to join and there's a 90-day trial period, with absolutely no risk. Twelve months of this coverage is specially priced at only $29.95 (regular $33.95) and second membership at no extra cost.

## AMERICAN AUTOMOBILE ASSOCIATION (AAA)
8111 Gatehouse Road
Falls Church, VA 22047
703-222-6000

Joining AAA will net you a myriad of benefits, including travel planning and road service for disabled cars. They also publish the *Handicapped Driver's Mobility Guide*, listing valuable resources, equipment modifications, hand-control manufacturers, and more.

## AVIS
800-331-1800

Special rates are given to members of AARP, CARP (Canadian Association of Retired Persons), Northwest's World Horizons program, and Mature Outlook, amounting to 5 to 10 percent off regular rates.

## CAMPING WORLD
800-626-5944; 502-781-2718 (in Hawaii)
502-781-2775 (Fax)
CK,MC,V,AE,D,DC
C

Whether you shop in any of their 17 locations coast to coast or order toll free from their catalog, if it's something for your RV, look no farther. Meet your friends on the road in style, when you hit the road in your RV. Your complete RV parts and supplies superstore offers a 10 percent (and more) savings incentive if you are a member of their President's Club super-saver program. An annual membership fee of $20 entitles you to save on all products, parts and services, "members only" sales and events, a quarterly newsletter, up to 83 percent on pharmaceutical needs, special discounts on tours and caravans, and a FREE, one-year KOA Value Kard.

## CREATIVE WORLD RALLIES AND CARAVANS
**606 N. Carrollton Ave.**
**New Orleans, LA 70119**
**800-732-8337**

Since 1976, this spinoff of Bill La Grange's full-service travel agency organizes both RV road rallies and caravans. In the United States, caravan participants drive their own RVs; while overseas, Creative World will book air transportation and arrange for an RV. You drive to a designated rendezvous point for a rally, pack, and proceed to enjoy all the planned activities. A caravan, on the other hand, is when you proceed from destination to destination, detouring to points of interest along the way. International itineraries are jam-packed with interesting sidebars and are priced all inclusive with airfare, lodging and campground fees, motorhome rentals, and special meals. Other resources to call upon for RV planning:

Family Motor Coach
8291 Clough Pike
Cincinnati, OH 45244
513-474-3622

Recreation Vehicle Industry Association
P.O. Box 2999
Reston, VA 22090
702-620-6003

Also, rent an RV nationally from Cruise America (800-327-7778) or Go Vacations, Inc. (800-387-3998), or check your local Yellow Pages under Recreational Vehicles—Leasing & Rental.

## CRUISE AMERICA
## MOTORHOME RENTAL & SALES
**800-327-7778; 800-327-7799 (in CAN)**

Join Cruise America's Holiday Club program ($49 introductory membership) and start saving 10 percent on the over two hundred motorhome rental locations in North America. Wheel in for savings, including a $100 award certificate toward a week's rental, their "Guide to Free Attractions" (retail $14.95), an Attractions Discount Book (two-for-one vouchers, value $250) and more. Hop aboard and get rolling.

## INTERSTATE TRAVELMATE
**c/o Whestter**
**800-531-0004**

This calculator-sized computer contains a state-by-state rundown on restaurants, motels, and services located off more than 13,000 major highway and interstate exits. Also, you'll have at your fingertips 24-hour gas stations and restaurants, hospitals, campgrounds, highway-patrol offices, and local numbers for road conditions and traveler's assistance. The cost is $99.95; $20 for yearly updating.

## KAMPGROUNDS OF AMERICA, INC.
**P.O. Box 31734 VCD**
**Billings, MT 59107-1734**
**406-248-7444**

KOA could stand for "Kids of All Ages" who have fun at their campgrounds in the U.S. and Canada. Now you can save 10 percent on camping at over 650 KOA Kampgrounds.

KOA offers readers of *Great Buys* their own special Value Kard for $3 (value $6), along with the following benefits: 10 percent discount on registration fees, express check-in service and the best available campsites, a money back guarantee within one hour of check-in time, and Hertz rental car discounts.

## RECREATION VEHICLE INDUSTRY ASSOCIATION (RVIA)
P.O. Box 2999
Reston, VA 22090
703-620-6003

This is an organization of manufacturers and suppliers whose members produce 95 percent of all RVs manufactured in the U.S. The RVIA library is packed with information of interest to RVers. Publications offer information on trade shows, buying or renting RVs, campgrounds, camping clubs, et cetera, and many of them are free.

## RECREATION VEHICLE RENTAL ASSOCIATION
3251 Old Lee Highway
Fairfax, VA 22030
800-336-0355; 703-591-7130
C $5

An annual subscription to *Rental Ventures* provides the ultimate where, when, why and how to go in your RV. Included are campgrounds, rentals, how to obtain the needed licenses, a directory of state travel offices; this is your source of travel RV tips. The comprehensive U.S. and Canadian directory of rates will also be sent.

**TELEMAP NAVIGATION SERVICES**
**1327 North Main Street, Ste. 101**
**Walnut Creek, CA 94596-4634**
**800-843-1000; 415-256-4560**
**$24/annual fee**

For a cost of $24 per year, this company will give you detailed directions for more than 10,000 cities in the U.S., Canada, Mexico, Puerto Rico, and the Virgin Islands. With one toll-free call (or you can have them faxed), you can forget looking for your glasses to read the road maps or wasting time and gas driving all over town looking for that desired restaurant, hotel, or landmark.

**TELETIRE**
**17642 Armstrong Avenue**
**Irving, CA 92714**
**800-835-8473**
**MC,V,D,CK,MO**
**B**

This multimillion-dollar dealer sells brand-new tires at 30 percent off. Whether you need one for your car, truck, van, or RV, you might as well take off for less. Price quote by phone or mail.

**THRIFTY RENT-A-CAR SYSTEM, INC.**
**World Headquarters**
**5330 East 31 Street**
**P.O. Box 35250**
**Tulsa, OK 74153-0250**
**800-FOR-CARS (800-367-2277) (worldwide)**

Thrifty Car Rental has always been one of the leaders in the car rental industry when it comes to discounts and "deals." But feast your eyes on this! For seniors who belong to AARP,

Thrifty offers the "Purchase Privilege Program," offering an additional 10 percent on already low Thrifty rates with an AARP member coupon. Thrifty has over 750 locations in 30 countries to choose from worldwide, so the next time you need the latest model, from subcompact to luxury, call Thrifty. Use the worldwide toll-free number to book your reservation.

**TITAN RUBBER INTERNATIONAL**
**One Bryan Drive**
**Wheeling, WV 26003-0137**
**800-443-8473**
**MC,V,D,CK,MO**
**PQ**

You'll never tire of recommending Titan Rubber (also called Tire America) for their first-quality savings of up to 50 percent on namebrand tires. Knowledgeable sales assistance by phone is available to help you make the right choice in every make and model of tire made. There's also a tire and wheel package available on some. Price quote available by mail with SASE.

**U.S. NATIONAL PARKS**
**Department of the Interior**
**Washington, DC 20240**

The Golden Age Passport permits persons 62 and older free lifetime use of all nationally held and operating park and recreation facilities and areas, in addition to a 50 percent discount on federal use fees for services such as camping, boat launching, and parking. All you need to do is show proof of age at any federally operated recreational areas when you arrive, but reservations for campsites may be made eight weeks in advance for individual campsites, such as the Grand Canyon or Yellowstone, by writing: Department R, 401 Hackensack Avenue, Hackensack, NJ 07601.

# TRAVEL—
# ARTS AND CRAFTS

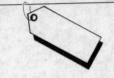

The following are opportunities for the "crafty" traveler to pursue his avocation and his vacation at the same time.

## ANDERSON RANCH ARTS CENTER
**P.O. Box 5598**
**Snowmass Village, CO 81615**

Renowned craftsmen visit this Rocky Mountain Retreat each summer (late May to September 16) and teach one and two week courses in furniture design, woodworking, ceramics and bookmaking, as well as photography and painting. Tuition was $280 for one week and from $425 to $475 for two weeks, with room and board of $235 to $325, depending upon room selection.

## ARROWSMITH SCHOOL OF ARTS & CRAFTS
**P.O. Box 567**
**Gatlinburg, TN 37738**

One mile from the entrance to the Great Smokey Mountain National Park, this visual arts complex, sometimes called the "woodworking capital of America" teaches crafts of all kinds. It is particularly noted for instruction in unusual techniques:

patination of metal, anodizing of aluminum, granulation of sterling silver, combining "media" on cloth. One and two week sessions offered in March, June, July, and August. The cost was $295 to $345 per week, all inclusive.

## JOHN C. CAMPBELL FOLK SCHOOL
**Brasstown, NC 28902**

Take your choice of mountains at this Folk School, with the Smokies on one side and the Blue Ridge on the other. While you enjoy the beauty of nature, you can also receive instruction in traditional and Appalachian crafts through one-week classes offered from February to mid-December. A fee of $300 per week covered everything, but an extra $100 may be charged for certain wood-burning and metal finishing courses.

## CRAFT WORLD TOURS, INC.
**6776 Warboys Road**
**Bryon, NY 14542**

Tour the studios of noted crafts people all over the world, and hope some of the talent will rub off on you. Write Craft World Tours for more information.

## NATIONAL REGISTRATION CENTER
  **FOR STUDY ABROAD**
**823 North Second Street**
**Milwaukee, WI 53201**
**C**

Request free catalogs for summer craft courses in Britain and Mexico.

## PENLAND SCHOOL
### Penland, NC 28765-0037

An hour's drive from Asheville, NC, Penland School is a sprawling complex of 50 buildings on 500 acres of Blue Ridge Mountain land. Classes are taught by experts and result in artistry with wood, clay, fibers, glass, iron, metal, and paper. Cost was $170 to $195 per week and room and board fees of $145 (dorm) to $270 (double with private bath) per person, per week.

# TRAVEL—
# BED AND BREAKFAST

**B & D de VOGUE INTERNATIONAL**
**P.O. Box 1998**
**Visalia, CA 93279**
**800-727-4748; 209-733-7119**

Ask your travel agent or write direct for your catalog, *Chateax 1990*, an association of the most exclusive, privately owned and family-occupied, breath-taking historic chateaux in France and Europe. Take the royal pain out of hotel stays and elevate your trip to king-size proportions.


**BED AND BREAKFAST (AND BOOKS)**
**35 West 92 Street**
**New York, NY 10025**
**212-865-8740**
**B**

Bed and Breakfast (and Books) is a reservation service for travelers looking for something besides the run-of-the-mill hotel/motel rooms in the Big Apple. This "network" of charming urban bed and breakfasts are a close kin to the wonderful country bed and breakfasts, but afford guests the opportunity to experience New York City as well as the people who live there. A wonderful alternative to traditional lodging, these accommodations will run 20 to 50 percent less than most city hotels, depending upon location. And whether you opt to rent a room in someone's home or go for a more private place, Bed and Breakfast's list of services promises you won't be disappointed with any of their out-of-the-ordinary offerings.

*Great Buys* readers bed down for 5 percent less than their regular retail rates.

## BED & BREAKFAST CONNECTION
**3324 Country Club Blvd.**
**Cape Coral, FL 33904**
**800-673-9566**

Call for your personalized invitation to experience the comfort and charm of a bed and breakfast inn anytime or everytime you travel. Be it for business or pleasure, call toll-free for your reservation at over 5000 bed and breakfasts in the U.S.A. All 50 states are represented from as low as $35 in middle America to $200 in the more expensive cities like San Francisco and New York. But can you imagine a luxurious suite overlooking Central Park West for under $100? Don't be discouraged if the line's busy—try, try, try again.

## BED AND BREAKFAST, SAN FRANCISCO
**P.O. Box 349**
**San Francisco, CA 94101**
**415-931-3083**

The American Family Inn offers the traveler a unique and comfortable alternative to traditional lodging, while not detracting from the charm and magic of San Francisco. Regular prices on rooms began at $75 per night with a private bath and full breakfast. American Family Inn represents over one hundred bed and breakfasts in the Bay Area.

Readers can obtain an additional 10 percent off the regular price of a one-night stay at their special "No Name Victorian" in the heart of the city, complete with hot tub and deck, simply by mentioning they read about it in *Great Buys*.

## THE EVERGREEN CLUB
**16 Village Green, #203**
**Crofton, MD 21114**
**301-261-0180**

If you're over 50, single, or a couple, and you like to meet new friends while saving money, this is the club for you. Make your home available to fellow club members traveling in your town for $10 to $15 a night. In return, you may stay in a club member's home at the same rate. Yearly dues are $40–$50, for which you'll get a directory of club members and quarterly newsletters. Send a SASE to the address above for more information.

## EYE OPENERS BED AND BREAKFAST
### RESERVATIONS
**P.O. Box 694**
**Altadena, CA 91001**
**714-684-4428; 818-797-2055**
**MC,V,CK,MO**

Like other bed and breakfasts, Eye Openers serves as a wonderful alternative to everyday hotels and lodging. For $30 to $160, you can enjoy Continental or full American breakfasts, a clean, comfortable, cozy, and private night's stay. All that is required to get you on your way is a $25 deposit and a $10 one-time membership fee. Allow seven days in case of cancellation, less a $10 bookkeeping charge.

Call and say you read about them in *Great Buys* and secure additional special savings as they are made available.

## HUDSPETH HOUSE
**1905 4th Ave.**
**Canyon, TX 79015**
**806-655-9800; 806-655-4111**

A health and fitness bed 'n' breakfast spa is just what the doctor ordered. Restore yourself to good health, rest, relax, and rejuvenate in the Victorian splendor of the Hudspeth House. Dave and Sally Haynie, the innkeepers, have maintained its beauty along with its designation as a historic landmark. Daily or weekly rates include gourmet breakfast in the Georgia O'Keeffe Dining Room, complimentary drinks upon arrival, a hot springs hot tub and exercise area, and period antiques to complement the ambience. Enjoy the Texas hospitality or sign on as a spa guest for weight loss and fitness restoration. Professional staff will guide you every "inch" of the way.

## NW BED & BREAKFAST TRAVEL UNLIMITED
**610 SW Broadway**
**Portland, OR 97205**
**503-243-7616**

Since 1979, NW Bed & Breakfast Travel Unlimited has been booking reservations to the over 300 bed and breakfasts, homestays and inns from British Columbia through Washington, Oregon, and California with limited service in Hawaii. All host homes are inspected and carefully monitored for maintaining continuing quality and value, and hosts pride themselves on their hospitality. Membership fee of $25 annually allows members to make as many reservations during that year without any additional service fee. Also available is help with any itinerary recommendations to seniors who have never been to the great Northwest.

*Great Buys* readers: special membership fee $10.

# Registries

A quick look at some interesting opportunities in Bed & Breakfast and Home Exchange:

**AT HOME ABROAD**
**405 East 56 Street**
**New York, NY 10022**
**212-421-9165**

For home rentals abroad.

**AT HOME IN ENGLAND**
**P.O. Box 104**
**Larchmont, NY 10538**
**914-834-8568**

Bed and breakfast in England and Scotland.

**BED & BREAKFAST/HAWAII**
**P.O. Box 449**
**Kapaa, HI 96746**
**808-822-7771**

Home exchange, home stays and rentals in Hawaii.

**BED & BREAKFAST LEAGUE**
**20 Nassau Street**
**Princeton, NJ 08540**
**609-921-0440**

Bed and breakfast in U.S. cities.

## CANADIAN BED & BREAKFAST REGISTRY, LTD.
**664 West 71st Avenue**
**Vancouver, BC V6P 3A1 CAN**
**604-321-1265**

Homestays with Canadian families.

## CANADIAN HOSTELLING ASSOCIATION
**333 River Road**
**Vanier City, Ottawa KIL 889 CAN**

Recreation and low-cost accommodations in Canada.

## CARIBBEAN HOME RENTALS
**P.O. Box 710**
**Palm Beach, FL 33480**

Inexpensive home vacations in the Caribbean.

## CITIZEN EXCHANGE COUNCIL
**18 East 41st Street**
**Suite 1800**
**New York, NY 10017**
**212-889-7960**

Arranges exchange visits between the U.S., Eastern Europe and the USSR.

## FRIENDS OVERSEAS
**68-04 Dartmouth Street**
**Forest Hills, NY 11375**
**718-544-5660**

Stay with a family in Norway, Sweden, Iceland, Denmark, and Finland with the help of Friends Overseas.

**INTERNATIONAL SPAREROOM**
**P.O. Box 518**
**Solana Beach, CA 92075**
**714-755-3194**

Rent or swap accommodations worldwide.

**VISIT/USA**
**356 West 34th Street**
**New York, NY 10001**
**212-760-5856**

This program of the YMCA offers low-cost accommodations worldwide.

**VISITING FRIENDS, INC.**
**A Round Robin of Hospitality**
**P.O. Box 231**
**Lake Jackson, TX 77566**
**409-297-7367**

Visiting Friends is a private group of people from all across the country that offers singles and couples the opportunity to use the guestroom in participating homes on a time-exchange basis as a means of staying with compatible people in other areas of the country. Although there are a few younger members, the large majority are past 50. The Friends network is an excellent supplement to other travel and can be used for short or long trips. The visits are individually arranged, and the privacy of each member is protected. Members are not expected to provide transportation, meals, or entertainment, though many hosts do ask their guests to join them for breakfast. A newsletter is sent at no charge to members two to four times per year. Registration for lifetime membership is $25 and first-time Host Home per trip (one to six nights) is only $20, with each additional Host Home on the same trip (one to six nights in each home) $15. These low charges are *per visit,* not *per night!*

Super *Great Buys* reader discount: 40 percent discount on registration for lifetime membership, PLUS 25 percent discount on first exchange fee.

# TRAVEL—COMPANIONS

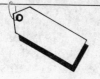

**GREAT EXPEDITIONS**
**P.O. Box 8000-411**
**Sumas, WA 98295-8000**

Through free classified ads in *Great Expeditions,* you could easily find a soulmate to join you on a backpacking trek through the Andes, or anywhere else for that matter. This is THE source for matching travel companions and out-of-the-way destinations, cultural conclaves and budget-minded possibilities. Subscription is $18 for six issues, $32 for twelve issues.

**ODYSSEY NETWORK**
**c/o Charles River Travel**
**118 Cedar St.**
**Wellesley, MA 02181**
**$20**

Join this members-only network to hook up with a traveling companion, thus avoiding costly "single" surcharges if you're traveling alone. You'll make up the fee and gain a friend at the same time.

## PARTNERS IN TRAVEL
**Miriam E. Tobolowsky, Publisher**
**P.O. Box 491145**
**Los Angeles, CA 90049**
**213-476-4869**

Looking for a "compatible" traveling companion? Look no further. For over nine years, Partners in Travel has been operating through its newsletter and special service, "Match Up!" to do just that, bring people together. Their goal is to make travel a happier experience for the single senior. Two additional services are also available to members; a Vacation-Home Exchange program and a guide to hassle-free travel, "To Your Good Health." Connections and sharing are what Partners in Travel is all about.

Readers of *Great Buys* may take a full 10 percent off any of their services.

## TRAVEL COMPANIONS EXCHANGE, INC.
**Jens Jurgen, President**
**P.O. Box 833**
**Amityville, NY 11701**
**516-454-0880**

"Matchmaker, matchmaker . . ." You won't have to sing alone anymore with the help of Travel Companion Exchange, a top-notch match-up service for travel minded singles.

For the *Great Buys* reader, not one, not two, but *three* special discounts are made exclusively for you: a full 50 percent discount off their one-year introductory membership rates; single, widowed or divorced MALES ages 65 and over who are interested in female travel companions or partners in their own age group may ask for a FREE six months' membership; a sample copy of Travel Companions Exchange newsletter for only $1 postage (normal charge is $4). Just mention *Great Buys* and the offer that interests you and you'll be sailing into new fun-filled, friend-filled activities.

# TRAVEL—CRUISES

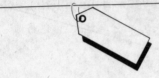

**ADMIRAL CRUISES**
**1220 Biscayne Blvd.**
**P.O. Box 080882**
**Miami, FL 33101**

Whether it's the Bahamas or Mexico, Admiral Cruises can get you there in style and comfort on one of their three or four-night super cruises, without making a dent in your pocketbook. Prices included all accommodations, meals and entertainment, and ranged in price from $425 to $895. Round-trip airfare is even included in most cases to the ship's port. Call your travel agent about special discounts in addition to the already low fares. And remember what they say: "Once is never enough."

**COASTWISE CRUISE LINE (CCL)**
**P.O. Box 1630**
**36 Ocean Street**
**Hyannis, MA 02601**
**800-322-1525**
**MC,V,D**

From 40-room mansions to 100-foot whales . . . cruise New England in the steamship tradition. Come explore the charm of intracoastal New England aboard the Pilgrim Belle. Discover ports rich in history as you tour Plymouth, Newport, and Provincetown, plus the islands of Nantucket and Martha's Vineyard. The experience of a lifetime is waiting for you on a seven-day Pilgrim Belle cruise. Relax in the grand elegance of superior service and exquisite cuisine as you explore New England like never before. Details available by writing or calling the toll-free number above.

**ELKIN TRAVEL/CRUISES ONLY!**
**28592 Orchard Hills Rd.**
**Farmington Hills, MI 48018**
**800-445-1666; 313-932-4400 (in Detroit area)**

If your sites are set on flights of fancy, but your budget's more earthbound, then call on this travel company to help you land. On sea, or in the air, too, whether it's a last-minute trip or one that is months in the planning, one call can net you great dividends. In service and savings, this company can orchestrate everything, from an African safari or elk hunt in the Canadian rockies, a spa-hopping get-away to a Hong Kong shopping excursion. With their division called Cruises Only! there are no watered-down cruise rates here. Oh, $H_2O$, what a deal! Set sail on any of the cruise options offered by this specialty cruise company, one of the largest in the world, and forget cabin fever and promenade the decks of any cruise line in the world. Need to stay on your diet, need special handicap accommodations, or want to splurge on an exotic escape aboard the *Passion Princess,* well, call Cruises Only! and anchors away. Expect a discount of $75–$500 and personalized service from a crew of experts.

*Great Buys* readers will receive a special $25 discount coupon per cabin.

## HUCKLEBERRY FINN UNIVERSITY
c/o Detour
1705 Second Avenue #422
Rock Island, IL 61201
800-269-3061; 309-788-8687 (in IL)

Taking a detour from tradition, two women from Rock Island built a forty-foot, twelve-passenger houseboat in honor of Mark Twain and now cruise down the Mississippi, for less, from May 25 to October 1. Rather than sleeping aboard, passengers stay at historic inns along the way between St. Louis and St. Paul. The average cost, $150 a day, includes the ride, lodging, and two meals daily. Call or write for more information.

## KELLY CRUISES, INC.
708-932-8810

Sail off into the sunset with that special person in your life on a Kelly Cruise. Discounts of 10 to 40 percent for seniors on your choice of exotic and exciting cruise destinations. If you're over 50 and planning a cruise for your next vacation, think Kelly Cruises, the "cruise specialists."

## LE MISTRAL
Port Isabel, TX
800-292-7022

Le Mistral is the "Riviera of the West" where a floating poker game is just the beginning. This 550-passenger, 257-foot cruise ship sails from Port Isabel, past South Padre Island's sand dunes and flawless beaches and into international waters in less than an hour. Then, the Lone Star Casino opens its doors to slot machines, craps, blackjack, poker, bingo (with jackpots as high as $20,000). British croupiers add to the fun and Vegas-type atmosphere. Cruises last six to eight hours and an all-you-can-eat buffet (from shrimp to salads), dancing, entertainment and access to the casino are all included in one low price. Special discounts for day tours on Wednesdays at 11:00 A.M., $44.95 (regularly $49.95) and Thursdays at 7:00 P.M., $44.95 (regularly $59.95). Allow two weeks advance reservation, and be sure to arrive one hour before sailing in comfortable clothes and shoes.

**PREMIER CRUISE LINES**
**P.O. Box 573**
**Cape Canaveral, FL 32920**
**800-327-7113; 305-783-5061 (in FL)**
**B**

Stay in shape aboard this ship as you sail away into the sunset. If you're 60 plus, you'll receive a 10 percent discount on cruise fares (actually everyone traveling in your cabin gets a discount, regardless of age). Write for free brochures to their two destinations, Nassau and Soft Key or Abbacl Islands (which includes Green Turtle Key, Man of War Key, Treasure Key, and Great Guana Key). Three night excursions begin as low as $445 with planned activities orchestrated by the ship's cruise director.

**REGENCY CRUISES, INC.**
**260 Madison Avenue**
**New York, NY 10016**
**212-972-4774; 212-687-2290**

Regency Cruises will allow you to see Alaska like no other. Ships are spacious and elegant with all the personal touches and amenities to make your stay as comfortable as possible. And if that's not enough to convince you, take a peek at the low, reasonable fares in their travel brochures. Included in the price of your ticket, you will get a larger-than-average stateroom, health spa, whirlpool, disco, theater, on-board shops and computer room/library, as well as a casino and other exciting entertainment. So there's never a dull moment. They even offer craft classes, computer instruction, French cooking demonstrations and dance lessons! Most cruises board at Vancouver and vary in length. Contact your travel agent or call Regency for details and other special offers.

**ROYAL CARIBBEAN**
**903 South American Way**
**Miami, FL 33132**
**800-327-6700 (individual reservations);**
   **800-327-2055 (group reservations)**
**800-245-7225 (in CAN)**

Whether you want to sit and relax by the pool or venture into hidden, undiscovered shopping areas on shore, you'll love the sophisticated, warm and friendly atmosphere aboard a Royal Caribbean cruise ship. Savor the fine dining, nightly entertainment, and sight-seeing in exotic ports of call, as well as an array of other activities complemented by the best service they know how to offer. Although rates vary according to the package you choose and your point of origination and destination, in most cases, all on-board services and airfare will be included in one reasonable fare. Call your travel agent for reservations or details on special senior rates that vary according to the package.

**TRAVLTIPS**
**Cruise and Freighter Travel Association**
**P.O. Box 188**
**Flushing, NY 11358**
**800-872-8584; 718-939-2400**

Where can I go on a freighter? What are the accommodations and what is the food really like? How much time will we have in port? What about visas, immunizations, age and health restrictions? These are some of the questions answered in a free pamphlet available from TravlTips. Freighter travel is not for everyone and shipping is always a freighter's main concern, with passengers "along for the ride." Nevertheless, freighter travel is becoming increasingly popular, as shown in the bi-monthly newsletter published by the association that features first-hand accounts of voyages worldwide, written by the members themselves. Leisurely and unregimented days, spacious accommodations, good food and the companionship of no more than a dozen passengers make freighter travel a delightful way to cross the Atlantic, and the cost—averaging about $100 per day per person—make it an excellent economical value for senior travelers with time on their hands . . . and a dislike for jet lag.

# TRAVEL—
# ENVIRONMENTALLY
# CONSCIOUS

With the increased emphasis in this decade on the environment and Earth Day activities and observances, along with a growing awareness of our ecological problems, more and more people are determined to do something, to make a difference and help preserve the planet for future generations.

The following entries are specially designed vacation packages for the environmentally conscious traveler, which combine the elements of fun and protection the environment.

**AUDUBON ECOLOGICAL CAMPS AND WORKSHOPS**
**National Audubon Society**
**613-K Riversville Road**
**Greenwich, CT 06831**
**203-869-2017**

Offering one to two week ecological camps at costs beginning from $450 for field ecology camps in Connecticut to $895 for a camp on the Olympic Peninsula in Washington or in Texas's Big Bend National Park, the Audubon Society is doing their part to encourage travelers to do their part!

**EARTHWATCH**
**680 Mount Auburn Street**
**P.O. Box 403**
**Watertown, MA 02172**
**617-926-8200**

Two week stints (plus transportation) cost $990 to $2,000. Opportunities include: preserving the Great Plains by surveying grasslands, Fort Collins, Colorado; humane trapping and monitoring of black bears, Asheville, North Carolina; humane capture and study of wild dolphins, Sarasota, Florida. Write or call for information regarding these and other ecologically sound vacations.


**SIERRA CLUB**
**Outings Department**
**730 Polk Street**
**San Francisco, CA 94109**
**415-923-5630**

At the low cost of $130 to $255 (plus transportation), more than 60 trips were planned by the Sierra Club for 1990. Some examples were: Kaena Point Nature Preserve alien-plant removal, Hawaii, and the Bog and Oswegatchie rivers campsite restoration, Adirondack Park, New York.

# TRAVEL—GUIDES

**AIRHITCH**
2901 Broadway
Suite 100
New York, NY 10025
212-864-2000
B

Hitch a ride to Europe and back if you want to save plenty of money but are willing to be flexible on the times—like being agreeable to leaving close to when you'd like to go. Though originally designed as a low-cost service for students, you need not be one to think like one. This service is ideally suited for the free-spirited, independent, and resourceful person looking at every possible way to cross the Atlantic cheaply. Certain restrictions and rules apply. Write for free brochure and application.

**AMERICAN JEWISH CONGRESS**
World Travel Guide
National Resource Center
800-221-4694; 212-879-4588 (in NY call collect)
516-752-1186

Not a travel agency, but a Jewish organization that designs, creates and oversees its own tours, from start to finish, providing quality at the best possible value. A unique combination of general travel with a Jewish interest twist, covering major sites as well as stops of Jewish cultural significance. Spectacular tours are chronicled in their free Travel Guide detailing the nature of the tour (special ones for singles), itinerary, airfare, accommodations and more.

**BUDGET HOST INNS DIRECTORY**
**2601 Jacksboro Highway**
**Caravan Suite 202**
**P.O. Box 10656**
**Fort Worth, TX 76114**
**817-626-7064**

Write today for your toll-free directory to Budget Host Inns from Alberta, Canada, to Wyoming, with all the others in between. An even greater incentive is their "bonus coupons," offering additional savings as well as their senior citizen discounts. The directory describes all the pertinent information on each inn, including amenities, rates, credit cards, the owner's name and what the specific discount would be via the coupon bonus.

**DIRECTORY OF LOW-COST VACATIONS**
  **WITH A DIFFERENCE**
**Pilot Books**
**103 Cooper Street**
**Babylon, NY 11702**
**516-422-2225**

Vacations, bed and breakfast stays, home exchanges, people, senior programs, study groups, and vacation work programs; a selection of different ways to travel are included in this directory to help you enjoy your leisure time. How do listings like "Above the Cloud Trekking," "Arrow Adventures," "Bicycle Africa," "Meet the Aussies," "Off the Deep End," "Volunteer for Peace," or "Worldwide Yacht Charters" sound for starters? Choose your spot from the alphabetical listings and make good use of this thoroughly usable guide for only $5.95, postpaid.

## THE DISCOUNT GUIDE FOR TRAVELERS OVER 55
by Caroline and Walter Weintz
$7.95 (published by E.P. Dutton)

Foreign countries as well as America (state by state) are covered in this comprehensive guide to senior discounts on all of your travel activities. Order direct from the publisher or check with your local bookseller.

## EMPLOYEE TRAVEL TIMES
904 Silver Spur Road
Suite 680
Rolling Hills, CA 90274
213-377-6248

This newsletter lists discounts and bargains on accommodations, car rentals, land packages and cruises. Many of the listings are for privately owned condominiums in vacation areas of the U.S., Mexico, the Caribbean, Canada, and Europe. Many of the lodgings are owned by airline personnel and available for rent at reasonable prices.

## GOING SOLO: THE NEWSLETTER FOR PEOPLE
   TRAVELING ALONE
P.O. Box 1035
Cambridge, MA 02238
$36 (one year subscription—8 issues)
$6 (sample copy)

How to avoid potentially uncomfortable, even dangerous situations if you're a woman traveling alone is just one of the subjects discussed in this newsletter. On the positive side are all the many benefits traveling alone fosters, such as how the locals will open their homes to a lone traveler or how a taxi driver will go the extra mile to show you the town.

## GUIDE TO BEST BUYS IN PACKAGE TOURS
Pilot Books
103 Cooper Street
Babylon, NY 11702
516-422-2225

This economical ($3.95) pocket-sized guide "lists and describes more than one hundred selected group tours that offer solid values for your travel dollar." This guide tells how to choose an agent; where to get accident, trip cancellation, or health insurance; gives a trip preparation checklist and shows ways to create package variations. It even tells how to file travel complaints. Included is a list of countries that require entry visas and a set of fundamental health precautions. Packages offered include a variety of tours for individual tastes—fly/drive packages, escorted tours, unescorted tours, cruise options, plus adventure, luxury, economy, and special interest tours.

## THE HALF-PRICE EUROPE BOOK 1991
800-334-4133
$70 ($55 to readers)

A hefty price for a book, you say, but you'll recoup your investment many times over with just one night's stay at the Hotel de la Tremoille in Paris. Almost 400 coupons and vouchers for 50 percent off every night of your stay at 3-, 4- and 5-star hotels across Europe, including Israel. Designed by American Marketing, Inc., of Paris for the sophisticated traveler who demands quality service at half the price. The book is sold by Paralelles, Inc., and includes restaurants, museums, theaters, and other sights to behold. You book your own reservations and save. There's no ID required to secure the discounts; just present the coupon, making it easy to share the savings with a friend.

Special to *Great Buys* readers: Save $15 off the price of the book; cost is $55, including postage and handling (it weighs a pound).

## INTERNATIONAL HEALTH GUIDE FOR THE SENIOR CITIZEN TRAVELER

**Pilot Books**
**103 Cooper Street**
**Babylon, NY 11702**
**516-422-2225**

This pocket-sized reference book by Dr. W. Robert Lange is a must-have for the senior or handicapped person planning a trip, particularly a foreign trip. One look at the statistics— approximately one traveler in four will experience an illness and most will be unprepared—should convince us of the need to take precautions. International travel always imposes some risks, which are only magnified for the senior or disabled traveler. This guide is intended to assist the seasoned as well as the less experienced traveler in relation to health matters with advice on minimizing health risks, disease prevention, medical preparedness and assistance. A helpful appendix lists Resource Organizations including health insurers and specialized travel agencies for the disabled. Available solely from the publisher for only $4.95 postpaid.

## INTERNATIONAL TRAVEL NEWS

**2120 28th Street**
**Sacramento, CA 95818**

Write for your free copy, and sample this meaty magazine-type digest of the best in packaged tours. Lots of first-person accounts of trips taken, with an emphasis on value. An excellent homespun source for monthly travel tips. A one-year subscription is $15; two years for $29.


**THE MATURE TRAVELER**
**P.O. Box 50820**
**Reno, NV 89513**
**702-786-7419**

Subscribers discover a bonanza in this publication with Gene and Adele Mallott as guides through a maze of travel offers, itineraries, special packages and, of course, discounts. With this treasure chest of travel bargains, you can learn how to jump ship on a Club Med cruise for half price or take a whole year's worth of trips with the grandkids. Inside the covers, we even found a discount for their book *Get Up and Go: A Guide for the Mature Traveler* (Gateway Books). There's no need to ever leave home without them. Subscription price $21.97.

Special subscription rate for *Great Buys* readers of only $19.97.


**MOBIL TRAVEL GUIDES**
**Rand/McNally Research Center**
**P.O. Box 7600**
**Chicago, IL 60680**

Available at bookstores nationwide, this guide, published in seven different regional editions, offers valuable information designed to save you money as you travel across America. In addition, each book contains discount coupons good toward lodging, attractions, and dining.

## NATIONAL COUNCIL OF STATE TRAVEL DIRECTORY
**Travel Industry Association**
**1133 21st Street NW**
**Washington, DC 20036**
**B**

The National Council's *Discover America* brochure features a listing of state and territorial offices in the U.S. By calling one of the travel offices listed in the brochure, you can receive free vacation information, maps, calendar, travel guides and brochures.

## NATIONAL DIRECTORY OF BUDGET MOTELS
**Pilot Books**
**103 Cooper Street**
**Babylon, NY 11702**
**516-422-2225**

Over 2,000 motels are described in this directory ranging from as low as $21 to $38 per night. Available for $4.95 postpaid from the publisher.

## NATIONAL TOUR ASSOCIATION, INC.
**546 East Main Street**
**P.O. Box 3071**
**Lexington, KY 40596-3071**
**B**

This association of tour companies provides a colorful comprehensive guide to all the agencies that offer escorted tours. National Tour Association also provides a Consumer Protection Plan of up to $100,000 per company, protecting you from unscrupulous or bankrupt operators who make off with your deposit.

## NATIONAL TRUST FOR HISTORIC PRESERVATION
1785 Massachusetts Avenue NW
Washington, DC 20036

For $2, you can request a list of 32 historic hotels in America where the coveted historic designation has been awarded. Rates were from $68 to $325, but history should not come cheap.

## PALM BEACH COUNTY CONVENTION
## & VISITORS BUREAU
1555 Palm Beach Lakes Blvd.
West Palm Beach, FL 33401
800-242-1774

Join others making the trek to Palm Beach Country and pocket $500 worth of Palm Beach County FREE. Call for this coupon book worth up to $500 or more on everything from sports to sightseeing, shopping to dining, from Boca Raton to Jupiter—with just one toll-free call.

## PAN FOR GOLD ON YOUR NEXT VACATION
Pilot Books
103 Cooper Street
Babylon, NY 11702
516-422-2225

"Gold is where you find it" goes the old saying, but you have to look for it, and what better way than on a unique vacation panning for gold? Visualize clear streams and skies, ghost towns and tall tales, bright campfires and, of course, the bonanza . . . gold! You will learn such things as what equipment to take and how and where to pan—some potentially profitable areas include Alaska, Arizona, Colorado, Idaho, et cetera. The gold you find can help pay for your trip or can be worn as jewelry, given as gifts or added to a mineral collection. The Suggested Reading section has listings of more intriguing titles on the subject. Available for $3.50 per copy, plus $1 for postage and handling.

## SENIOR CITIZEN'S GUIDE TO BUDGET TRAVEL/U.S. AND CANADA
**Pilot Books**
**103 Cooper Street**
**Babylon, NY 11702**
**516-422-2225**

Niagara Falls, Grand Canyon, Disneyland, Grand Old Opry, Prince Edward Island, the Canadian Rockies, French speaking Quebec. . . . Love to travel and want the best possible deals on transportation, accommodations and meals? Check out the hundreds of useful facts and travel tips in this guide compiled by Paige Palmer. You'll find out where to get free information about outstanding attractions in the 50 states and Canada. Also, one section is devoted to keeping you fit and healthy in order to better enjoy those exotic locales!

For readers of *Great Buys*, this book can be purchased for $3.95 and the usual shipping charge of $1 will be waived.

## TRAVEL AMERICA AT HALF PRICE
**Entertainment Publications**
**1400 North Woodward**
**Birmingham, MI 48011**

This coupon book, published annually, offers up to 50 percent discounts at hotels and motels, tourist attractions and the like. The company is currently expanding its discounts to certain European locales, as well. Write for more information.

## TRAVEL EASY: THE PRACTICAL GUIDE FOR
##   PEOPLE OVER 50
**AARP Books**
**400 East Edward Street**
**Mount Prospect, IL 60056**

"Older people have never been younger," or so says author Rosalind Massow in the preface to this handy, fact-filled guide to helping seniors plan trips that maximize both time and money spent. Beginning with the basic, but oh-so-important steps to choosing a destination, she goes on to discuss various means of travel, and includes sections on evaluating tours, health and dental concerns, rights and redress, and tips for traveling overseas, all for only $8.95. Other books available through the association of AARP with Scott Foresman are *The Essential Guide to Wills, Estates, Trusts and Death Taxes; What to Do with What You've Got: The Practical Guide to Money Management in Retirement;* and *The Over Easy Foot Care Book,* just to name a few. All orders must be prepaid. Write or call AARP for more information and a complete list of books.

# TRAVEL— HANDICAPPED

**ACCESS FOUNDATION**
800-876-2882
$25

If you are handicapped, don't let a physical disability keep you down. This nonprofit organization is your compass to companionship and travel worldwide.


**ACCESS TRAVEL: AIRPORTS**
**Consumer Information Center**
**Pueblo, CO 81009**

This free 39-page booklet lists facilities and services for the handicapped at over 500 airport terminals in 62 countries.


**ADAPTIVE DRIVING PROGRAM**
**Mike Shipp, Manager**
**Louisiana Tech University**
**P.O. Box 10426**
**Ruston, LA 71272-0046**

*Adaptive Driving Devices and Vehicle Modification* is a basic, illustrated guide for drivers with disabilities. Wheelchair lifts are pictured and described, along with automatic door openers, power seats that move the driver into a functional position, elbow switches, hand controls, left foot acceleration and a host of other modifications for any vehicle. Another booklet compiled by Louisiana Tech is *Disabilities and Their Implications for Driving.* Either of these is available upon request from the university at the address above.

**AIR TRANSPORTATION OF
  HANDICAPPED PERSONS
(AC No. 120-32)
Department of Transportation
Distribution Unit TAD 443-1
Washington, DC 20590**

This booklet identifies the problems facing handicapped air travelers and provides guidelines on how to alleviate them.

**ANSAID TABLETS
GUIDE TO TRAVELING WITH ARTHRITIS
P.O. Box 307-D
Coventry, CN 06238
B**

Traveling with arthritis can be a royal pain, but this 8-page travel booklet from the Upjohn Company may offer some relief to the over 37 million sufferers. Useful tips for planning vacations, how to navigate the airlines, and how to stay fit while on the road are all yours for the asking.

**"CALL ME CARDS"**
**800-222-0300**
Call Me Cards are available free from AT&T, simply by calling the toll-free 800 number above. People with disabilities can call home, even if they are unable to use a pay phone. The card is good *only* for calling home, so it is worthless if lost or stolen.

**THE DIABETIC TRAVELER**
**P.O. Box 8223 RW**
**Stamford, CN 06905**
**203-327-5832**

*The Diabetic Traveler* is a great newsletter that offers information for people with diabetes who are interested in safe travel; for example, insulin adjustments for air travel, storage cases for insulin, and how to carry medical history. Each issue features a different destination (regular subscription, $19.95 per year). Another publication, *Traveling Healthy*, is a bi-monthly newsletter offering information for people (especially seniors or others with health restrictions) to help plan safe, happy, and comfortable travel. It includes a health advisory and other information from the U.S. Public Health Service (regular subscription, $24 per year). Send $1 for sample back issue to the address above.

*Great Buys* readers: Receive one year of *Diabetic Traveler* for $14 or *Traveling Healthy* for $19.

## DISABILITY BOOKSHOP
"Directory of Travel Agencies for the Disabled"
P.O. Box 129
Vancouver, WA 98666
800-637-2256
$14.95

Over 350 agencies in the United States, Canada, and other countries specializing in travel for people with disabilities are listed in this valuable resource guide. Price includes shipping.

## FLYING WHEELS TRAVEL
P.O. Box 382
Owatonna, MN 55060
800-535-6790

For over 20 years, this company has specialized in travel for the physically disabled. Besides tours to national parks, Disneyworld, French-speaking Canada, New England, and Europe, they also offer cruises where staterooms are even wheelchair accessible.

## IAMAT (INTERNATIONAL ASSOCIATION FOR MEDICAL ASSISTANCE TO TRAVELERS)
417 Center St.
Lewiston, NY 14092

The nightmare of getting sick outside the country is over. This association provides you with a FREE membership card (donations are welcome, though) that entitles you to the directory of participating worldwide medical doctors. All were trained in an English-speaking country and have passed stringent guidelines. All have agreed to an established set fee of $30 per office visit, $40 per hotel visit ($50 at night). In addition, you'll receive a record of your medical history, informative travel and medical-related brochures, and a world immunization chart.

## PORT AUTHORITY OF NEW YORK AND NEW JERSEY
One World Trade Center
New York, NY 10048

The Port Authority of New York and New Jersey welcomes travelers to Kennedy International, Newark International, and La Guardia airports with a brochure especially prepared to inform the disabled traveler of accessible airport facilities. The Port Authority ensures that barrier-free facilities are constructed at each of the airports for the elderly, disabled, or otherwise mobility-restricted traveler. The brochure includes "Tips for Making Reservations," "Questions to Ask," "Getting to the Airport," "Facilities for Departing/Arriving Passengers," parking information and signs and symbols to look for. There is also a detailed overhead map of each airport, as well as detailed maps of the interiors with information on how to find medical assistance. Check your local airports for their own disabled traveler's procedures and their facilities.

## TRAVELING NURSE'S NETWORK
P.O. Box 129
Vancouver, WA 98666
206-694-2462

Author and registered nurse Helen Hecker has founded a service for anyone seeking medical assistance while traveling. Expertise in all areas including diabetes, dialysis, respiratory, spinal cord injuries, wheelchair bound, and psychiatric. Costs vary depending upon needs. Also, the network can assist with travel agencies that specialize in the disabled, equipment rental, specially equipped vans, group tours, and more.

Though headquartered in Vancouver and Portland, Oregon, the Traveling Nurse's Network can provide nurses anywhere in the world.

## TRAVELIN' TALK
P.O. Box 3534
Clarksville, TN 37043-3534

This free network of people sharing handicapped travel information, tips, and services throughout the United States is the brainchild of Rick Crowder, the founder. Write for their quarterly newsletter to get on board.

## WHOLE PERSONS TOURS, INC.
P.O. Box 1084
Bayonne, NJ 07001-1084
201-858-3400
C

Tours for travelers with handicaps are organized for set destinations by Whole Persons Tours and are all inclusive except airfare and lunches (though airfare can be arranged). Open to travelers with any disability, tours to Ireland, England, Germany, France, Hawaii, Western Canada are just a taste of tour options. Along with their packages, Whole Persons Tours also publishes a terrific magazine, titled *Itinerary*, featuring the latest travel opportunities for persons with disabilities, how-to articles and new products.

*Great Buys* readers will receive free gift(s) upon departure.

# TRAVEL—LODGING

## Discount Hotels and Motels

Many hotels and motels across the country and around the world offer attractive discounts for seniors, as well as other amenities. Here is a listing of some of them:

**BEST WESTERN**
**800-528-1234**

For 55+, Best Western offers a discount of 10 percent with proof of age via AARP membership card.

**BUDGETEL INNS**
**800-528-1234**

If economy is your buyword, be sure to check out Budgetel Inns located in 20 states, mainly in the South and Midwest. Check when you make your reservations if they are one of the over half that will give you a 10 percent discount if you're over 55.

**DOUBLETREE HOTELS**
**800-528-0444**

If luxury's your style and saving's your game, join the Silver Leaf Club and receive about 15 percent off (varies at each location). Call for more information.

## DRURY INNS, INC.
**10801 Pear Tree Lane**
**St. Ann, MO 63074**
**314-429-2255**

Nothing dreary about the Drury Inns nationwide, as they offer 10 percent discounts off regular room rate if you are over the age of 50. Plain and simple.

## EMBASSY SUITES
**800-362-2779**

Over 100 Embassy Suites nationwide offer a normal discounted rate of 10 percent off room rates to AARP members.

## EXCEL INNS
**800-356-8013**

These Inns serve the Midwest and Texas and offer a 10 percent discount for seniors over the age of 55.

## HILTON HOTELS
**800-445-8667**

The Senior Hilton Honors Program offered through Hilton Hotels to those 60 plus provides a choice of three levels of membership: (1) Annual domestic, at participating hotels in the U.S.; fee $25. (2) Annual worldwide; fee $50. (3) Lifetime worldwide; fee $150. The Hilton Honors Program brings discounts of up to 50 percent, or the same as the lowest published rate, and includes a 20 percent discount on dinner in participating restaurants. Spouse is free. Hilton Honors members can earn points and are entitled to other benefits including late, instant checkout; free newspaper; complimentary Health Club use; and special consideration during sold-out periods.

## HOLIDAY INNS
## 800-HOLIDAY

Seniors can save 20 percent on rooms and 10 percent on meals at more than 1200 participating Holiday Inns. Members of AARP and other senior groups can take advantage of other savings by presenting their membership card.

## HOSPITALITY INTERNATIONAL
## 800-251-1962

Hospitality International represents the growing franchise of over 300 motels/hotels shared by Scottish Inns, Master Hosts, and Red Carpet Inns. With their new Identicard program, seniors can enjoy a 10 percent discount off the room rate at participating hotels (be sure to check, since not all hotels/motels in the organization recognize the discount) and 10 percent off on Hertz rental cars.

## HOWARD JOHNSON
## 800-654-2000

The majority of Howard Johnson locations offer 15 percent off to seniors, though some do not, so be sure to check first.

## LA QUINTA INNS
## 800-531-5900

Be a member of the Senior Class at La Quinta Inns and get a 20 percent discount off room rates, receive newsletters with coupons, and earn credits for overnight stays—10 credits are worth one night FREE. There is a $10 annual fee and you must be 60+. Your Senior Class card will identify you when you call and hold your reservations for after 6 P.M. arrival.

## MARRIOTT
**800-228-9290**

In conjunction with TWA and Eastern Airlines, the Marriott offers seniors a very special Leisure Life program with savings of 50 percent on rooms, 25 percent on food, and even 10 percent on purchases in their gift shop. Call for details and brochure.

## OMNI HOTELS
**800-THE-OMNI**

Just for being a member of AARP, you can secure a 50 percent room discount at Omni hotels and a 15 percent discount on food and nonalcoholic beverages. Not to mention the other benefits that come to AARP members!

## QUALITY INNS
**800-228-5151**

Prime Time senior discount of 10 percent off room rate at participating Quality Inns. Senior Saver discount is also available and will save you 30 percent off room rate, if you reserve the room at least 30 days in advance with a major credit card and cancel at least 30 days in advance. Both discounts are available only at participating inns, so be sure to call first.

## RAMADA INNS
**800-228-2828**

At participating Ramada Inns coast to coast, the Best Years Program offers members of AARP a 25 percent discount; or if not a member, you must be 65.

## RED LION/THUNDERBIRD
**P.O. Box 1027**
**Vancouver, WA 98666**
**800-547-8010**

If you're a member of AARP, *Mature Outlook*, or *Silver Pages*, you can take 20 percent off your room rate based on availability. Call for your free directory of locations.

## RESERVE-A-HOST
**800-251-2962**

Reserve-A-Host serves three major hotels in handling reservations for Red Carpet Inns, Scottish Inns, and Master Host Inns. The normal discount is 10 percent for 55+, but this can vary according to locations, so be sure to check when making reservations.

## ROADWAY INNS
**800-533-2100**

Discount to seniors is 10 percent for age 55+ or to members of AARP.

## SANDMAN HOTELS
**800-663-6900**

It doesn't cost a dime to join the Senior Citizens program at this hotel chain. You just have to call if you're 55 plus. Discounts may vary per location.

## SEPTEMBER DAYS/DAYS INN
**800-241-5050**

Travelers 50 and older are entitled to savings of up to 50 percent on Days lodging, travel, and more by applying for the September Days Club. Membership entitles you to a subscription to *Travel—Holiday* magazine, complete with club benefits and discounts, trips and tours at discount rates, travel agency services, $100,000 free flight insurance, discounts on Alamo rental cars, and a host of other offerings and savings. Call for an application.

## SHERATON HOTELS
**800-325-3535**

Seniors can get a 25 percent discount on room reservations at all Sheraton hotels, based on occupancy. AARP members are entitled to the same discount.

## SONESTA HOTELS
**800-343-7170**

Members of AARP are generally offered a discount of 15 percent, but this varies from one hotel to another, so be sure to check first.

## SUPER 8 MOTELS
**800-848-8888**

When booking reservations, use this special reader number (#S8M 186) to insure an exclusive 10 percent discount off established rack rates at participating motels. Other reader benefits include a National Car Rental discount and a $50 check-cashing privilege per visit backed by a major credit card.

## THE VAGABOND INNS
**800-522-1555; 800-468-2251 (in CANADA)**

Call toll free for Vagabond's Club 55 information and application. You'll get 10 percent off regular rates and their quarterly travel newsletter. They even allow four people in a room for the price of one. For every nine nights you stay at a participating Vagabond Inn, you'll get one night free. Extras at no extra charge include a continental breakfast, coffee and tea, local phone calls, weekday newspaper, fresh fruit, cable TV, in-room VCRs, and FAX machines. "Get back to normal" in a Vagabond Inn only in CA, NV, AZ, NM.

## VALUE INN BY NENDELS
**800-547-0106 (or call your travel agent)**

Since 1934, this company has maintained its warmth and standards with their inns and hotels in the West. From large metropolitan complexes in major West Coast cities to small, intimate retreats in country towns, you're sure to find what you're looking for. Whether it's a basic economical room, a full-scale facility, or a suite with cooking facilities, if you go West, young man, call on a Nendel property. Special senior discounts for Golden Escape Members. Call for more information.

# Home Exchange Services

**GLOBAL HOME EXCHANGE & TRAVEL SERVICE**
**P.O. Box 2015**
**South Burlington, VT 05403-2015**
**802-985-3825**

West coast office:
2600 10th Street #436
Berkeley, CA 94710
415-848-3056

**HOME EXCHANGE INTERNATIONAL**
**22458 Ventura Blvd., Suite E**
**Woodland Hills, CA 91364-1581**
**818-992-8990**

## INTERVAC INTERNATIONAL:

INTERSERVICE HOME EXCHANGE
P.O. Box 87
Glen Echo, MD 20812
301-229-7567

INTERNATIONAL HOME EXCHANGE SERVICE
P.O. Box 3975
San Francisco, CA 94119
415-435-3497

## VACATION EXCHANGE CLUB
**12006 111th Avenue, Unit 12**
**Youngstown, AZ 85363**
**602-972-2186**

## WORLDWIDE EXCHANGE
**1344 Pacific Avenue, Suite 103**
**Santa Cruz, CA 95060**
**408-425-0531**

## EDGEWATER BEACH RESORT
**P.O. Box 9850**
**Panama City Beach, FL 32407**
**800-874-8686; 904-235-4044 (in FL)**

The beauty, warmth, and serenity of the Florida coast, combined with the service, hospitality, and affordable, luxurious accommodations at Edgewater Beach Resort sure can compete with anyone's description of the perfect vacation. Edgewater Beach Resort is described as "a Caribbean-like condominium resort of unsurpassed beauty," and it can be enjoyed year-round. Both the facilities and the amenities combine to take the edge off ensuring a successful vacation.

## INTERHOME, INC.
**Swiss Chalets**
**201-882-6864**

This New Jersey–based company is linked by computer to Switzerland and can book reservations to more than 3,000 Swiss chalets and condos in major resort areas. From budget-priced studios to more expensive villas, they can also handle your reservation at over 100 Swiss hotels.

## GLEN EAGLES FARM
**P.O. Box 7**
**Deep Gap, NC 28618**
**704-262-5002**

If you long for the "good old days" and would feel right at home in a horse and buggy, the pastoral life of the country at Glen Eagles Farm is for you. Nestled along the famous New River in the Blue Ridge Mountains, Glen Eagles is the home of champion steeplechaser "Thrice Worthy." It offers deluxe guest apartments, private riding instruction, buggy rides, golf, shopping, nature walks, picnics in the woods, river explorations, or simply a breathtaking setting in which to relax and unwind. Rates are as low as they can possibly be for what is offered by Glen Eagles Farm, and they just may surprise you.

## SENIOR SHOPPER DISCOUNT TRAVEL PASSBOOK
**Discount Travel Passbook**
**26600 Telegraph Road, Ste. 1200**
**Southfield, MI 48034**
**313-357-5300**
**CK,MO**

Save big bucks—50 percent on over 400 hotels and cruises year 'round at participating hotels such as the Hyatt, Hilton, Loew's, Sheraton, Radisson, Embassy Suites, Marriott, Guest

Quarters, and Doubletree, among others. From elegant vacation resorts like the Ikekai in Honolulu to a night's rest at a Days Inn, you can sleep cheap. Drive other bargains of up to 50 percent off on select tourist attractions, restaurants, sports attractions, retail stores, and more across the USA and Canada. If you take advantage of just *five* of the *hundreds* of money-saving opportunities, you could pocket as much as $500.

Similar books cost $39.95 and more—but for *Great Buys* readers, this book is FREE (though it costs $4.95 for postage and handling). Offer limited to one FREE book per household. Additional passbooks are $14.95 for *Great Buys* readers only (includes postage and handling).

**SWAMP FOX TOWERS**
**2311 South Ocean Blvd.**
**P.O. Box 1307**
**Myrtle Beach, SC 29578-1307**
**800-222-9894; 803-448-8373**

Swamp Fox Towers offers everything the Myrtle Beach vacationer could possibly want under one roof. Famous for its beaches and family activities, Myrtle Beach now offers affordable, luxury lodging right on the ocean. Rates vary according to need and type of room desired, but they offer a 10 percent discount to AARP members and a variety of in-hotel activities, services, and amenities to make any stay in Myrtle Beach a time to be remembered.

# TRAVEL—LUGGAGE

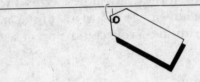

**ACE LEATHER PRODUCTS**
**2211 Avenue U**
**Brooklyn, NY 11229**
**800-DIAL-ACE; 718-891-9713 (in NY)**
**CK,MC,V,AE**
**C $1 (refundable with purchase)**

Ace stacks the cards in your favor by selling namebrand handbags, luggage, small leather goods and accessories, briefcases, and gifts at 20 to 40 percent less than the baggage handlers around town. Over a quarter of a century of sales, service, and savings, Andy and Ira deal you a winning hand with brands like SAMSONITE, ANDIAMO, HARTMANN, and ETIENNE AIGNER. Their 30–40-page color catalog is one of the leaders of the pack. Orders shipped the same day they're received, and exchanges are made within 10 days of purchase.

FREE travel clock with purchase of over $100 to all *Great Buys* shoppers.

**A TO Z LUGGAGE**
Dept. GB
4627 New Utrecht Ave.
Brooklyn, NY 11219
800-DIAL-011; 718-435-2880 (NY residents)
CK,MC,V,AE,DC,CB
C

How do you spell relief? S-a-v-i-n-g-s! We found everything from attachés to zippered manicure sets at one of their eight stores in New York. Christmas comes just once a year, and when it comes, it brings A to Z's only catalog. (But don't miss their periodic sale fliers). The brimming book contained all kinds of luggage and travel accessories from famous makers such as HARTMANN, ZERO, HALIBURTON, ROLF, TUMI, LACOSTE, and SAMSONITE. Discounts were 20 to 40 percent. Their imported attaché items represented a particularly good buy. If you're looking for something special, send a detailed description (including style and/or manufacturer's number) of the item you want, along with a SASE, and they will give you a price quote. Their catalog represents only a portion of the A to Z inventory. By calling the company before placing the order, we found out which catalog items were on sale for further reductions. Most orders arrive in about 10 days.

An additional 5 percent will be deducted from the bill if you mention you read about them in *Great Buys*.

**BETTINGERS LUGGAGE**
80 Rivington Street
New York, NY 10002
212-475-1690; 212-674-9411
CK,MC,V,AE
PQ,SASE

"Betting" you can't pass up a deal like this! Pack 30 to 40 percent off on attachés, briefcases, garment bags, luggage, small leather goods, and trunks. Brands like SAMSONITE,

---

**ASTA**
**Fulfillment Department**
**1101 King Street**
**Alexandria, VA 22314**
"Packing Tips." Tips to help you plan your packing *before* a trip, from choosing luggage to planning your wardrobe. Security tips for protecting your luggage in transit. This is *must* reading.

---

HARTMANN, SKYWAY, AMERICAN TOURISTER, and LARK should get you there in style. Minimum purchase is $25 plus $5 shipping and handling. Orders in about 15 days.


**CREATIVE HOUSE**
**100 Business Parkway**
**Richardson, TX 75081**
**800-527-5940; 214-231-3461 (in TX)**
**CK,MC,V,AE**
**C,PQ**

It doesn't take a creative genius to realize the savings of 30 to 60 percent on moderately priced luggage and attachés here. Pack 'em in—in SAMSONITE, AMERICAN TOURISTER, and AMELIA EARHART. Choose from many styles and colors of attachés, leather luggage, and garment bags. Handbags, wallets, and other leather items are also part of this house's inventory. All aboard!

Free leather business-card case or credit-card case with purchase of $50 or more to all *Great Buys* shoppers who identify themselves as a reader.

# TRAVEL—
# PACKAGES AND TOURS

**AARP TRAVEL SERVICE**
**100 North Sepulveda Blvd.**
**Suite 1020**
**El Segundo, CA 90245**
**800-227-7737 (tours & packages)**
**800-227-7885 (cruises)**

This value-packed service is provided exclusively to members of AARP, offering a variety of travel "hosted" opportunities, such as holidays to Europe for as low as $1,298 per person, including air, hotel or apartment accommodation, English-speaking host and more, and cruises that won't sink your pocketbook. Write for their easy-to-read information-packed brochures detailing the various destinations from Alaska to the U.S. Waterways, complete with itineraries, featured meals, and hotel descriptions.

**AMITY TOURS**
**2710 El Camino Real**
**Redwood City, CA 94063**
**800-523-8406; 800-227-6928 (in CA)**

Many tours for seniors featuring such intriguing extras as mineral baths and treatments and folk-dancing demonstrations. The Soviet Union and Eastern Europe are specialty locations, and tours depart from either coast. You may book your tour through a travel agent or write directly to Amity at the address above for a catalog.

## AVC TRAVEL CONSULTANTS
**177 Beach & 116th Street**
**Rockaway Park, NY 11694**
**800-221-5002; 718-945-5900 (in NY)**

If escorted tours on a *leisurely* basis are your "bag"—well, pack and go for 15–22 days. Specializing in Israel, Switzerland, and Italy, the 50 Plus Club is your ticket to discounted fares.

## BREEZE TOURS
**2750 Stickney Point Rd.**
**Sarasota, FL 33581**
**800-237-5630; 800-282-5630 (in FL)**

Travel with the wind behind your back with Breeze Tours. Specializing in the mature traveler, you can enjoy Hawaii, Australia, New Zealand, or England. Call for more information.

## MAYFLOWER TOURS, INC.
**1225 Warren Avenue**
**P.O. Box 490**
**Downers Grove, IL 60515**
**800-323-7604; 708-960-3430 (in IL)**
**(or call your travel agent)**

Owners Mary and John Stacknik have been taking travelers down the road filled with "Miles of Smiles" since 1979. Packed full of fun, destinations are varied but all brimming with value, convenience, companionship, and security. Making your travel easy, there will always be a tour director, local guides, complete transportation, lodging, baggage handling, sightseeing, several meals, taxes and gratuities included. Yes, air fare is included in the price. Tour pick-ups begin in the Chicago and surrounding areas but wind up at Disneyland, Epcot Center, Universal City or MGM Studios, Phoenix, Las Vegas, a tour of Texas called the Texas Fiesta, trips to New Orleans, Hawaii, Washington, D.C., Cape Cod by train, an Alaskan Odyssey, a Colorado Rockies Adventure—even a Mystery Tour. Swing to the magic of the 1930s and 1940s with a journey back in time to the big band era and USO shows by signing up for the California Stardust Tour.

## ORIENT FLEXI-PAX TOURS
**630 Third Avenue**
**New York, NY 10017**
**800-545-5540; 212-692-9550**

Call for your all-inclusive (air and land) super value pax trip to the Orient. From Classic China to the Exotic Orient, say "hi" to Bali or "aloha" to Hawaii; these tours offer a multitude of options to fit your interests and budget. Worry-free travel by these experienced travel leaders is their strength and byword.

Special to *Great Buys* readers: Save $100 per couple ($50 per person).

## PLEASANT HAWAIIAN HOLIDAYS
**2404 Townsgate Road**
**Westlake Village, CA 91361**
**800-242-9244**

If you're 60 years of age or older, you can take advantage of reduced fares on some of the most popular Hawaiian Holidays. All you have to do is send for the brochure, pick one of the spectacular holiday packages with choice of accommodations and, voilá, you're almost there. Check with your travel agent and be sure to bring along proof of age. This package is meant to be used in conjunction with air transportation by Delta, Hawaiian Air, or United.

## SAGA HOLIDAYS
**120 Boylston Street**
**Boston, MA 02116**
**800-343-0273**

Saga Holiday's "Travel Bulletin" gives "sneak previews" of coming attractions (forthcoming tours). It also brings updates on their Lecture Tour Programs, now expanded to include the United Kingdom and Europe as well as the U.S., Canada, and Mexico. Saga's specialist teams are ready and waiting to answer your questions and book your holiday at the toll-free number above.

## SENIOR ESCORTED TOURS, INC.
**P.O. Box 400**
**Cape May Courthouse, NJ 08210**
**800-222-1254; 609-465-4011 (in NJ)**

Senior Escorted Tours works in conjunction with services like Amtrak and ARC Carriers to bring seniors the best deals in tours to places like Orlando and Hawaii. Write for more information about special packages (cruises, train trips, bus trips, et cetera), terms and rates. Send in your deposit at least six months early and receive two nights before or after your trip at a deluxe hotel—free. Can you afford to miss out on an offer like that?

*Great Buys* readers discount: $25 off, except for the Catskills or Cape May/Wildwood tours.

## SINGLEWORLD
P.O. Box 1999
Rye, NY 10580
800-223-6490
C

See the world with other "singles" without missing a single beat. Hop aboard any one of Singleworld's loveboat cruises (Norwegian, Carnival, or Royal Caribbean lines) or take a land tour in summer to Europe. They are one of the country's largest tour and cruise operators and you can sail away not only on one of the best (and cheapest all-inclusive) vacations you've ever had, but maybe land a love connection, too. No marrieds allowed. The Singleworld escort helps orchestrate activities, all in the name of love, of course. Write Singleworld for their free 32-page catalog or call your travel agent for details.

## SUN HOLIDAYS

Call your travel agent and have fun in the sun off the coast of Spain. You must stay for at least one month (or longer) during the winter months to save, save, save. Jump in for as little as $769 per person for a Wednesday departure from Newark via Air Europa charter (slightly more from other cities). Price includes round-trip air, hotel transfers, furnished studio apartment with fully equipped kitchenette and any other assistance you may need for a month.

## TRAFALGAR TOURS
21 East 26th Street
New York, NY 10010
800-854-0103 (reservations); 212-689-8977 (in NY)

Trafalgar Tours is the #1 tour operator to Europe and Great Britain. Join other English-speaking passengers and hit the road, Jack. Take the worry out of traveling with optional trip-cancellation insurance, travel insurance, and a guaranteed price. Tour prices included a first-class hotel, sightseeing, most meals, airport transfers and the services of an experienced tour guide. Their "Cost Saver" program offered a 30 percent savings over the same tour if you planned it yourself.

## TRANS-NATIONAL TRAVEL
2 Charlesgate West
Boston, MA 02215-3552
800-225-7678; 617-262-9200 (in MA)

For fifteen years, TNT has been working to pass on savings to its seniors through such organizations as Mature Outlook, North Carolina Senior Citizens, and the National Association of Retired Federal Employees. TNT acts as a wholesaler, obtaining a discounted rate from the vendor to block space for cruises. Members of one of the above mentioned organizations can take advantage of wonderful savings on trips to destinations from Moscow to the Caribbean. All it takes is a phone call to one of the member organizations or to the address above.

## TRAVEL AVENUE
800-333-3335; 312-876-1116 (in IL)

A money-saving alternative to the traditional commission-based travel agency (with the exception of planning an in-depth vacation package or around-the-world tour), this company charges an $8 service fee for domestic flights and rebates an 8 percent check off airfare price with ticket. International flights: $20 service fee and you'll get a 8–15 percent rebate. Receive an additional check (even after posted discounts) of 5 percent with proof of hotel stay or car rental. Tours and cruises, save 8 percent and a fee of $20 (for cruises less than $1000) and $40 (for cruises over $1000). Guaranteed lowest published fares and rates. Ask about specials called "The Ultimate Deal."

Call on the travel expert, Pat Mallory, for the best deals on customized tours to paradise. There are over 2,000 islands that offer an untouched, unspoiled tropical view of the blue Pacific. Besides the splendor and seclusion, you can see the world's tallest mountain (Guam), and experience the world's most steady climate (Saipan). Veterans who formerly served in Guam and Yap during WWII are particularly nostalgic and excited about a return vacation visit. A stopover in Hawaii can also be planned.

*Great Buys* readers need only ask for Pat and identify themselves as readers of this book to receive 10 percent off the regular price for scheduled or customized tours.

**WORLDWIDE COUNTRY TOURS**
**5925 Country Lane**
**Greendale, WI 53129**
**B**

Embark on a New England Craft Tour, bypassing cities for unforgettable stretches of beach and mountains. Browse craft shops to your heart's content. Not satisfied with offering only one section of the country, WorldWide has planned a total of almost two dozen different tours with country emphasis for 1991. A detailed brochure is available for each trip planned.

# Trip Cancellation Insurance:

**ACCESS AMERICA**
600 Third Avenue
P.O. Box 807
New York, NY 10163
800-284-8300

**TRAVEL GUARD INTERNATIONAL**
1100 Center Point Drive
Stevens Point, WI 54481
800-826-1300

**TELE-TRIP COMPANY**
3201 Farnam Street
Omaha, NE 68131
800-228-9792

**WORLDCARE TRAVEL ASSISTANCE
  ASSOCIATION**
2000 Pennsylvania Avenue NW
Suite 7600
Washington, DC 20006
800-521-4822

**TRIP 'N TOUR**
P.O. Box 150806
Irving, TX 75015
800-348-0842; 214-252-7233
B

## YUGOTOURS
## "PRIME OF YOUR LIFE" VACATIONS
**350 Fifth Avenue**
**New York, NY 10018**
**800-223-5298; 212-563-2400**

If you're 60 years old and have a companion, you can take advantage of the wonderful travel packages available through Yugotours to Yugoslavia. Fees and deposits vary, however, with each package, but you can count on first class hotels with meals included, and round-trip transfers are provided from the airport by motorcoach or private car. Whatever city you choose to visit, your trip should be memorable, as well as reasonable.

# TRAVEL—SPECIALTY

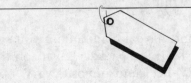

**ALL AMERICAN SPORTS**
**45 Kensico Dr.**
**Mt. Kisco, NY 10549**
**800-223-2442; 914-666-0096 (in NY state)**

Want to vacation in a beautiful spot and come away with a
"guaranteed improvement" in your tennis game? Special
rates for "40s Plus Week" and "Seniors Week," along with
an evaluation of your level of play, instruction, practice,
videotape playbacks, strategy sessions, and lots of time play-
ing (both singles and doubles). Sounds like heaven for the
tennis enthusiast, but if your spouse doesn't play, take heart.
The home front can still be 40-love when you see the other
offerings at these gorgeous resorts. The guarantee even
entitles you to a free tennis program (accommodations not
included) if you feel your game has not improved at any of
the resorts within six months!

**AMERICAN YOUTH HOSTELS, INC.**
**P.O. Box 37613**
**Washington, DC 20013-7613**
**202-783-6161**

You don't have to be a kid to enjoy the ultra-cheap accommodations of a hostel nationwide. No, they're not located
just in the boonies, either. In fact, you'd be surprised at how

central some are: Washington, D.C., Boston, Chicago, San Francisco, New York City, and Los Angeles (the LA facility has 200 beds). Travel for cost-cutting seniors via the hostels is a way to cut costs, but not the fun or friendship along the way.

**AMTRAK**
**800-USA-RAIL**

Special 25 percent discount fares are available for seniors, but these are most advantageous when used for one-way travel. The savings for a round trip would be minimal (in comparison to their already low round-trip fares). On board, you'll find wide, reclining seats, tasty snacks, terrific dining, and, of course, spectacular scenery.

**AUDUBON ECOLOGY CAMPS**
**National Audubon Society**
**613 Riversville Rd.**
**Greenwich, CT 06831**
**213-869-2017**

If natural history is your thing, check out these programs located in Connecticut, Maine, and Wyoming. Sessions vary in length from 6 to 12 days, and all are geared for the over-50 adult.

## Bicycling Today

Bicycling is fast becoming the most popular sport in America today. People are finding great pleasure in riding more than just to the corner store and back. Biking isn't just for the kids; there are now many tours and clubs in the U.S. and

Canada designed especially for the over 50s. For more information contact:

- American Youth Hostel Bike Tours (AYH), Dept 855, P.O. Box 37613, Washington, DC 20013-7613; (202) 783-6161.
- Bicycle Touring for Women Only, Outdoor Vacations for Women Over 40, P.O. Box 200, Groton, MA 01450; (617) 448-3331.
- The Ontario Masters Cycling Association, RR #3, Caledon East, ON L0N 1E0, Canada; (416) 880-5136.
- Bicycle Racing, USFC, 1750 E. Boulder St., Colorado Springs, CO 80909; (303) 578-4581.
- The Cross Canada Cycle Tour Society, 1200 Hornby St., Vancouver, BC V6Z 2E2, Canada.
- Wandering Wheels, P.O. Box 207, Upland, IN 46989; (317) 998-7490
- THE TOURFINDER is a guide to bicycle tours in the U.S. and around the world. Available from League of American Wheelmen, 6707 Whitestone Rd., #209, Baltimore, MD 21207.

**THE BIG SKY GAMES**
**P.O. BOX 2318**
**BILLINGS, MT 59101**

The Big Sky State Games are held in Billings, Montana, each July, for people over 55. Write for more information.

**DISCOUNT TRAVEL INTERNATIONAL**
**215-668-7184; 215-668-2182**
**MC,V,CK**

For those not blessed with a brother-in-law in the business, meet Discount Travel International, the national clearinghouse for unsold trips. For $45 per year, Discount Travel

## BritRail

If you're traveling to England, remember to buy your BritRail Pass *before* you leave, as they're not sold in England. This is a fantastic way for the over-60 traveler to obtain 8-day, 15-day, 22-day, or month-long unlimited travel at a discounted rate.

## Disney's Magic Years Club

Join Disney's Magic Years Club (60+) for discounts at both Disneyland and Walt Disney World and receive discounts on parking, meals, shops, some Hilton Hotels, and some National Car Rentals. You'll also receive a quarterly newsletter and travel packages. Write to Disney's Magic Years Club, P.O. Box 4709, Anaheim, CA 92803-4709; or call 714-490-3250.

International members have access to a toll-free hotline number giving up-to-the-minute information on all available trips where hopping aboard (with one to eight weeks notice of departure) can save you up to 70 percent, plus 5 percent off regularly scheduled airlines (domestic or international), 7 percent on tours, 7 percent on charters, 7 percent on cruises, savings on car rentals, suite vacations and, wait, there's more—50 percent off at such participating hotels as Sheraton, Hilton, Westin, Holiday Inns, Quality Inns, Best Western, Radisson, and more. But who could ask for anything more? How about the opportunity for a free trip to Paris if you don't save double your Discount Travel International membership fee?

Attention *Great Buys* readers: Get the regular $45 membership for only $29.95—that's a third off.

## EURAILPASS
P.O. Box 325
Old Greenwich, CT 06870

Before leaving the United States, be sure to buy your EURAILPASS for unlimited first-class train travel in 16 European countries. If your group numbers three or more, you can qualify for a EURAIL SILVERPASS for even greater savings. Write for more information.

## GRAND CIRCLE TRAVEL, INC.
347 Congress Street
Boston, MA 02210
800-221-2610; 607-350-7500 (in MA)

Grand Circle has been working for over thirty years to bring the best opportunities and deals in travel to active, mature Americans. Whether it's a trip to Europe or the Galapagos Islands, Grand Circle Travel can get you there with money to spare. And with twelve cruise destinations, you'll need more than a coin to decide where you should go first. Write or call—maybe they can help you decide.

## HIDEAWAYS INTERNATIONAL
800-822-9798; 800-486-8955 (in MA)
508-486-8252 (FAX)

Hideaways International, as its name implies, represents the little-known, out-of-the-ordinary secret escape where vacations are etched with indelible memories. This full-service travel resource specializes in premier villa and condo rentals, yacht charters, special cruises, intimate inns and resorts . . . even castles and ranches. Your membership entitles you to the quarterly newsletters giving the "inside scoop" on new places, a personal travel service for airfares, and money-saving discounts. From Antigua to Wyoming, Grenada to Quebec, this is the way to go in style. The guide details handicap access, whether your pets are welcome, plus a myriad of details on every property.

Free 4-month trial membership for readers of *Great Buys*.

**INTERNATIONAL HOME EXCHANGE SERVICE**
**INTERVAC U.S.**
**P.O. Box 190070**
**San Francisco, CA 94119**
**415-435-3497**
**415-956-3447 (FAX)**
**B**

Choose a home exchange from a list of thirty countries, including Japan, Brazil, Australia, Morocco, Poland, Zimbabwe, and New Zealand. And your home can be a rewarding experience for someone from another country or some other part of the U.S., in return. Membership is $35 per year, plus postage and handling. The current brochure gives information about home exchange, subscription form and listing deadlines. To expedite membership, exchange information can be sent by Fax. When a Fax is used, payment must be with Visa or Mastercard, but photos may not be sent by Fax.

Note: Home exchange is possible anytime during the year, including summer, Christmas, and Easter vacations.

## ITALIAN STATE RAILWAYS
**666 Fifth Ave.**
**New York, NY 10103**
**212-397-2667**

For those planning extensive train travel in Italy, you would
be well advised to purchase a travel-anywhere pass (available
to all ages) called a BLTC, valid for unlimited travel for 8,
15, 21, or 30 days. It is relatively inexpensive and must be
purchased in the United States, as it is not available in Italy.
If you won't be traveling quite as much, you might want the
*Carta d'Argento* (Silver Card), which is valid for one year and
a bargain at $5. This entitles men age 65 plus and women
age 62 plus to a 30 percent discount on Italian railway travel.
It can be purchased at railroad stations in Italy at the special
windows (*Biglietti Speciali*). Throw your coins in the fountain
and plan on returning year after year.


## MOMENT'S NOTICE
**Discount Travel Club**
**40 East 49th Street**
**New York, NY 10017**
**MC,V,AE,CK**

Moment's Notice is a short notice travel clearinghouse,
offering unsold space to its 17,000 members at discounts
ranging from 15 to 45 percent off brochure prices. Annual
membership fee is $45. Travel opportunities are 99 percent
international—cruises, Caribbean packages, European tours,
and airfares are their primary focus. Occasionally, they even
offer African safaris and trips to the Orient and the South
Pacific.

*Great Buys* reader offer: the opportunity to access the
members-only travel special hotline and receive quarterly
travel updates. Forward your request in writing to Ellen
Baum, Director of Marketing, address above.

**OMNI SENIOR RAIL TOURS**
**800-962-0060**

Let Omni book your next get-away for a leisurely, relaxed, enjoyable trip by rail. Amtrak, United Airlines, and local motorcoach sightseeing combine to let you relive the forgotten pleasure of actually being able to see what you've missed. If your sights are set on Texas, Florida, California, the great national parks, Nevada, or New Orleans, then Omni can fill the bill, but you have to foot it!

# Special Interests

Choose a vacation with a special focus from the following annotated list.

**ACTS INSTITUTE**
**P.O. Box 10153**
**Kansas City, MO 64111**

A retreat for writers, scientists and scholars.

**ADVENTURE CENTER**
**1311 63rd Street**
**Suite 200**
**Emoryville, CA 94608**
**800-277-8747**

Camping vacations.

**AMERICAN FRIENDS SERVICE COMMISSION**
**1501 Cherry Street**
**Philadelphia, PA 19102**

The Religious Society of Friends (Quakers) offers a variety of volunteer work opportunities.

## ARCHAEOLOGICAL INSTITUTE OF AMERICA
P.O. Box 1901
Kenmore Station
Boston, MA 02215

Publishes a list of excavations that take volunteers.


## OUTWARD BOUND USA
384 Field Point Road
Greenwich, CT 06830
800-243-8520

Ready, set, Outward Bound! Leave the comforts of home for the unfamiliar and adventurous in the most spectacular wilderness areas in the world, and discover your own capabilities under challenging conditions. Almost 20,000 people, ages 14 to 77, have participated in over 600 course offerings last year, most of them with little or no experience in the wilderness. Special courses are offered for teens, women over 30, adults over 55, as well as for family members, couples, and parents with children. Recent catalog listings include: backpacking, canoe expeditions, horsetrailing, western Alpine mountaineering, sailing and sea kayaking, cycling, whitewater rafting and dog sledding!


## SPECIAL TRAVEL INDEX
305 San Anselmo Avenue
Suite 217
San Anselmo, CA 94960

For just $6 ($2 off the regular price), senior travelers can receive two idea- and activity-packed issues of *Specialty Travel Index,* spring/summer and fall/winter issues. You can choose from thousands of unusual activities and vacations worldwide at the touch of your fingertips. Whether it's cooking schools or gourmet tours to France, to hiking and river-rafting in far-off exotic places, you'll want to read about each one, then choose the best trip for your particular interests and needs.

## STEAMBOATIN' PLUS AIR
**c/o The Delta Queen Steamboat Co.**
**800-543-1949**
**B**

If you're cruisin' for a bargain, consider round-trip plane ride, airport transfers, and a cruise down the Mississippi. Special airfares have been negotiated in conjunction with the Mississippi Queen or the Delta Queen steamboat cruises. It's recommended you arrive a day in advance to insure you don't miss the boat. (And promise you'll sit down if you start rockin' the boat!) Prices vary based on your departure city. Call for brochure and more information.

## TRAIL BLAZER LLAMAS
**Don Johnson**
**7819 NE 154th Street**
**Vancouver, WA 98662**
**206-573-1159**

Trail Blazer Llamas makes it easy for you to see the back country of the Pacific Northwest. Gentle, surefooted llamas carry your gear while you walk unburdened through alpine meadows and evergreen forests of southern Washington and northern Oregon. For two, three, or four days you can camp amid unrivaled scenery, fish in sparkling mountain streams, and enjoy the meals provided by Trail Blazers. What's not to like? Special consideration is given to the novice hiker, including easy trails with many rest breaks if needed. Groups of three to eight can be reserved exclusively for seniors and seniors can take 25 percent off the price of custom trips, such as the Lewis River three-day trip for $200, or the Indian Heaven three-day trip for $210. They'll provide the tents, canteens, sleeping pads, rain gear and all food and utensils!

*Great Buys* readers can receive an additional 15 percent discount (minimum two people) on overnight camping trips.

## TRANSITIONS ABROAD
**18 Lulst Road**
**P.O. Box 344**
**Amherst, MA 01004-9970**

For the often overlooked learning vacation, Professor Clayton Hubbs of Hampshire College in Amherst created a bimonthly 62-page magazine, *Transitions Abroad,* devoted to trips that are designed to allow you to experience the realities of the culture of the country you choose to visit. Independent travelers wishing to "live" the life rather than just *"pass through"* would really enjoy making this transition abroad. A one-year subscription was $15; two years a bargain at $20; and three years for $39.

# TRAVEL—TIMESHARES

Want a luxury vacation but don't want to spring for luxury prices? The solution is a timeshare! This industry has come a long way from its fragmented beginnings 25 years ago. Today, some of the finest names in hospitality—like Marriott, Divi, Fairfield, and Rank—operate over 2,000 timeshare resorts around the world. These properties sell vacation time by the week, and the majority offer a lifetime deed to your portion of the property. Once you are an owner, the staff at your home resort will become almost family; they will, as the song says, "Know your name." Today, over two million families are timeshare owners.

The two main benefits that timeshare owners talk about most are (1) the incredible value of having a luxury, fully furnished townhome or condominium all to yourself at far less than the cost of a cramped hotel room, and (2) the "exchange" privilege. As an owner, your resort will most likely be affiliated with one of two major exchange companies—RCI or II. Both provide the service of arranging vacation exchanges to other of their affiliate resorts as part of the benefits of ownership. Thus you can own a timeshare in one place—say, South Padre Island—but exchange it, one year for Hawaii and the next for the Poconos. In other words, a timeshare purchase is really a ticket to many luxury vacations just about anywhere on earth!

The trade association for timeshares is the American Resort and Residential Development Association (ARRDA), based in Washington, DC. These folks have really cleaned up the acts of small-time developers who gave the industry a bad name in its early days. By mandating rules and regulations for timeshares and enforcing a strict code of ethics among their 1,000 developer-members, you can rest easy in a timeshare resort. As a matter of fact, they have put together a booklet of consumer guidelines that can be had just by calling their toll-free number (1-800-695-ARDA). To make sure you're dealing only with a member, look for the ARRDA logo when choosing a resort. If the resort also displays the AEI seal of achievement, this means that their staff, procedures, and facilities reflect the very highest standards in the industry.

Many timeshare resorts fill their unsold inventory with vacation rentals. If you meet their qualifications and are willing to take the time to tour their property (usually a very pleasant experience), they will allow you to take a mini-vacation at almost unheard-of prices. Talk about a bargain! Following are several who have extended a super special offer to the over-50 *Great Buys* reader. Be sure to identify yourself.

**FAIRFIELD BAY**
**Fairfield Bay, AR**
**800-643-9790**

Visitors and residents of this Ozark paradise enjoy one of the finest resort-retirement communities in America. Located on a 40,000-acre lake, one of the nation's cleanest, there are two 18-hole golf courses, fishing, boating, tennis, indoor and outdoor pools, a complete shopping center, senior hobby groups, and more.

*Great Buys* special offer: $49.95 per person per night, based on double occupancy, with continental breakfast and free greens fees (cart not included). Includes a 90-minute resort presentation and tour.

## FAIRFIELD FLAGSTAFF
**Flagstaff, AZ**
**800-526-1004**

This resort-retirement community is between 20–30 degrees cooler than Phoenix in the summer. Just 80 miles from the Grand Canyon, it offers two 18-hole golf courses, two heated pools, tennis, and winter skiing at Snowbowl, 14 miles away.

*Great Buys* special offer: $49.95 per person per night, based on double occupancy, with continental breakfast and free greens fees (cart not included). Includes a 90-minute resort presentation and tour.

## FAIRFIELD GLADE
**Fairfield Glade, TN**
**800-251-6778**

A paradise for senior vacationers and residents. *Four* 18-hole championship golf courses, 11 lakes for fishing and boating, dozens of community-center social groups, shopping, and more.

Special offer to *Great Buys* readers: $49.95 per person per night, based on double occupancy, with continental breakfast and free greens fees (cart not included). Includes a 90-minute resort presentation and tour.

## FAIRFIELD MOUNTAINS
**Lake Lure, NC**
**800-438-9631**

Beautiful, tranquil Lake Lure is the centerpiece of this gorgeous resort-retirement community. It offers two 18-hole golf courses criss-crossed by trout streams, marina, indoor and outdoor pools, fitness center, tennis, and more. Near historical and picturesque Asheville.

Special offer to *Great Buys* readers: $49.95 per person per night, based on double occupancy, with continental breakfast and free greens fees (cart not included). Includes a 90-minute resort presentation and tour.

Other Fairfield locations that will honor *Great Buys* specials:

- Edisto Island, SC (800-845-8500)
- Myrtle Beach, SC (800-833-7048)
- New Bern, NC (800-327-3747)
- Pagosa Springs, CO (800-523-0479)
- Sapphire, NC (800-438-3421)
- Williamsburg, VA (800-777-1776)

## LAWRENCE WELK'S DESERT OASIS GOLF AND TENNIS RESORT
**Cathedral City/Palm Springs Area**
**619-485-8063**

Bask in the sun, marvel at the mountains, and enjoy the fabulous "27" holes of challenging golf, 10 tennis courts (7 lighted for night-time play), pool, spa, restaurant, lounge—all situated in the world's most famous desert playground. This Palm Springs/Coachella Valley resort area is offering a GRAND OPENING SPECIAL for *Great Buys* readers: 4 days/3 nights accommodations (space available), including a required minimum sales presentation and tour of resort, with FREE greens fees (cart mandatory): $79.99 per family (maximum 2 adults/2 children).

## ROYALE BEACH AND TENNIS CLUB
**South Padre Island, TX**
**800-292-0204**

Luxuriate in the year-round sun at one of America's ten best beaches. This property features efficiency, one- and two-bedroom (1250 sq. ft.) luxury condominiums complete with beach frontage, swimming pools, jacuzzis, tennis courts, and access to golf. A 3 day/2 night stay is $79.00 per couple (excluding airfare); a 5 day/4 night stay is $129.00 per couple (excluding airfare), including a 90-minute sales presentation and tour of resort as part of this *Great Buys* reader special.

# TRAVEL— FOREIGN TOURIST BUREAUS

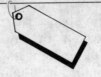

**AUSTRALIA TOURIST COMMISSION OFFICE**
489 Fifth Avenue
New York, NY 10017


**AUSTRIA NATIONAL TOURIST OFFICE**
500 Fifth Avenue
New York, NY 10010


**BAHAMAS TOURIST OFFICE**
150 East 52nd Street
New York, NY 10022


**BARBADOS BOARD OF TOURISM**
800 Second Avenue
New York, NY 10151


**BERMUDA DEPARTMENT OF TOURISM**
310 Madison Avenue
New York, NY 10117

## BRITISH TOURIST AUTHORITY
40 West 57th Street
Suite 320
New York, NY 10019-4001
212-581-4700

Request the booklet *Affordable Britain,* the gateway to bargains and discounted travel in the United Kingdom. It even includes a glossary of English expressions such as "bill," the equivalent of the American "check," and "turf accountant," better known in this country as a "bookie"!

## BRITISH VIRGIN ISLANDS TOURIST BOARD
370 Lexington Avenue
New York, NY 10017

## CAYMAN ISLANDS DEPARTMENT OF TOURISM
420 Lexington Avenue
New York, NY 10017

## CHINA
## PEOPLE'S REPUBLIC OF CHINA EMBASSY
2300 Connecticut Avenue NW
Washington, DC 20008

## DENMARK TOURIST BOARD
655 Third Avenue
New York, NY 10017

## EGYPTIAN GOVERNMENT TOURIST OFFICE
630 Fifth Avenue
New York, NY 10111

## FRENCH GOVERNMENT TOURIST OFFICE
610 Fifth Avenue
New York, NY 10020

**GERMAN NATIONAL TOURIST OFFICE**
747 Third Avenue
New York, NY 10017

**GREEK NATIONAL TOURIST ORGANIZATION**
168 North Michigan Avenue
Chicago, IL 60601
312-782-1084

Select reductions are granted to passengers over 60 upon presentation of passports or identity cards that entitle the bearer to additional discounts. Seniors are given 30 to 50 percent off railways in many European countries. Write for free details.

**HAITI TOURIST BUREAU**
630 Fifth Avenue
New York, NY 10020

**HONG KONG TOURIST ASSOCIATION**
548 Fifth Avenue
New York, NY 10036

**IRISH TOURIST BOARD**
757 Third Avenue
New York, NY 10036

**ISRAEL GOVERNMENT TOURIST OFFICE**
350 Fifth Avenue
New York, NY 10118

**ITALIAN GOVERNMENT TRAVEL OFFICE**
630 Fifth Avenue
New York, NY 10111

**JAMAICA TOURIST BOARD**
866 Second Avenue
New York, NY 10017

## JAPAN NATIONAL TOURIST ORGANIZATION
630 Fifth Avenue
New York, NY 10111


## KENYA TOURIST OFFICE
424 Madison Avenue
New York, NY 10017


## MEXICO NATIONAL TOURIST COUNCIL
405 Park Avenue
New York, NY 10022


## NETHERLANDS BOARD OF TOURISM
355 Lexington Avenue
New York, NY 10017
212-370-7360; 212-370-7367

Write for brochure and information on the Holland Leisure Card, a discount card for travelers to the Netherlands, and discover this country full of surprises, great folklore, art, world-famous flowers, and, of course, windmills.


## PHILIPPINE TOURISM
50 Biscayne Blvd.
Miami, FL 33132


## PORTUGUESE NATIONAL TOURIST OFFICE
590 Fifth Avenue
New York, NY 10036-4704
212-354-4403; 212-764-6137

Study the rich history and architecture of Portugal with its medieval cities or enjoy its bustling modern nightlife. Seniors are afforded a 40 percent discount on public and rail transportation.

## SCANDINAVIAN TOURIST BOARD
**655 Third Avenue**
**New York, NY 10017**
**212-949-2333**

Take your pick from among five of Europe's most beautiful countries for your next trip. Whether it's Denmark, Finland, Iceland, Norway, or Sweden, you'll find competitive rates and helpful people anxious to acquaint you with the unique charm of Scandinavia. Discounts for seniors exist in the form of railway discounts, but this is the transportation of choice in much of Europe.

## SOUTH AFRICA TOURIST CORPORATION
**747 Third Avenue**
**New York, NY 10017**

## SPANISH NATIONAL TOURIST OFFICE
**665 Fifth Avenue**
**New York, NY 10022**

## SWISS NATIONAL TOURIST OFFICE
**Swiss Center**
**608 Fifth Avenue**
**New York, NY 10020**
**212-757-5944**

Check out the discounts offered to seniors at many of the 440 hotels throughout Switzerland. Ladies over 62 and men over 65 need only present a passport or ID card at the hotel desk upon arrival. Or you can write for the "Season for Seniors" listing of participating hotels from the Swiss National Tourist Office, and be sure to request some of their colorful brochures of breathtakingly beautiful countryside.

**TAHITI TOURIST BOARD**
12233 Olympic Boulevard
Los Angeles, CA 90064

**USSR**
**INTOURIST**
630 Fifth Avenue
New York, NY 10111

**VENEZUELAN GOVERNMENT TOURIST BUREAU**
7 East 51st Street
New York, NY 10022

**YUKON BUREAU OF TOURISM**
P.O. Box 2703
Whitehorse, YT CAN Y1A 2C6
403-667-5340

The magic and mystery of the Yukon will be at your fingertips
in this colorful guide available from Yukon Tourism.

# TRAVEL—U.S.
## TOURIST BUREAUS

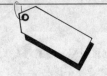

**ALABAMA BUREAU OF TOURISM AND TRAVEL**
532 South Perry Street
Montgomery, AL 36104
800-252-2262; 800-392-8096 (in AL); 205-261-4169

**ALASKA TOURISM MARKETING COUNCIL**
P.O. Box E-501
Juneau, AL 99811
907-465-2010; 907-586-8399

The Alaskan Tourism Council has information about individual hotels, cruise lines, airlines, and tours and special offers for seniors, so be sure to inquire before you plan your trip to our northernmost state.

**ARIZONA OFFICE OF TOURISM**
1480 East Bethany Home Road
Phoenix, AZ 85014
602-255-3618

**ARKANSAS DEPARTMENT OF PARKS & TOURISM**
One Capitol Mall
Little Rock, AR 72201
501-682-1191

With its natural springs and variety of lakes and rivers, Arkansas is great for canoeing, boating, fishing, and camping, to name a few. But the best way to inquire about special deals for seniors and activities tailored to your particular needs is to write to the Arkansas Department of Parks & Tourism or call the number above.

**CALIFORNIA OFFICE OF TOURISM**
**1121 L Street**
**Sacramento, CA 95814**
**800-446-7275; 916-322-1396**

**CARLSBAD, NM**
**Chamber of Commerce**
**P.O. Box 910**
**Carlsbad, NM 88220**
**800-221-1224; 505-887-6516**

Carlsbad wants seniors to know that in addition to their famous caverns and beautiful mild weather, they also have an extremely low crime rate, low taxes, and a number of senior activities and year-round attractions. Consider a visit, and you might just like it enough to stay. Many people have done just that.

**COLORADO TOURISM BOARD**
**1625 Broadway**
**Denver, CO 80111**
**800-255-5550; 303-799-4900**

**CONNECTICUT DEPARTMENT OF ECONOMIC**
    **DEVELOPMENT, TOURISM DIVISION**
**210 Washington Street**
**Hartford, CT 06106**
**800-243-1685; 800-842-7492 (in CT); 203-566-3948**

**DELAWARE STATE TRAVEL SERVICE**
P.O. Box 1401
99 Kings Highway
Dover, DE 19901
800-441-8846; 800-282-8667 (in DE); 302-736-4271


**DISTRICT OF COLUMBIA**
**WASHINGTON CONVENTION AND VISITORS ASSN.**
1575 Eye Street NW
Washington, DC 20005
202-789-7000


**FLORIDA DIVISION OF TOURISM**
Visitor Inquiry Section
107 West Gaines Street
Tallahassee, FL 32301
904-487-1462


**GEORGIA TOURIST DIVISION**
P.O. Box 1776
Atlanta, GA 30301
404-656-3590


**HARLINGEN, TX**
Chamber of Commerce
P.O. Box 189
Harlingen, TX 78551
800-531-7346; 800-292-7272 (in TX)

Texans know Harlingen for its close proximity to Padre
Island and to Mexico. With an average year-round temperature of 74°, it's no wonder people often think of it first,
especially when planning winter getaways or looking for a
mild, temperate climate in which to retire. Call or write
today and discover this treasure deep in the heart of Texas.

**HAWAII VISITORS BUREAU**
Waikiki Business Plaza
2270 Kalakaua Avenue
Honolulu, HI 96815
808-923-1811

**IDAHO TRAVEL COUNCIL**
Statehouse, Room 108
Boise, ID 83720
800-635-7820; 208-334-2470

**ILLINOIS TOURIST INFORMATION CENTER**
310 South Michigan Avenue
Suite 108
Chicago, IL 60604
800-223-0121; 800-252-8987 (in IL); 312-793-2094

**INDIANA TOURISM DEVELOPMENT DIVISION**
One North Capitol Avenue
Indianapolis, IN 46204
800-292-6337; 800-858-8073; 800-622-4464 (in IN);
  317-232-8860

**IOWA STATE DEVELOPMENT COMMISSION**
Tourism and Travel Division
200 East Grand Avenue
Des Moines, IA 50309
515-281-3100

**JEKYLL ISLAND, GA**
Convention & Visitors Bureau
P.O. Box 3186
Jekyll Island, GA 31520
800-841-6586; 800-342-1042 (in GA)

The historic eastern seaboard with its cities of Savannah and
Jekyll Island is among the best-kept secrets in the U.S. Since
the 1500s, people have been drawn by the beautiful beaches,

green marshes, and wildlife, but one of the main attractions has always been the year-round mild climate that lends itself perfectly to golf, swimming, fishing, and outdoor activities. Be sure to ask about senior rates on tours and at area hotels.

**KANSAS TRAVEL & TOURISM DIVISION**
503 Kansas Avenue
Topeka, KS 66603
913-296-2009

**KENTUCKY DEPARTMENT OF TRAVEL
DEVELOPMENT**
Capitol Plaza Tower
Frankfort, KY 40601
800-225-8747; 502-564-4930

**LOUISIANA OFFICE OF TOURISM**
Inquiry Department
P.O. Box 94291
Baton Rouge, LA 70804
800-231-4730; 800-535-8388; 504-925-3860

**MAINE STATE PUBLICITY BUREAU**
97 Winthrop Street
Hallowell, ME 04347
207-289-2423

**MARYLAND OFFICE OF TOURISM DEVELOPMENT**
45 Calvert Street
Annapolis, MD 21401
301-269-2686

**MASSACHUSETTS STATE DEPARTMENT OF
COMMERCE**
Division of Tourism
100 Cambridge Street
Boston, MA 02202
800-624-MASS; 800-632-8083 (in MA); 617-727-3201

## MICHIGAN TRAVEL BUREAU
P.O. Box 30226
Lansing, MI 48909
800-543-2937; 517-373-1195

## MINNESOTA OFFICE OF TOURISM
250 Skyway Level
375 Jackson Street
St. Paul, MN 55101
800-328-1461; 800-652-9747 (in MN); 612-296-5029

## MISSISSIPPI DIVISION OF TOURISM
P.O. Box 22825
Jackson, MS 39205
800-647-2290; 800-962-2346 (in MS); 601-359-3414

## MISSOURI STATE DIVISION OF TOURISM
Truman Building
308 East High Street
Jefferson City, MO 65102
800-325-0733 (surr. states); 800-392-0711 (in MO);
   314-751-4133

## MONTANA TRAVEL PROMOTION BUREAU
1424 9th Avenue
Helena, MT 59620-0411
800-548-3390; 406-449-2654

## NEBRASKA TRAVEL AND TOURISM DIVISION
P.O. Box 94666
301 Centennial Mall South
Lincoln, NE 68509
800-228-4307; 800-742-7595 (in NE); 402-471-3796

## NEW HAMPSHIRE OFFICE OF VACATION TRAVEL
P.O. Box 856
Concord, NH 03301
800-258-3608; 603-271-2343

**NEW JERSEY STATE DIVISION OF TRAVEL &
   TOURISM**
CN 826
Trenton, NJ 08625
609-292-2470

**NEW MEXICO COMMERCE & INDUSTRY
TOURISM & TRAVEL DIVISION**
Bataan Memorial Building
Santa Fe, NM 87503
800-545-2040; 505-827-6230

**NEW YORK STATE DEPARTMENT OF COMMERCE**
Division of Tourism
99 Washington Avenue
Albany, NY 12245
800-CALL-NYS; 800-342-3810 (in NY); 518-474-4116

**NEW YORK STATE HOSPITALITY & TOURISM
   ASSOCIATION**
505 Eighth Avenue
Suite 902
New York, NY 10018
212-564-2300

Discover all there is to love about the Big Apple from beautiful, colorful brochures available upon request from the New York State Hospitality & Tourism Association. Also included in the promotional package is a tourism map and a travel guide with map of New York State.

**NEVADA STATE DEPARTMENT OF ECONOMIC
   DEVELOPMENT**
Commission on Tourism
Capitol Complex
600 East Williams Street
Carson City, NV 89710
702-885-4322

**NORTH CAROLINA STATE TRAVEL &
TOURISM DIVISION**
430 North Salisbury Street
Raleigh, NC 27611
800-847-4862; 800-438-4404; 800-334-1051 (in NC);
919-733-4171

**NORTH DAKOTA TOURISM PROMOTION**
Liberty Memorial Building
Capitol Grounds
Bismarck, ND 58505
800-437-2077; 800-472-2100 (in ND); 701-224-2525

**OHIO OFFICE OF TRAVEL & TOURISM**
P.O. Box 1001
Columbus, OH 43216
800-282-5393; 614-466-8844

**OKLAHOMA TOURISM &
RECREATION DEPARTMENT**
Literature Distribution Department
215 N.E. 28th
Oklahoma City, OK 73105
405-521-3831

**OMAHA, NE**
Convention & Visitors Bureau
1819 Farnham
Suite 1200
Omaha, NE 68183
800-332-1819; 412-444-4660

Omaha offers a variety of shopping, entertainment, and
dining prospects, as well as outdoor and sports activities for
you to choose from. Also among its attractions are the
country's largest 4H exhibition and rodeo and the Henry
Doorly Zoo with its collection of rare white tigers. For more
information, contact the Visitors Bureau.

**OREGON STATE TOURISM DIVISION**
595 Cottage Street N.E.
Salem, OR 97310
800-547-7842; 800-233-3306 (in OR); 503-378-3451

**PANAMA CITY BEACH, FL**
Convention & Visitors Bureau
P.O. Box 9473
Panama City, FL 32407
904-233-6503

The Gulf Coast of northwest Florida boasts 25 miles of some of the world's most beautiful beaches. Panama City is also known for a number of tourist attractions, offers delectable fresh seafood during the fall months, and boasts an average temperature of around 70°. Discounts and rates vary, so be sure to inquire and find the best bargains for a pleasant stay in sunny Florida.

**PENNSYLVANIA STATE BUREAU OF
    TRAVEL DEVELOPMENT**
Department of Commerce
416 Forum Building
Harrisburg, PA 17120
800-847-4872; 800-233-7366; 800-237-4363

**RHODE ISLAND STATE TOURIST PROMOTION
    DIVISION**
Department of Economic Development
7 Jackson Walkway
Providence, RI 02903
800-556-2484; 277-2601

**SOUTH CAROLINA DEPARTMENT OF PARKS,
    RECREATION AND TOURISM**
P.O. Box 71
Columbia, SC 29202
803-734-0122

**SOUTH COUNTY, RI**
Tourism Council
P.O. Box 651
Narrangansett, RI 02882
800-548-4662; 401-789-4422 (in RI)

South County is a place where dreams are made and the perfect place to enjoy a bed and breakfast retreat or a summer stroll along a private beach. One look at the colorful brochure and you'll agree you'll want to plan your next getaway vacation in South County.

**SOUTH DAKOTA STATE DEPARTMENT**
   **OF TOURISM**
711 Wells
Pierre, SD 57501
800-843-1930; 800-773-5243 (in SD); 605-773-3301

**SOUTHEASTERN CONNECTICUT**
Tourism District
P.O. Box 89
New London, CT 06320
800-222-6783; 203-444-2206

A whole new world awaits you in southeastern Connecticut, where you can treat yourself to one of their quaint bed and breakfasts or stay at one of several hotels in the region. Write or call for more information about historic places like New London, Salem, or Mystic.

**TENNESSEE TOURIST DEVELOPMENT**
P.O. Box 32170
Nashville, TN 37204-3170
615-741-2158

Try Tennessee for your next vacation and soak up all that southern tradition. Visit the Great Smoky Mountains or Cumberland Gap, discovered by Daniel Boone, or venture over to Chattanooga, famous for its Civil War battlefields. Write or call for specific information regarding senior-related events, lodging and activities.

## STATE DEPARTMENT OF HIGHWAYS AND PUBLIC TRANSPORTATION TRAVEL & INFORMATION DIVISION
P.O. Box 5064
Austin, TX 76763-5064

A request to the Texas Department of Highways will bring to your door an absolutely beautiful, full-color 248-page publication with sections on cities, lakes, state parks, national forests, hunting and fishing, rocks and minerals, flowers, birds, and climate. In addition, it has a section on Mexico, a list of city convention and visitor's bureaus with addresses and phone numbers and a very thorough index.

## TEXAS TOURIST AGENCY
Employees Retirement System Building
P.O. Box 12008
Austin, TX 78711
512-463-7400

## UTAH STATE TRAVEL COUNCIL
Council Hall, Capitol Hill
Salt Lake City, UT 84114
801-533-5681

## VERMONT SKI AREAS ASSOCIATION
P.O. Box 368
Montpelier, VT 05601
802-223-2439; 802-229-6917

Seniors over 65 can ski the slopes of Vermont at most resorts for up to 50 percent off the regular price. If you're over 70, well, it's almost always free! Opportunities to ski exist from October well into May, but if skiing is not your cup of tea, then check out one of their bed and breakfasts, relax, and let yourself drift, enjoying the incredible scenery.

**VERMONT TRAVEL DIVISION**
134 State Street
Montpelier, VT 05602
802-828-3236

**VIRGINIA DIVISION OF TOURISM**
Interstate 77
9915 Vandor Lane
Manassas, VA 22110
703-361-2134

From its deep, underground caverns to its white, sandy beaches, Virginia will welcome you with an array of things to see and do. Write for a free copy of "Virginia Wineries Festival and Tour Guide." Most hotels and tours offer senior discounts.

**WASHINGTON STATE TOURISM INFORMATION**
Department of Commerce & Economic Development
101 General Administration Building
Olympia, WA 98504
800-541-9274; 800-562-4570 (in WA)

**WEST VIRGINIA STATE TRAVEL**
  **DEVELOPMENT DIVISION**
Office of Economic & Community Development
1900 Washington Street East
Capitol Complex
Charleston, WV 25305
800-225-5982; 304-348-2286

**WILLIAMSBURG, VA**
800-446-9244

Seniors are special people in Williamsburg and there's a special brochure to prove it ("Senior Time")—not to mention the special offers and rates at hotels, motels, attractions, restaurants, campgrounds, shops, and other businesses throughout the area. Other promotional materials upon request will help you plan your trip to Virginia.

**WISCONSIN STATE DIVISION OF TOURISM**
123 West Washington Avenue
Madison, WI 53703
800-372-2737 (in the Midwest); 608-266-7621

**WYOMING STATE TRAVEL COMMISSION**
Frank Norris Jr. Travel Center
Cheyenne, WY 82002
307-777-7777

# VOLUNTEERING

**ACTION**
1100 Vermont Ave., NW
Washington, D.C. 20526
202-634-9349 (Foster Grandparents)
202-634-9351 (Foster Companions)

Two of the most successful volunteer efforts to date are the
Foster Grandparents (loving children is easy, especially those
who have special needs) and Foster Companions (helping
someone who would benefit from independent living rather
than institutionalization). Call or write to get involved in this
worthwhile effort.


**AMERICAN HIKING SOCIETY HELPING OUT**
1015 31 Street NW
Department 18
Washington, DC 20007

A publication of the American Hiking Society, "Helping Out
in the Outdoors" is a list of volunteer projects and jobs in
the U.S. parks and forests in all 50 states, and how you can
apply for them. Some of the organizations that sponsor the
projects include the Appalachian Mountain Club and the
Sierra Club. Copies of the directory are $3 and checks or
money orders should be made out to "AHS Helping Out"

at the address above. Publication dates are February and August.

## COMMISSION ON VOLUNTARY SERVICE AND ACTION
P.O. Box 117
New York, NY 10009
212-581-5082

Get involved with children and youth, or the aged in community service projects around the world with this Commission that lists over 40,000 placements for full-time volunteers through almost two hundred agencies like Project Hope and the YMCA. Volunteer to help with trades, crafts, counseling, health care, organizing, and teaching.

## 50 SIMPLE THINGS YOU CAN DO TO SAVE THE EARTH
Earthworks Press
P.O. Box 25
1400 Shattuck Avenue
Berkeley, CA 94709

A practical look at how each of us can help save the planet for our children and grandchildren. Sample suggestions: (1) Don't choose plastic or paper at grocery checkout stands. The book recommends using string bags and tells where to find them. (2) Choose goods packaged in either recycled paper or recyclable material rather than plastic. (3) Avoid polystyrene products altogether; rumor has it they'll still be around in 500 years! This book is dedicated to the "not yet born" and is available in paperback for $4.95 from bookstores or directly from the publisher (add $1 shipping and handling).

## FOSTER PARENTS PLAN
### 800-556-7918

Reach out and you will touch a child for the rest of his or her life. A desperately poor child who struggles alone can be educated, cured of nutritional deficiencies or health diseases, whatever it takes to provide a fighting chance to grow up and survive. Sponsor a child and receive a photo, family history, progress reports and a free subscription to their magazine. Choose children from Africa, Asia or Latin America and make a gift (which can be deducted monthly from your checking account) for as low as $22 per month.

## HOW TO MAKE THE WORLD A BETTER PLACE
### Jeffrey Hollender
### William Morrow $9.95

One hundred and twenty "quick and easy actions" aimed at "Making the World a Better Place!" Reduce everything—from hunger, to homelessness, to violence on television. Sometimes all it takes is time and a commitment to do something! It's $9.95, plus postage and handling, from William Morrow, or check with your local bookstore.

## LITERACY VOLUNTEERS OF AMERICA, INC.
### 5795 Widewaters Parkway
### Syracuse, NY 13214

Help fight the tragedy of illiteracy by offering some of your time through one of the many volunteer literacy organizations. For the name, address, and phone number of the literacy program nearest you, contact the address above.

## NATIONAL FISH & WILDLIFE SERVICE
### VOLUNTEERS
**1849 C Street NW**
**Washington, DC 20240**
**202-208-5634**

Write for a list of places you can volunteer and for answers to any questions you might have.

## NATIONAL PARK SERVICE

Call a national park, historic site, or a National Park Service regional office in Boston, Philadelphia, Washington, D.C., Atlanta, Omaha, Denver, Santa Fe, San Francisco, or Anchorage, and ask for a copy of the brochure "Volunteers in Parks," which includes an application form. Then send the completed form to the park or site where you would like to volunteer.

## OFF OUR ROCKERS
**Senior Citizens of Greater Dallas**
**214-823-5700**

If you love children and have a desire to help, then consider "Off Our Rockers," a group that places senior volunteers into schools simply to be one-on-one to love the children. By spending one hour a week in one of the area schools helping a student work a puzzle or play games, older adults can develop close relationships that are priceless. Ultimately, the association builds strong self-confidence in the child and pays for itself in the form of gratification and great personal rewards for the senior involved. It's also a chance for the senior to have fun and share a little of themselves. Check with the school districts in your community to see if similar opportunities are available and volunteer to help.

**PEACE CORPS**
**1990 K Street NW**
**Washington, D.C. 20526**
**800-424-8580 ext. 293**

Since 1961, thousands of senior volunteers have served in the Peace Corps, sharing their wealth of education, experience, and wisdom in developing countries in Latin America, Africa, the Caribbean, Asia, and the Pacific. Why remain idle in retirement? Help others to help themselves. Skills are sought from agriculture, forestry and fisheries, trades such as carpentry or plumbing, education, community development, home economics and nutrition, engineering, math, and science. Continued attention is paid to volunteers' safety, training, travel, good health care, and a monthly living stipend is provided.

**TIME DOLLAR**
**c/o Essential Information**
**P.O. Box 19405**
**Washington, D.C. 20036**
**B**

The old adage "what goes around, comes around" provides the foundation for Edgar S. Cahn's innovative concept of the Time Dollar. This former dean of Antioch Law School in Washington, DC, has created a system of credits that one can earn by performing chores for others. Simply put, it's a bartering system for seniors that can practically eliminate the need for nursing homes. "If you cook my dinner tonight, I'll take you to the mall tomorrow." Service credits are tax exempt. For more information, write for free brochure. Enclose $1 in a SASE for postage and handling.

## U.S. ARMY CORPS OF ENGINEERS
**20 Massachusetts Avenue NW**
**Washington, DC 20314-1000**

Write to Volunteers, U.S. Army Corps of Engineers, for more information or apply at one of the 472 projects or 34 district offices.


## U.S. FOREST SERVICE
## VOLUNTEERS IN FOREST SERVICE
**P.O. Box 96090**
**Washington, DC 20013-0690**

Apply at the Forest Service in your area, or contact the address above for more information and details regarding local addresses.


## VOLUNTEER
**The National Center**
**1111 North 19th Street**
**Suite 500**
**Arlington, VA 22209**
**703-276-0542**

Who says the best vacation has to be all play and no work? Volunteer to run a camp, help build a church, or work on a research project while you travel to an out-of-the-way vacation destination. Often, lodging will be provided, and those who prefer giving may receive much more in return. Sample possibilities include maintaining trails in Colorado's national forests on weekends during summer months, building a shelter along the Appalachian Trail, or repairing low-income housing in Kansas City. For further information and volunteering opportunities, contact the National Center.

# CATEGORY INDEX

# COMPANY INDEX